STUDIES IN ANCIENT TECHNOLOGY

VOLUME VI

STUDIES
IN ANCIENT TECHNOLOGY

BY

R. J. FORBES

VOLUME VI

HEAT AND HEATING
REFRIGERATION
LIGHT

WITH 39 FIGURES AND 5 TABLES

SECOND, REVISED EDITION

LEIDEN
E. J. BRILL
1966

CONTENTS

PREFACE

This little volume attempts to set out our present knowledge of the ancient means of producing heat, cold and light. It is shown that there is a severe lack of essential data on these basic elements of ancient daily life. Our vague data on ancient furnaces and heating devices sometimes make it impossible to establish the techniques of certain arts and crafts, in which the temperatures attainable or needed play such a large part. Archaeologists should make more precise plans of the remains of such furnaces and kilns which experts can then easily determine. More attention should also be given to remains of ancient fuel, charcoal, etc., a factor which is but too vaguely described upto now and which, again, is essential to draw conclusions on the heat obtainable and the processes used by the ancient craftsmen. It is hoped that these summaries of our present knowledge will lead to more careful reporting of details on the essential and basic factors of ancient technology.

April 1958.   R. J. FORBES

PREFACE TO THE SECOND EDITION

Helpful suggestions and corrections from various readers and a number of new references have helped to bring this edition uptodate.

January 1966   R. J. FORBES

CHAPTER I

HEAT AND HEATING

1. *Introduction*

Man was scarcely man till he came into the possession of fire, which is the basis of all modern forms of production, manufacture and transportation. In the words of Pliny (1):

> "We cannot but marvel at the fact that fire is necessary for almost every operation. It takes the sands of the earth and melts them, now into glass, now into silver, or minium, or one or other lead, or some substance useful to the painter or the physician. By fire minerals are disintegrated and copper produced; in fire iron is born, and by fire it is subdued: by fire gold is purified: by fire stones are burned for the binding together of walls of houses. It is sometimes profitable to heat a substance several times, and a single material may give different products on its first, second, and third ignitions. For example, it is only when ignited and quenched that charcoal itself acquires its characteristic powers, and only when it seems to have perished that it becomes endowed with greater virtue. Fire is the immeasurable, uncontrollable element, concerning which it is hard to say whether it consumes more or produces more. Fire itself is not without medical importance. It is recognised that the plagues which afflict men when the sun is darkened are alleviated in many ways if fires are kindled... By this we see that benefit is to be derived from things so despised and so unimportant as charcoal and ashes."

For already in the days of Pliny the all-encompassing properties of fire were fully appreciated. We have now archaeological proof that the "taming of fire" took place at a very early stage in the history of mankind. We do not know whether the earliest uses of fire, the Sinanthropi of Peking, actually made fire but they could certainly maintain it when naturally ignited. As the Choukoutien hearths date from the second glaciation, it is obvious that Europe lagged behind for the earliest traces of fire go back to Mid-Acheulian (second interglacial) sites such as Torralba in our continent. In Africa there were no signs of fire before late Acheulian sites of the last interglacial period. We have no proof that any of the living primitive tribes never knew fire, only the Andaman islanders do not have it, but it is highly probable that they lost the art of making fire in the course of the centuries. All primitive tribes take great care in avoiding the necessity of kindling fire anew, they often go as far as carrying it in clay hearths in their canoes when travelling.

Fire was the first element which man harnessed and he turned it into one of the giant powers of this earth (2). He used it not only to warm his body and his shelter or cave but, in possession of a properly heated home, he could increase the area of human inhabitation on this globe. Fire taught him to cook food which had been uneatable in his earlier days, it aided and shortened his digestive process and increased the range of foodstuffs considerably. As he changed his way of life from hunting to a sedentary existence he was capable with the help of fire to increase the density of population. He used it to extend the pasture for his grazing herds and used the ashes of the forest fires to manure the cleared spaces. Such a "fire vegetation" belongs to the culture pattern of the aborigines of the Great Plains of North America. Phytotherapy and cooking and sterilization of food were not the only benefits he derived from his fire. It became the basis of his technology and engineering, of the crafts he developed when attempting to model, shape and transform the materials and products which Nature provides for him. From the kitchen range he proceeded to the baking oven and then to the pottery kiln and the metallurgical furnace.

We need not wonder that this powerful element, fire, occupied a large place in the mind of the inhabitants of the pre-classical and the classical world. It was no doubt a gift of the gods, a supernatural power snatched from heaven, an element endowed with the power of purification, destructive and helpful, a shield against the wild animals and the evil powers, ghosts of the dead and demons. Fire was the male principle in life, a spark could impregnate a virgin. Vesta and Vulcan embody these opposite aspects of the heavenly fire. Fires were already lit over the bodies of the dead Neanderthal people. The dead of pre-historic days were buried near the hearth to warm them or special fires were lit over their bodies. In fact the roots of the ritual fire and of cremation go back far into prehistoric days. There is no need to discuss here the part which fire played in ancient magic or religion (3), this has been amply discussed. We would, however, like to draw the attention to the many metaphors in ancient languages to denote "fire".

Thus the ancient Egyptians have three common expressions denoting "fire" but a host of metaphors (4) such as "the executioner", "the red one", "the angry one", "the useful one", "the living one", "the planned", "the devoured one", "the mighty one", "the burning", "the beautiful", "the withering one", or the "scorching one". The Egyptian word for fire or disaster shows a picture of a burning city (5) and thus all the aspects of fire in human life are illustrated in these terms. No wonder that the first scientists speculated on the nature of fire and after them the Greeks, the alchemists and the phlogistonists until Lavoisier and his generation solved the mysteries of combustion.

Nearly all primitive and early peoples avoided rekindling fire and took all trouble to preserve it. Charles the Great in his Capitulare de Villis still ordered a fire to be kept burning in each inhabited house. Upto the eighteenth century bells were rung when the evening fell, this was called "cur-few" (French couvre-feu, Italian copri-fuoco). Rains have been known to stop battles, as the fuses of fire-arms became wet and no fire could be made!

In ancient Rome the rekindling of the fire kept in the Temple of Vesta involved a ceremony in which a fire drill figured. "If the fire in the temple of Vesta is extinguished, the Vestal maidens are flogged by the Pontifex Maximus. Afterwards they rekindled the fire (with the help of the Pontifex?) by turning a hole in a slab of fruit-bearing wood, which one of them then carried into the sacred building in a bronze sieve" (6).

Fire had to be kept over until the next day. Did not Homer describe Odysseus' sleep after the storm (7) "as when some swain hath hidden deep his torch beneath the embers, at the verge extreme of all his farm, where, having neighbours none, he saves a seed or two of future flame?" And did not Plautus say (8) "you can always get fire, even by asking your enemy for it?" Cutting off somebody from water and fire, "aqua et igni interdicere", was the equivalent of banishing. Leopold (9) tells us how in Southern countries even in the twentieth century tobacconists had a burning fuse attached to their doorpost, matches and the like still being scarce in these regions.

Hence we hear much of the difficulties of keeping fires burning and if the encamped army spread out over a large area, fire was carried to the outposts from a central campfire in earthenware pots (10). When kings travelled in the Near East fire was carried before them (11) and even in Greece. This was a Spartan custom (12) of offering to Zeus the Leader and consulting the oracles before engaging in battle. We are also told that Alexander the Great had planted a torch in front of his tent, the fire of which was visible during the night and the smoke during the daytime (13). The Scythians swore by the hearth of the king (14) whose duty it was to watch that the fire was never extinguished. His health was often said to depend on this fire. Hence on certain days the Vestal Virgins address the rex sacrorum with these words "Vigilasne rex? Vigila!" (15). In the course of time not only was the life of the king believed to be dependant on this fire, he was even identified with it (16). These and many other beliefs of the relations between the celestial powers, the king, the state and the upkeep of the holy fires resulted in the many "eternal fires" kept in such Greek cities as Athens, Argos and many others, and also in famous temples like that of Jupiter Ammon and Vesta (17).

In the following pages we will have to discuss the origins and production of fire, the fuels used in Antiquity and the different forms of heating in the home and in the workshop.

2. *Origin and Production of Fire*

Has man originally lighted his first firebrand with the help of a fire induced by Nature or did he start by devising artificial means of producing fire? In all ages authorities agreed that man first used the fire which Nature provided in one way or another. We all have heard the story of how Prometheus snatched fire from heaven, but a late version of this story makes Prometheus light his firebrand at a volcano. His firebrand was the branch of "narthex", the pith of Ferula Narthex, which together with the powder of Cirsium Eriophum was often used to catch the sparks of a strike-a-light (18).

The ancient authorities waver between a forest ablaze when struck by lightning or by the friction of boughs moved by the wind. Thus Diodor (19) says: "For once, when a tree on the mountains had been struck by lightning and the forest nearby was ablaze, Hephaestus went up to it, for it was winter-time, and greatly enjoyed the heat; as the fire died down he kept adding fuel to it, and while keeping the fire going in this way he invited the rest of mankind to enjoy the advantage which came from it". The other hypothesis is supported by Lucretius (20):

"For we see many things flare up, kindled by flames from heaven, when a stroke from the sky has brought the gift of heat. Yet again, when a branching tree is lashed by the winds and sways to and fro, reeling and pressing on the branches of another tree, fire is struck out by the strong force of the rubbing, anon the fiery heat of flame sparkles out, while branches and trunks rub against the other. Either of these happenings may have given fire to mortals. And then the sun taught them to cook food and soften it by the heat of flame since they saw many things among the fields grow mellow vanquished by the lashing of his rays and by the heat."

Pliny (21) does not take any decision in this matter but states: "Moreover, as this one element has a fertile principle that engenders itself and grows out of the smallest sparks, what must be expected to happen in future among all these funeral pyres of the earth? ... add the fires of man's making and also those implanted in the nature of stone and timber rubbing against itself, and again the fire of the clouds, and the sources of thunderbolts—and doubtless all marvels will be surpassed by the fact that here had even been a single day on which there has not been a universal conflagration, when also hollow mirrors facing the sun's rays set things alight more easily than any other fire."

We have no idea when the domestication of natural fire started but it must have been early in the story of mankind as the Sinanthropus of Peking certainly tended fires in his caves. We have the impression that for a considerable period man did not yet know to produce fire. Yet by the time that archaeology begins to shed more light on his history "keeping fires" had already made place for "making fires". The Palaeolithic and Mesolithic cave-dwellers in most parts of the world have left us proof that they used lumps of flint and pyrites as strike-a-lights. It seems that fire-drills or ploughs came later and some tribes like the mammoth-hunters of Kostenki living in the tundras did not produce fire by rubbing two kinds of wood together but they used bones.

The development of fire making has been carefully studied and many data have been collected from ethnological evidence supplied with the results of archaeology (22). These data allow us to establish the following table of the means of producing fire (23):

Principle	*Apparatus*

A. *Friction of wood* (across the grain)
   1. Drilling   Fire drill: (a) Two-stick drill
                         (b) Strap drill (four parts)
                         (c) Bow drill (four parts)
                         (d) Compound or pump drill

	2. Sawing	(a) Friction saw
		(b) Fire thong
	3. Planing	Fire-plough
	(with the grain)	
B.	*Percussion* Strike-a-light:	(a) Pyrites and pyrites
		(b) Pyrites and flint
		(c) Steel and flint
		(d) Bamboo and pottery or flint
C.	*Physical methods*	(a) Fire-piston (compressed air)
		(b) Lenses and mirros (sun's rays)
		(c) Electric sparks and current
D.	*Chemical methods*	Matches

There is no doubt that both electricity and matches were not used before the early nineteenth century (24) but the ancients already possessed a variety of means of producing fire (25) even if they always took great care to tend a fire and not to let it extinguish. Some authors have tried to establish a natural series of fire-making appliancies. Thus Hough believes this evolution to be represented by the following series: Volcano in action — lightning — campfire — fire saw — fire thong — fire plough — fire drills and pump drill — strike-a-light. However, we have already seen that archaeology tends to show that strike-a-lights came before fire drills and anyhow it is doubtful whether such a logical evolution as represented by Hough's series can be established at all when in different regions of the world materials and conditions may have promoted evolution along very special lines. Both the earliest preclassical and classical civilizations are already too far advanced to establish such lines of evolution with any precision.

If we turn to the Old Testament we find the preservation of fire standing foremost in the mind of the ancient Israelites. "Abraham took the wood of the burnt offering ... and he took the fire in his hand and they went both together" (26). A potsherd served "to take fire from the hearth" (27) or a "live coal he took with tongs (melḳâḥájim) off the altar" (28). "And the fire upon the altar shall be burning in it, it shall not be put out" (29). Lightning is the source of fire in several cases, "now when Solomon had made an end of praying, the fire came down from heaven, and consumed the burnt offering and the sacrifices" (30) and again "there came a fire out from before the Lord, and consumed upon the altar of the Tabernacle the burnt offering and the fat" (31).

The fire of the second Temple was lighted with naphtha (32): "For when our fathers were led into Persia, the priests that were then devout took the fire of the altar privily, and hid it in a hollow place of a pit without water, where they kept it sure, so that the place was unknown to all men. Now after many years, when it pleased God, Neemias, being sent from the King of Persia, did send of the posterity of those priests that had hid it to the fire; but when they told us they found no fire but thick water. Then he commanded them to draw it up, and to bring it; and when the sacrifices were laid on, Neemias commanded the priests to sprinkle the wood and the things laid thereupon with the water. When this was done, and the time came that the sun shone, which was afore hid in the cloud, there was a great fire kindled, so that every man marvelled". Again after the Syrian sacrilege (33) "having cleansed the temple they made another altar, and striking stones they took fire out of them, and offered a sacrifice after two years". "Foreign fire" was forbidden (34) and the strike-a-light seems to have been the prescribed means of relighting the fire on the altar. Tradition tells us that Adam struck or rubbed two stones pointed out to him by the Lord (35).

Jewish Law forbade the production of fire on the Sabbath and other holy days from wood, stones, dust ('âphâr), and water. Maimonides (36) calls naphtha "the sharpest of liquids" which catches flame when shaken; and also "a vessel with water can fire flax, if the sun shines on it". The "dust" mentioned above was probably sulphur (gophrît) which "the Lord rained upon Sodom and upon Gomorrah" and "which shall be scattered upon his habitation" (37) to destroy it utterly.

Whereas the Jewish Law therefore seems to hold that the strike-a-light is the earliest fire-making appliance and mentions the fire drill for profane uses only, the Greeks held the fire drill to be the primary and most primitive instrument. Both the Latin "ignariai" and the Greek "pyreia" denote the two pieces of wood used to produce fire (38). Their knowledge is said to have come down from prehistoric times (39). The term "pyreia" is sometiems also applied to the flints from which sparks are struck (40). In a slightly changed orthography, "pyri" denote burning-mirrors used to produce fire (41), but this does not hold good for the term "igniaria". Latin authors affirm that the igniaria are mostly in the hands of shepherds or army scouts (42) who would not find fire everywhere on their way. Townsmen usually employed strike-a-lights of one kind or another. On the other hand they are careful not to extinguish the fire in their hearths and keep them burning by covering them with ashes (43). Should one need fire, one could always go to one's neighbours to fetch it. Even the armies preserved fire carefully and sent glowing embers to their advance parties in pottery vases (chytrai) (44).

We must therefore start our discussion with the *strike-a-light*. Though Pliny (45) attributes the discovery of "fire from flint to Pyrodes, son of Silix, the storing of fire in a fennel-stalk to Prometheus" we know that such stories concocted much later were wrong. Nodules or pyrites with well marked grooves were found in Magdalenian deposits of the Upper Palaeolithic Age and pieces of flint and pyrites, which evidently made strike-a-lights were found in many a Neolithic settle-

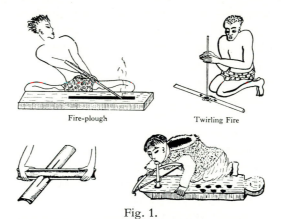

Fig. 1.

Primitive methods of kindling the fire
(Fire-plough, twirling fire, fire-saw and fire-drill) (After Lips).

ment. The ancient Egyptian language has a word for "firestone" (46) or flint. A hard fine-grained pyrites is the most suitable type of stone, the kind which Latin authors call "live pyrites" (47).

Classical authors agree that stone striking stone came first (igniarius lapis) (48). The combination of pyrites and steel came much later for we should realize that the "iron" used was in reality steel. Wrought iron or soft steel make bad strike-a-lights, the best steel for this purpose is a hardened high-carbon steel with about 3—4% of carbon (or a modern steel with 0.8% of carbon and 0.3% of magnanese). Thus the Trojans sought "the seeds of the flame which is hidden in the veins of the flint" (49), but only later could "stone strike on stone or on iron; for then a flash leaps out and fire scatters abroad bright sparks" (50). The

method is never mentioned by Greek authors and we are led to conclude that it is not earlier than about 300 B.C. when the appropriate
steel was manufactured, nails being sometimes mentioned (51).

The spark was absorbed in sulphur dust, dried mushrooms (fungi
aridi) or dry leaves, the flame being fed with chips of wood (assulae),
sprigs (cremia) (52) or small twigs (ramalia) (53). Flint and steel continued to aid mankind, mechanization setting in in the seventeenth
century, so that about 1700 pistol and wheel tinder-boxes were available to the general public, and continued into use until our own times.

We now turn to the *fire drill* and similar forms of friction-heat produced by two kinds of wood. By boring or drilling one piece of wood
into another, by rubbing or ploughing along the grain or by sawing
across the grain, fire may be produced. Here again, we cannot say
whether the fire drill was an earlier invention than the fire saw or the
fire plough, each of these forms being more or less peculiar to a
particular region. The prime requisitive was the choice of the right
kind of wood; thoroughly seasoned and very dry. Soft finegrained
woods were preferably used and hard woods should be rejected.
Usually the drill was of the same wood as the hearth, but some tribes
preferred a harder wood for the drill.

There were two distinct operations: the first was the preparation of
a smouldering spark or ember; the second the transformation of this
ember into a flame with the help of tinder (fine dry vegetable fibres,
bark, grass or moss, inner chestnut bark or vegetable down). The drill
used almost exclusively in the ancient world was also used in the whole
of North America and in practically all Africa. The essential feature
of all fire drills is that one piece of wood, cylindrical or flattened in
form, which is spoken of as the base or hearth, is held horizontally on
the ground whilst another piece, always circular (about $1/4$—$5/8''$ in
diameter) and some 14—30 inches long, often called the drill stick, is
twirled rapidly with its lower end pressed into a shallow pit or depres-
sion made ih tne hearth. The wood-dust and tinder in the hearth is
ignited by the heat produced by the friction. Sometimes the drill stick
has a socket for downward pressure. The slot in the hearth is an invention of great importance as it permits the air to contact the hot
wood dust. Both parts of the apparatus must be very dry, and sometimes the parts where the friction occurred were intentionally charred
beforehand. The time needed to produce fire varied from eight seconds
to two minutes.

We have no proof that the fire drill antedated the New Stone Age.

The ancient Sumerian god of the fire, Gibil (54) was the god of the fire drill. Pictures of fire drills occur in Third and Fourth dynasty tombs in ancient Egypt and the fire drill may owe its origin to experiments in drilling holes in bone and flint and such materials. The Egyptian pictogram clearly shows the drill stick and the hearth (55).

The ancients claimed that the fire drill was invented by Prometheus (56) or by Hermes (57): "and he brought together much wood and sought after the art of fire. A fair bough he took and smoothed it to a point with iron and therewith drilled, for well it fitted his hand till a hot breath arose. Yes, Hermes first of all produced firesticks and fire. And much dry wood he took, in a trench in the earth, in bundles he laid it in great abundance and the flame gleamed, shooting forth afar a jet of fire that is mickle of might". The Argonauts, we are told (58), "moved the fire drills with the hands" or better still "moved the fire drills to and fro" (59) though some authors say that "they obtained fire from rubbed rocks to leaves and fed it with the friendly sulphur" (60). The Greek writers of "Robinson Crusoe" stories like Lucian always provide their hero with a fire drill (61). Zeus himself is called "promantheus" (fire drill, compare the Sanskrit pramantha) (62) and in Homer's story the eye of the cyclop is the pit or hearth in which the fire drill awakens fire. Hence Odysseus is also called Itahkos (the man who causes fire to glow) (63) and that is why he calls himself Aithoon when he wants to remain incognito (64).

We have no precise description of the way in which the ancient Greeks worked with the fire drill, for even such stories as that of Lucian remain vague in this respect but we can fill up the gaps in our knowledge by data taken from Hindu and other religious ceremonies. The fire stick, called trypanon or teretron (65), is a piece of fairly hard wood. It is introduced into a hole in the base or hearth, called eschara (66) and then rotated quickly either by hand or by means of a cord wound once or twice around it. The other end of the trypanon is pushed on to the base by the operator.

Inflammable matter such as dry leaves or mushrooms is placed in the hole in the base to receive the fire (67) which is then fanned (68) to enliven it. This is what Pliny has to tell us about the type of wood to be used for the fire drill and what the correct "fomes" (tinder) is:

> "Other hot woods are mulberry, laurel, ivy and all those used for making fire sticks (igniaria). This has been discovered by experience in the camps of military scouting parties and of shepherds,

because there is not always a stone at hand to strike fire with; consequently two pieces of wood are rubbed together and catch fire owing to the friction, and the fire is caught in a lump of dry tinder, fungus or dead leaves catching most readily. But there is nothing better than ivy wood for rubbing against and laurel wood for rubbing with; one of the wild vines (not the claret-vine), which climbs up a tree like ivy, is also spoken well of".

Theophrastus (Hist. Plant. V. 9.7) has a more detailed passage on the choice of the correct wood for the fire drill:

"Fire sticks are made of many kinds of wood, but best, according to Menestor, from ivy: for that flares up most quickly and freely. They say also that a very good fire stick is made of the wood which some call traveller's joy: this is a tree like the vine or the wild vine which, like these, climbs up trees. The stationary piece should be made of one of these, the drill of bay; for the active and passive parts of the apparatus should not be of the same wood, but different in their natural properties to start with, one being of active, the other of passive character. Nevertheless they are sometimes made of the same wood, and some suppose that it makes no difference. They are made in fact of buckthorn, kermes oak, lime and almost any wood except olive; which seems rather surprising, as olive wood is rather hard and oily; however, it is plainly its moisture which makes it less suitable for kindling. The wood of the buckthorn is also good, and it makes a satisfactory stationary piece; for, besides being dry and free from sap it is necessary that this should also be of rather open texture, that the friction may be effectual; while the drill should be one which gets little worn by use. And that is why one made of bay is best; for, as it is not worn by use, it is effective through its biting quality. All fire sticks take fire quickly and better in a north than in a south wind, and better in an exposed spot than in one which is shut in".

The Greek authors agree that the trypanon should be made of a hard type of wood but that the hearth should be chosen from a less dense timber such as "kittos" (69), purging buckthorn (70), "ramnos", the kermes oak (prinos) or the limetree (philyra). The wood of the olive-tree was considered too dense and holding too much water (71). They were never quite clear on what happened when the fire drill worked, though they understood that it did not work in a humid atmosphere (72). Notably, Theophrastus could not understand how sparks could be produced by striking two stones, two cold things! Neither can Lucretius (73) explain how heat is caused by friction. "If in logs flame lurks hidden, and smoke and ash, it must need be that the logs are composed of things alien in kind, of alien things, which rise up out of the logs ... But often on mighty mountains it comes to pass, you say, that the neighbouring tops of tall trees rub together, until at last a flowery flame gathers, and they blaze with fire. And yet you must know that fire is not implanted in their wood, but there are many seeds of heat, which when they have flowed together through rubbing, create fires in the forests. But if the flame had been hidden away, ready-made, in the forests, the fires could not have been concealed for any time, they would consume the forests one and all, and burn the trees to ashes."

The other forms of fire drills were not used in fire-making in the Mediterranean region. The *strap* or *cord drill* belonged to the Eskimo civilization and that of Siberia and some other parts of Asia. The *bow drill*, not known in Japan and in Africa, was used for drilling wood, bone and ivory, but not for fire-making by the ancients. The *pump drill*, unknown to them is used for fire-making in Asia and North America. The principle of obtaining fire by sawing is applied in a region where a special material suitable for such operations is found, the bamboo. A piece of bamboo with a sharp edge is sawed or rubbed rapidly back and forth in the notch of a split piece of bamboo. Like the related *sawing thong*, the *fire saw* is characteristic of the Malay region of south-eastern Asia and certain parts of India.

Coming to the physical methods of fire production we have the *fire piston* of Malaya. It works on the same principle as the Diesel engine, that is on the fact that air when compressed gives off heat. The fire piston is used in Malaya and Indonesia by peoples of a relatively low stage of culture and it is curious to note that the same principle was observed, independently, in Europe in 1801 and 1807 and a patent for a fire piston for domestic uses was based upon this discovery! It was never used in Aintquity.

Lenses and mirrors may have played some part in fire-making in Antiquity. Lenses were rare, but the concentration of the sun's rays by a glass sphere filled with water was observed by Pliny (74) and burning glasses are also mentioned in a few cases (75). It was, however, more common to use concave mirrors (specula concava) to light a fire

(76), the bronze mirrors covered with a silver or lead foil known to the ancients. Plutarch claims that the sacred fire of Vesta was thus re-lighted, but Festus seems right in saying that the fire sticks were used, for mirrors did not go back to the time when the worship of Vesta was established and it is hard to believe that such a newfangled thing as a mirror would be introduced in the ancient cult of the Goddess. We have of course the story that Archimedes set the Roman fleet afire with concave mirrors at Syracuse, but this seems technically impossible. Still mirrors must have been used from time to time for Euclid is quite positive that "with concave mirrors set against the sun fire is lighted" (77).

3. *Fuel in Antiquity*

The materials burned in Antiquity to produce heat were of animal, vegetable and mineral origin. In the early stages of human history, when open fires were burned in caves and open spaces in the forests wood was the common fuel but a great variety of other fuels could be used in open fires with a minimum confinement between walls. As there was still hardly any specific heating device for buildings or special requirements for the furnace of kilns used for a certain craft every group used the fuels within its reach. Thus in the regions along the North Sea whale-bones were used, more particularly the small ones, according to Olaus Magnus, a usage which likewise finds parallel among the mammoth hunters of Upper Palaeolithic times. Fresh creta-cean bones were still used as an alternative to peat in the Faeroes, certainly upto the early years of the present century. This use goes back to prehistoric times here too for an ash-heap, overlying and in front of a fire-place of a Skara Brae (Scotland) hut, consisted principally of a mass of charred whale-bones mixed with burnt shells and bones (78).

As architecture developed and took different forms in various regions on earth and as various devices for heating such houses were developed the right choice of the fuel used, its kind, size, etc. became more important. Now we observe the rudiments of the manufacture of fuel. Wood, the most ancient fuel, could be made smokeless by stripping its bark and drying it for some days after wetting it. It could also be rubbed with oil or the pulp of olives, it could be slightly charred by passing it through a flame. With the advent of metallurgy and other crafts charcoal became more important and its manufacture was developed into an art of choosing the right type of wood and subjecting it to an incomplete combustion in order to obtain charcoal of the correct porosity and strength. As charcoal also came to be used for heating the home in many regions the discovery of the making of charcoal should be recognized as one of the most important inventions after the making of fire. For a very long period the world's advance in fire utilization and other arts and crafts depended upon charcoal. It was soon recognized that each technical operation required a special fuel, more or less free of volatile constituents, capable of bearing certain loads in the fire or producing a high flash heat, special requirements which each craft had to work out itself by experimenting (79). Hence we may expect a large variety of fuels used in a civilization where no temperature measurements or testing of calorific value was known, where no theory of heat could guide the craftsman or the designers of stoves, kilns and furnaces.

If we postpone our discussion of the main fuels, wood and charcoal, and turn to Egypt we find that here, as in the other parts of the Ancient Near East (and indeed in the entire modern world at the present time) farm wastes played a large part in fuel economy. Chaff, straw, reeds, rushes and sedges and the dried dung of cows and asses were used extensively. Even the modern Arab children still collect grass and dung and mixing them dry the flat cakes in the sun to sell them as fuel. The ancient texts do not speak of the collection of such fuels in particular. We learn much more from the Old Testament and Jewish documents.

Thorny shrubs (sîrîm, hamâsîm) (80) and withered sticks and twigs were collected and the Law even specified certain plants (81). Collecting this fuel was called "gibbêb" and it was used for the "tannûr" (baking furnace), cooking stoves and baths. Straw, either hacked straw (tében) or long straws or stubble (ḳaš) (82) were used in making bricks (83), and heating the baking oven, the bath and cooking stoves. The pulp of olives is not mentioned in the Old Testament but it was certainly used in those days in the same way as the "géphet" of the Law (84) which was applied in baking, cooking and heating stoves as were the dregs of the pressings of sesame-seed in Babylonia. We also hear of the remains of fat (ḥêleb), date kernels (gal'înîm) and palmtwigs (ḥarijjôt) being used as fuels. The dung of cattle was sometimes used for fires but the Law was doubtful whether this "gelêlê behêmâ" (zébel) was equivalent to other fuels (85). The bones of fishes, birds and animals were sometimes used (86).

In ancient Mesopotamia date kernels were used by the smiths as a substitute for charcoal (87). Thorny desert shrubs called "ašâgu" were collected in considerable quantities and the farm waste such as chopped straw and reeds and the cameldung still used as a cheap fuel by potters and lime-burners must have figured largely.

The ancient craftsmen were well aware of the different properties of such fuels as straw, faggots and good wood for specific processes (88) and they knew how to select the proper type of *wood*, their main fuel. The ancient Egyptians had two special terms for firewood (89) but their specific meaning is not quite clear to us. Theophrastus (90) tells us that the "Egyptians use the root of the papyrus plant instead of wood for burning, for it is abundant and good". Remains of mimosa wood have been found which together with the wood of the tamarisk and the nabak-tree is still used by the smiths of Cordofan. The use of olive wood and the charcoal produced therefrom is attested in late Hellenistic Gnostic papyri.

We have much more information on ancient Palestine (91). Here logs of wood (êṣîm) were necessary for offerings (92) and for baking (93) they were as essential as charcoal (94). Fire was considered essential for life (95), it burned when wood (stacked in heaps) (96) was available. Wood was used for the kitchen range (medûrâ) (97) and the altar (98), though the chips from the carpenter's shop would also serve (99). Logs were cut with an axe (garzen) made of steel (100), but it was also collected (mekôšêš) (101) or torn from the earth (tâlaš) (102). The wood used for the fires of a building was stored in the court-yard or in a special shed (dîr, bêt hâ-'êṣîm) which might be situated outside the village (103). The Temple had a special chamber for wood (liškat hâ'êṣîm) (104) with a special official in charge and also a chamber where the wood was inspected for damage by insects. This wood was used to heat ordinary cooking stoves, baking furnaces, stoves and the heating chamber of the Temple. Wood from cedars, laurels (ôren), cypresses and fig-trees was preferred (105). On the altar in the Temple twigs (but no pieces of the stem) of the fig-tree, the walnut-tree, and the spruce were burnt. The wood of the olive and the vine were expressly forbidden (106) and some added that of the sycomore, carob-tree, date-palm, oak and sâtûr. As wood damaged by insects was taboo, it was always to be cut before the 15th day of the month Ab (107) when the sun began to lose its strength and the insects began to damage the trees. The wood of old figs and olives might be used (108) but the Ordinance of Joshua laid down that only the wood collected on one's own field was meant (109), though this did not apply to enemy fields in wartime (110). Logs were to be split with the heavy double-axe (ḳardôm) (111) into smaller logs called "gizzêrîn" (112). At present only the wood of the storax-tree and the wild almond are not cut but other firewood is cut quite freely in Palestine. Tar ('iṭrânâ) and resin (ṣarwâ) were sometimes used to light the fire (113).

In Mesopotamia the general form of fuel was the brushwood, thorny twigs, shrubs and reeds or the like which were collected in swampy regions and the desert areas (113a). The firewood (ú) collecting was an arduous task and reserved for men as proverbs such as "My wife should not carry firewood for me" or "When his firewood is to be carried, he carries it himself" go to show. The word-lists give us various expressions for types of firewood such as wood shavings (giš-ḫaš = ḫiṣibtu, ḫiṣbu), mouldy firewood (giš-gibil = iṣu erru), dry firewood (giš-laḫ = iṣu šâbulu), cut-up firewood (giš-kud = niksu), carbonised wood (gumâru) and ashes (dè, dè-dal = didilu, ditallu, dikmênu).

Good quality wood was almost entirely used for the manufacture of charcoal (AN.DUB, DUB.DIR, KI.NE, or U₃.TU.BA = pêndu, pêntu, ass.pe'tu, pe'ettu, pettu), for industrial purposes and for the temples. The most common wood turned into charcoal for glass manufacture was "ṣarbutu-wood", which was almost certainly cut from the most common tree in Lower Mesopotamia, the "Euphrates poplar" (ᵍⁱˢasal = ṣarbatu). It was cut up into logs (kurû) in the hot month of Api and the logs were not bound up in bundles but stored under hides, if they were not turned into charcoal almost immediately·

We have an interesting letter in the correspondence of the famous king Chammurabi (114) addressed to his servant Sin-idinnam. It deals with the supply of "healthy", "green" wood (isum warqum) suitable to be turned into charcoal ("carbonized in the charcoal-heap" = ana šikir maqqari, as the text says) for the metallurgists. The type of wood mentioned (ᵍⁱˢA.BA = kušabku wood) was also imported from Meluhha for the manufacture of furniture according to Salonen (Möbel, pag. 213). The text of the letter runs as follows: "To Sin-idinnam say, thus speaks Chammurabi: Logs of AB-BA wood for the manufacture of charcoal for the metal-workers of Bad-tibira or where they may be, should be selected for you. They shall cut for you 7200 logs of ... wood of a volume of 10, 20 and 40 cubic centimetres(?) and of a length of 1 m., 1.50 m. and 2 m. Every lot of 300 logs shall be loaded into a freighter and ... brought to Babylon. Among the firewood that will be cut, there shall be no wood that died in the forest. They shall cut green wood only. This firewood shall be brought quickly lest the metal-workers sit down empty-handed".

In the classical period all kinds of firewood were used but as charcoal became the main fuel for heating the home on braziers and for industrial uses better selection is obvious from the texts. Thus we have a long law regulating the sale of charcoal and wood in the third century from the island of Delos where these commodities were imported from Macedonia and sold to other Greek communities in large quantities. The text runs (115):

"No one who does not use the public wood-scales is to sell charcoal or logs of wood; nor is anyone who buys in Delos or on board ship in the harbour to sell any of these products. Only he who was registered in his own name may sell, nor when goods have been announced for sale may he be seated while conducting sales, nor may he sell wood, logs, or charcoal that is the property of another. No one except the importers themselves is allowed to sell, and they are not permitted to sell at either a higher or a lower price than the one they have registered with the customs collectors. Before selling the importers are to register their goods also with the superintendents of the market at the same price as they register them with the customs collectors. If anyone makes a sale contrary to the regulations, he is liable to a fine of fifty drachms, and any citizen that wishes may denounce him to the superintendents of the market. The superintendents of the market are to bring these denouncements before the Thirty-One in the course of the month in which the denouncement was made. He who makes the denouncement is to deposit pay for the court. If the accused is convicted he is to return the pay to the one that deposited it, and is to give him two-thirds of the fine stipulated, and to give the other third to the public treasury. The superintendents of the market are to exact payment from him within ten days after conviction, and cannot be called to account for this action. If they are unable to do so, they are to take oath, and are to surrender him and his property to the denouncer and are to record this on the tablet with their other written statements and are to give this to the council to be deposited in the public archives. When the men that are immune from taxes import wood or logs or charcoal to be sold according to the public woodscales, they are to register with the superintendents of the market before they sell, the price

at which they are going to sell, and they are not to be permitted
to sell for either more or less than the price registered. If any of
them do not obey the regulations, the superintendents of the
market are to refuse them the use of the scales and of the charcoal
measures, and they are to pay the city as rent for the place in which
their wood or charcoal or logs are stored one drachme a day until
they are removed. The superintendents of the market are to exact
payment from them and cannot be called to account for this
action."

We also know of taxes at Cos for the domestic consumption of
wood. In Egypt there remained a dearth of good firewood in classical
times though tree-planting was carried on by the administration on the
canal embankments. Everything up to the cutting down of trees was
strictly regulated there. In Cyprus like in other Mediterranean regions
there was deforestation by the Greeks and the Phoenicians but protection by the city kings of the fourth century, exploitation by the
Seleucids, Antigone and Demetrius, and management of the forests
by the Ptolemies, who were anxious to acquire proper supplies of
wood for mining and shipbuilding locally and for building materials
to be exported to Alexandria. Still in Roman times Strabo could exclaim (116): "In ancient times plains of Cyprus were thickly overgrown
with forests, and therefore were covered with woods and not cultivated. The mines helped a little against this since the people would cut
down the trees to burn the copper and the silver and the building of
the fleets further helped".

It is often said that many regions were deforested by the cutting of
the trees for the manufacture of industrial and domestic charcoal and
this may be true for the Karst Mountains which were formerly thickly
overgrown with forests. However, there were certainly other and
more important factors at work which stimulated deforestation and
one of these was the number of goat-herds kept all over the Mediterranean region. It can be said without exaggeration that the goats de-
nuded many a fertile region in Greece, Malta and other parts of the
ancient world.

Still in the neighbourhood of mining regions charcoal burning did
much harm. The best iron ore of the Roman world was to be found
on the island of Elba but the local wood and charcoal industry had
apparently given out before the days of the Roman Empire and the ore
had to be transported after some initial roasting to the town of Popu-

Ionia on the mainland to be smelted there as wood and charcoal could be easily obtained from the Ligurian mountains. Pliny complains (117): "The effect of the shortage of fuel on the roasting operation is particularly noticeable in Gaul, where the second roasting is carried out with charcoal instead of wood" and he also comments on the shortage of fuel for the Campanian metallurgists (118). Modern metallurgical engineers such as Mr. L. U. Salkield of the Tio Rinto Mines supplied us with a fairly accurate estimate of the fuel consumption of ancient smelting activities by their study of the slags and other remains of such smelting sites. In the Rio Tinto region the Romans mined and smelted a chalcopyrite with about 8% of copper by means of a complicated chain of roastings, smeltings and refining to be discussed when we deal with the story of copper. The fuel requirement would be some 71,840 Kcals per kilogram of copper for the roasting processes and a further 132,760 Kcals per kilogram of copper for the smelting and refining. This would imply that for every kilogram of copper 21,8 kilograms of wood was needed for the roasting and another 68.5 kilograms of wood for the smelting (one third of which in the form of wood, two thirds in the form of charcoal, 5 parts of wood having the same calorific value as one part of charcoal), hence a total of 90.2 kilograms of wood.

Tests at Rio Tinto have shown that the average rate of growth of oak trees in 40 years is some 300 kilograms (max. 781) of wood suitable for charcoal and some 75 kilos of small branches (max. 156) that might serve for roasting. The climate was wetter in Roman times and assuming 900 kilograms per tree and 125 trees per acre, some 112.5 tons of wood would be produced per acre every 40 years. For the production of one Ton of metallic coper at least 0.8 acre of wood would have to be cut down and an annual production of a ton of copper a day would absorb the fuel grown in the form of wood of some 12,000 acres (40 square kilometers). For silver smelting, Salkield calculated, some 1.5 acre of forest needed to produce 50 Tons of silver slag as found in the large dumps on the spot. These figures show that the production of silver from jarositic material at Rio Tinto and the later smelting of copper pyrites by the Romans must have been limited by the availability of fuel, as the natural supplies of ore were abundant and have even gone to supply many decades of modern industrial mining and smelting activities. There is therefore some truth in the statement that the rising industries, notably metallurgy, had something to do with the deforestation of the Mediterranean.

However, we must remember that the industrial and domestic use of wood and charcoal was still very small as compared with modern fuel consumption. Hence the supplies of wood and charcoal seem to have remained ample even if here and there cheap local resources gave out. This simply meant obtaining such fuel from a larger distance and may have added to the fuel bill but it did not yet create the vast difficulties inherent in modern fuel supplies.

We can discuss the types of firewood used by the ancients best when we turn our attention to the manufacture of *charcoal* for most of the ancient texts discuss both. In ancient Egypt charcoal was extensively burned in the eastern desert and the Sinai peninsula. Samples of charcoal have been found in Early Dynastic tombs at Naga el-Deir in a First Dynasty tomb at Saqqarah and in the storerooms of the pyramid temple of Menkaurê. The "charcoal furnace" identified by Petrie at Tell el-'Amarna (119) is very loosely described and looks more like a furnace belonging to a glass factory as the author also states that straw was used in this factory. The Egyptians had a special term for charcoal (120) and a second one which seems to denote "quenched charcoal" (121) such as described by Pliny (122) and considered a superior quality: "It is only when ignited and quenched that charcoal itself acquires its characteristic powers, and only when it seems to have perished that it becomes endowed with greater virtue". The charcoal in Egypt was measured with a special measure (123) also used for milk, and hence some kind of vessel. Theophrastus tells us "that their smiths use the root of the sari grass, for it makes excellent charcoal because the wood is hard" (124). This root of the sari grass is a producer of good hard charcoal, which burns with an intense heat, as does accacia charcoal also used by them. The Egyptian gold-smelters also used chaff and straw, for Strabo tells us (125): "Gold is preferably melted with chaff-fire, because the flame, on account of its softness is suitable to a substance that yields and fuses easily; but the charcoal fire consumes much of it, it overmelts the gold and carries it off as a vapour". The latter statement is certainly not correct.

In ancient Mesopotamia charcoal had already been used as a pigment on prehistoric pottery, and charcoal, "pentû", was a common fuel for the craftsmen. It was manufactured of storax, mulberry, palm or abbas wood and the mountainous regions to the north exported it.

In ancient Palestine charcoal (pehâm) was used by the smith (126), it was transformed into glowing embers (gehâlîm) (127). It was also used in the portable stove or brazier in the King's palace (128) and probably also in the "coal fire" in the court of the High Priest's palace (129). Nothing is to be charred on the Sabbath not even a wick of a lamp, but only when making a knife for circumcision may one cut wood and make charcoal on this day (130). Charcoal was a costly fuel which is compared with pearls in some texts (131).

In ancient Greece charcoal was mentioned already by Homer (132) and burning it was an important trade carried out in kilns. Oak and box wood were avoided if possible. It was the common fuel for industrial furnaces and made in the centuries-old manner of burning logs of wood stacked in conical piles and heaped over with sods or turf. It was easy to regulate the draft and to obtain the desired degree of carbonization which, together with the choice of the wood, determined largely the quality of the product obtained. In zones where timber was rare carbonized peat may have been used either alone or in combination with charcoal as it still was in parts of Jutland down to about 1870 (133).

Pliny has a passage dealing with the suitability of oak for the manufacture of charcoal (134):

"As charcoal it (the broad-leaved oak) only pays to use it in a copper-smith's workshop, because as soon as the bellows stop it dies down and has to be rekindled repeatedly; but it gives out a great quantity of sparks. A better charcoal is obtained from young trees. Piles of freshly-cut sticks are fitted closely together with clay, and the structure is set fire to, and the shell as it hardens is prodded with poles and so discharges its moisture.

The worst kind both for charcoal and for timber is the one called in Greek the "sea-cork" oak, which has a very thick bark and trunk, the latter usually hollow and spongy; and no other variety of oak is so liable to rot, even while it is alive... An additional reason among others for its being disregarded for religious ceremonies is that its charcoal goes out during the course of a sacrifice."

but a long passage by Theophrastus (135) is much more revealing:

"Next we must state in like manner and endeavour to determine the properties of each kind of timber in relation to making fire. The best charcoal is made from the closest wood, such as aria (holm oak) oak, arbustus; for these are the most solid, so that they last longest and are the strongest; wherefore they are used in silver-mines for the smelting of the ore. Worst of the woods mentioned is oak, since it contains most mineral matter, and the wood of older trees is inferior to that of the younger, and for the same reason that of really old trees is specially bad. For it is very dry, wherefore it sputters as it burns; whereas wood for charcoal should contain sap. The best charcoal comes from trees in their prime, and especially from trees which have been topped: for these contain in the right proportion the qualities of closeness, admixture of mineral matter and moisture. Again better charcoal comes from trees in a sunny dry position with a north aspect than from those grown in a shady damp position facing south. Of, ir wood used contains a good deal of moisture, it should be of close texture; for such wood contains more sap. And, for the same reason, that which is of closer texture either from its own natural character or because it was grown in a drier spot is, whatever the kind of tree, better. But different kinds of charcoal are used for different purposes: for some uses men require it to be soft, thus in iron-mines they use that which is made of sweet chestnut when the iron has been already smelted, and in silver-mines they use charcoal of pine-wood: and these kinds are also used by the crafts. Smiths require charcoal of fir rather than of oak: it is indeed not so strong, but it blows up better into a flame, as it is less apt to smoulder: and the flame from these woods is fiercer. In general the flame is fiercer not only from these but from any wood which is of open texture and light, or which is dry: while that from wood which is of close texture or green is more sluggish and dull. The fiercest flame of all is given by brushwood; but charcoal cannot be made from it at all, since it has not the necessary substance.

They cut and require for the charcoal heap straight smooth billets: for they must be laid as close as possible for the smouldering process. When they have covered the kiln, they kindle the heap by degrees, stirring it with poles. Such is the wood required for the charcoal heap.

In general damp wood makes an evil smoke, and for this reason green wood does so: I mean the damp woods which grow in marshy ground, such as plane, willow, abele, black poplar: for even vine-wood when it is damp, gives an evil smoke. So does palm-wood of its own nature, and some have supposed it to give the most evil smoke of all; whence Chaeremon speaks of "veins issuing underground from roots of palm with its malodorous smoke".

Most pungent is the smoke of fig-wood, whether wild or cultivated, and of any tree which has a curdling juice; the reason lies in the sap; when such wood has been barked and soaked in running water and then dried, it gives as little smoke as any other, and sends up a very soft flame, since its natural moisture has also been removed. The cinders and ashes of such wood are also pungent, and especially, those of almond-wood. For the crafts requiring a furnace and for other crafts various woods are serviceable according to circumstances. For kindling fig and olive are best: fig, because it is tough and of open texture, so that it easily catches fire and does not let it through, olive, because it is of close texture and oily."

The details about the conical "meta" or the furnace in which this charcoal is made are given in the passages about the making of pitch (picem coquere) (136) which describes the tar-kilns (pissougein, picaria) (137) used to produce tar from resinous types of wood, the most interesting of which is that by Theophrastus (138) which we cite here:

"This is the manner in which they make pitch by fire (in Macedonia and in Syria): — having prepared a level piece of ground, which they make like a treshing-floor with a slope for the pitch to run towards the middle, and having made it smooth, they cleave the logs and place them in an arrangement like that used by the charcoal-burners, except that there is no pit; but the billets are set upright against one another, so that the pile goes on growing in height according to the number used. And they say that the erection is complete, when the pile is 180 cubits in circumference and fifty, or at most sixty, in height; or again when it is a hundred cubits in circumference and a hundred in height, if the wood happens to be rich in pitch. Having then thus arranged the pile and having covered it in with timber they throw on earth and completely cover it, so that the fire may not by any means show through, for if this happens, the pitch is ruined. Then they kindle the pile where the passage is left, and then, having filled that part up too with the timber and piled on earth, they mount a ladder and watch wherever they see smoke pushing its way out, and keep piling on the earth, so that the fire may not even show itself. And a conduit is prepared for the pitch right through the pile, so that it may flow into a hole about fifteen cubits off, and the pitch as it flows out is now cold to the touch. The pile burns for nearly

two days and nights; for on the second day before sunset it has
burnt itself out and the pile has fallen in; for this occurs if the
pitch is no longer flowing. All this time they keep watch and do
not go to rest, in case the fire should come through; and they
offer sacrifice and keep holiday, praying that the pitch may be
abundant and good. Such is the manner in which the people of
Macedonia make pitch by fire. They say that in Asia in the Syrian
region they do not extract the pitch by cutting out of the tree the
wood containing it, but use fire to the tree itself, applying an
instrument fashioned on purpose with which they set fire to it.
And then, when they have melted out the pitch at one place, they
shift the instrument to another. But they have a limit and indications when to stop, chiefly of course the fact that the pitch ceases
to flow. They also, as was said before use fire to get pitch out of
the terebinth; for the places where this tree grows do not produce
the fire. Such are the facts about resin and pitch."

Pliny in a short passage (139) discusses the making of tar (or pitch)
in ovens and the further treatment of the crude tar:

"In Europe tar is obtained from the torchpine by heating it, and
is used for coating ships tackle and many other purposes. The
wood of the tree is chopped up and put into ovens and heated
by means of a fire packed all round outside. The first liquid that
exudes flows like water down a pipe; in Syria this is called "cedar-
juice", and it is so strong that in Egypt it is used for embalming
the bodies of the dead. The liquor that follows is thicker, and
now produces pitch; this in its turn is collected in copper cauld-
rons and thickened by means of vinegar, as making it coagulate,
and it has been given the name of Bruttian pitch; it is only useful
for casks and similar receptacles, and differs from other pitch by
its viscosity and also by its reddish colour and because it is greasier
than all the rest. It is made from pitch-resin caused to boil by
means of red-hot stones in casks made of strong oak, or, if casks
are not available, by pilling up a heap of billets, as in the process
of making charcoal. It is this pitch which is used for seasoning
wine after being beaten up into a powder like flour, when it has
a rather black colour. The same resin, if rather gently boiled with
water and strained off, become viscous and turns a reddish colour;
this is called "distilled pitch" ("cocta"). For making this the inferior parts of the resin and the bark of the tree are usually set aside.

Another mixing process produced "intoxication resin": the raw flower of resin is picked off the tree with a quantity of thin, short chips of the wood and broken up in a sieve, and then steeped in water heated to boiling. The grease of this that is extracted makes the best quality of resin, and it is rarely obtainable, and only in a few districts of Italy near the Alps. It is suitable for medical use: the doctors boil $^3/_4$ of a gallon of white resin in $1^1/_2$ gallons of rainwater—though others think it pays better to boil it without water over a slow fire for a whole day, and to employ a vessel of white copper, or to boil resin from the turpentine-tree in a flat pan on hot ashes, as they prefer this to other kinds."

In the next three paragraphs Pliny discuses the correct way of tapping resinous trees for resin and "pitch" and during what season billets of wood should be cut to obtain the best pitch by slow combustion in the heaps or furnaces described above.

The tar and pitch thus produced either as a by-product of charcoal-making or as a speciality for certain regions such as the Alpine districts or Northern Italy and Bruttium is used for the "pitching" of wine-vessels and amphorae (picata dolia, picata vase fictilia) (140), for the careening of ships (141) and for the waterproofing of flat roofs and walls "for some localities like Carthage possess no other stone but tufa. It is devoured by the sea spray, crumbled into dust by the wind, and destroyed by the lashing of rain. Walls made of tufa are safeguarded by covering them with pitch, for the stone is attacked even by lime-plaster, and a wit has remarked that the Carthaginians treated their walls with pitch and their wines with lime, for they use the latter substance for tempering new wine" (142). Pitch also served for the manufacture of a lampblack used as pigment by painters (143), for the coating of metal objects to protect them from corrosion (144) and it was used in pharmacy and medicine as well as on the farm.

If the tar and pitch were the products aimed at, the choice fell on resinous types of wood like pine, cypresses, juniper-trees and terebinth-trees. For the production of charcoal there was a wider choice of base materials as illustrated by the passages quotes above.

The members of the *coal* family were known but seldom used on a large scale except locally. This is of course partly due to the fact that the rich coal strata are mostly deeply buried below the earth's surface. Still there were certain outcrops which could easily have been mined. Strangely enough, we have proofs that coal was used far back in pre-

historic times by the mammoth hunters encamping at Ostrava-
Petrkovice (Czechoslovakia) on the left banks of the Oder. The Ostra-
va coal measures come to the surface there quite close to this camp,
and the hunters learnt enough about the properties of this carbonaceous material to prefer it for fuel for their fires to the scanty supply of
pine logs. Pliny (145) does not recognize the *peat* burned by the
inhabitants of the Low Countries and simply states that "the Chaucians
dry the mud collected with their hands more by the wind than by the
sun and therewith warm their limbs stiff of the northern colds".

Certain types of lignite and bituminous earth were also known. Thus
Theophrastus (146) tells us that "there is a stone called spinos, which is
found in mines. If this is cut up and the pieces are piled in a heap, it
burns when exposed to the sun, and it does this all the more if it is
moistened and sprinkled with water". Caley and Richards (147) in
their valuable commentary on this difficult text of Theophrastus argue
very plausibly that this is a kind of natural asphalt or bituminous lignite
identical with the Thracian stone mentioned by several later classical
authors, which is said to be ignited by water and quenched by oil.
Theophrastus here describes for the first time an example of spontane-
ous combustion and does so in a reasonably matter-of-fact manner.
The same treatise refers to other similar substances (148): "Among the
substances that are dug up because they are useful, those known simply
as coals are made of earth, and they are set on fire and burnt like charcoal. They are found in Liguria, where amber also occurs, and in Elis
as one goes by the mountain road to Olympia; and they are actually
used by workers in metals. In the mines at Scaptê Hylê a stone was
once found which was like rotten wood in appearance. Whenever oil
was poured on it, it burnt, but when the oil had been used up, the
stone stopped burning, as if it were itself unaffected. These are roughly
the differences in the stones that burn". Caley and Richards deem it very
probable that Theophrastus here refers first to the lignite or brown
coal which is fairly common in Greece and later on to the well-known
brown fibrous lignite, which in appearance and in other respects very
often closely resembles rotten wood. Lignite of the kind to which he
apparently refers often contains in its natural state as much as 20 per
cent of water. Thus it cannot be readily ignited, though it is combustible when it is properly dried out, and this soon happens if, for
example, it is placed on a bed of glowing coals.

Archaeology has shown that lignite was locally exploited near Aix en
Provence, in the Ruhr and the Sarre districts and near Velem St. Vid

in Hungary, but it never became of prime importance. Theophrastus (149) also mentions that briquettes could be made by pressing together charcoal mixed with pitch and tar, but this was expensive and only used occasionally for the smelting of metals.

In China coal was used at an early date, for Marco Polo found (Book II, Chap. 23): "all over Cathay there is a kind of black stone existing in beds in the mountains, which they (the Chinese) dig out and burn like firewood. If you supply the fire with them at night, you will find them still alight in the morning; and they make such capital fuel that no other is used throughout the country". Ibn Batutta was also struck by this general use of coal in China.

The proper value of coal was not fully appreciated by the Romans, they neglected the out crops of Esterel andClermont-Ferrand (150). We should, however, remember that for many generation the characteristics of the different types of coal were not yet fully appreciated, many of them gave off volatile sulphurous fumes and low-boiling components which were apt to spoil the industrial products heated in kilns and furnaces fired with coal. Coal achieved its prime importance as a fuel only when the manufacture of coke was discovered during the XVIIIth century and the coking properties of the different types of coal appreciated. Still Pliny reports (151) that the so-called Campanian bronze was produced by "additional smelting with coal (carbo!) because of the shortage of wood". Though "carbo" occasionally denotes charcoal, we can be sure that coal is meant here.

However, coal did come into its own in Roman Britain (152). We have seen that coal was used locally in Europe in very early times. Only recently Klima discovered coal-cinders under the younger loess associated with a Bohemian Gravettian industry of Late Palaeolithic date (153). It was also used for a Bronze Age cremation burial in South Wales (154). For some Romans coal still remained a marvel in the third century A.D. Solinus commenting on the perpetual fire in the temple of Minerva at Bath is astonished by this fuel, which "never whitens into ash but as the flame fades turns into rocky balls (coke)."

It is not always easy to determine the real age of old mines. Thus at Benwell near Newcastle-on-Tyne shafts have been found some 40—45 yards apart, sunk at a depth of twelve to fifteen feet in a two-foot coal seam, which have been worked in every direction from the shaft bottom. These were always held to be Roman in the past but careful examination in 1858 failed to uncover any undoubted Roman object. Roman coal was, however, found at Wilderspool by

May, who claimed that "mineral coal was well-known to have been in general use throughout the Roman encampments along the lines of the Walls of Hadrian and Antonine, and elsewhere". At Castlecary considerable quantities of small coal, not more than one cubic inch in size, was found outside the granary walls. At Bar Hill a stratum 6 inches thick covered the bottom of a 6 by 5 feet hole, which therefore contained some 15 cubic feet of coal. These and many more examples show that coal was systematically worked and carted to Roman forts, where it was used in the furnaces of baths, iron-forges and elsewhere from the middle of the second century A.D. onwards. We do not know whether this coal was perhaps mined under military control.

Altogether Webster (156) was able to tabulate 51 sites where coal was found in Roman Britain. Two samples were found in association with cooking ranges, one with corn drying, ten with smithies or metallurgical operations, one with a cremation pyre and three with a hypocaust. Most of the finds probably represented the application of coal for some form of domestic heating. It seems that there were three coal-using areas in Roman Britain:

1. The towns and settlements of Wroxeter, Caerwent, Wilderspool, Tiddington and Heronsburg near Chester used local coal for domestic and industrial purposes.

2. Outlying villas and villages of Gloucestershire, Somerset and Wiltshire used coal for heating hypocausts and for domestic purposes. The chief coal field providing this fuel comprised the easily-worked deposits in Somerset, within the reach of the highly civilised half of Britain. This field was extensively worked and its produced was consumed over a large area, even in the poor villages of the hardly Roman peasants some twenty to thirty miles away from the workings. This phenomenon may be connected with the progressive exhaustion of the natural woods on the chalk uplands from the Bronze Age downwards.

3. The Fens formed a special case, the nearest coal field being that of central England. The absence of forests in the region necessitated supplies of coal being brought by the Roman canal, the Car Dyke, for the drying of corn in the richest corn-growing country of Roman Britain. Possibly coal was brought down by sea from the north too, but for this hypothesis we have no proof.

Only few [instances of the use of petroleum for heating purposes are known, its use in the thermae of Byzantium, discussed on page 85 of Volume I of these series, is a notabable exception to this rule.

4. *Heating the Home*

The first proofs that man used fire in the Old Stone Age to heat his cave and cook his food were found back in 1908 (157) and many more proofs have been found since though the arrangement of these open fires is not always carefully reported. Some of these fires were kept in a hole in the ground, others were enclosed by a line of stones. The basin or pocket holding the fire may often have been formed by the continual elimination of ashes.

As man started to build houses and huts the place of this fire in his enclosed dwelling space became a point of prime importance. This was definitely the case in northern latitudes, where the oldest arrangement with a central fire with a hole in the roof to draw off the smoke did not satisfy in the long run. As the fire was placed on one side or in a corner the ventilation of the room and the outlet for the smoke and combustion gases, the chimney, became important problems (157a).

In the open fire there is a natural draught caused by the uprush of the heated gases drawing in below displaced air. However, in the enclosed hearth, in which stones around the fire protected it from sudden gusts of wind and facilitated its keeping, proper draught had to be induced by other means. The placing of the fuel had much to do with the contour of the *hearth*. Then came a new invention to raise the fuel above the fire-bed and to promote combustion by inducing the draught. This could be achieved by setting stones in the fire and by pilling on the fuel regularly. In the primitive hearths we observe at a late stage these three stones or bosses of mud placed in the fire and also serving as a resting place for the cooking vessels. Next trivet bosses of baked clay fashioned in one piece are found.

Such primitive tripods and andirons were the rude beginnings of the stove and of a proper conquest of the principle of induced draught. Posts around the fire with cross sticks could be used to dry, roast or smoke the foodstuffs collected by the hunters or provided by the farmers.

By placing the fuel in a confined vessel on a tripod over the fire-bed and by piercing holes on the bottom of the vessel a better regulation of the combustion could be achieved, the space below the grate or hearth-stones forming an air-chamber. Here we have the rudiments of the later stove. It must be realised that the open fire heated only by radiation and that even a fire provided with a grate has only about 20% efficiency, that is most of the heat of the fuel escapes in the smoke which has to be drawn off in an enclosed dwelling space. In the case of the stove a 70—80% efficiency is attained.

However the introduction of stoves had to wait for the proper evolution of ventilation and chimneys. In Western Europe stoves are not in common use before 1400. In 1864 E. Harris claimed that chimneys had not been introduced before 1400 but this is not correct, for as we shall see the rudiments of chimneys existed already in the Roman hypocausts. However, it is quite true that the chimney plays no part

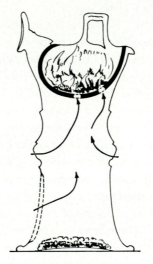

Fig. 2.
Greek portable stove.

in ancient heating devices for the home which for centuries were confined to the hearth, portable hearths and braziers or fire-pots. Heating systems such as we now know are all inventions of the eighteenth and nineteenth centuries. The stove of the Middle Ages was much improved in the days of Franklin. In some regions of Europe warm-air furnaces were in use. Then the early nineteenth century brought the introduction of steam as a heating medium; steam heating systems, notably the two-pipe systems, and hot water heating followed each other in rapid succession, gas and electricity were introduced as domestic fuels.

In the Mediterranean region there was of course little need for heating, and thus these simple heating devices could satisfy mankind for many centuries. Still the heating of larger public buildings and the extension of classical civilisation to northern regions forced the Hellenistic and Roman engineers to devise more efficient means of heating which though discontinued after the fall of the Roman Empire contained many elements which survived and which appear later in other combinations and applications of which the Romans did not yet dream.

Though hearths with wood fires were of course used in Antiquity, charcoal was much more popular. Charcoal marked a great advance on wood, this manufactured smokeless fuel was equivalent to an epoch-making discovery, it evaded the necessity of building a chimney or other ventilating and smoke-dispelling device, though it meant an inroad into the forests. Unless properly treated and selected wood is apt to cause much smoke and soot, and though Neuburger is probably wrong in believing that "atrium" is related to the term "ater" (black) because of the smoky fire which burnt there, we observe that wood was mainly used for industrial purposes and that charcoal was preferred for domestic use.

We will now review the types of hearths in use in the ancient civilisations of the Mediterranean region setting all types of cooking ranges and industrial furnaces apart for later discussion. In Egypt we know that a fire (158) was made and kept alive by fanning, this was probably a charcoal fire. Of old a type of hearth on raised stones was used (159) as shown clearly in the ideogram accompanying this sign for "fire". We also have a late word for "fire" (160) in which the ideogram shows a fire enclosed by a semi-circle of stones, but this type of hearth has something to do with ritual use in the temple for its name is closely related to a term meaning "to burn incense". In the hot climate of Egypt proper ventilation of the house was of more importance than heating. For this purpose the Egyptians used the prototype of the modern "mulquf" or wind-conductor (161) still so common in eastern towns. It was open to the wind and a constant stream passed down the slope of its two arms. The mulqufs of modern Egypt are directed only towards the prevailing north wind and consist of strong framework, to which several planks of wood are nailed, according to the breadth and length proposed; and if required of cheaper materials, the place of planks is taken by reeds or mats, covered with stucco, protected and supported by wooden rafters. Now such crude windmill-fans are supplanted by vents in the ceilings and windcatchers sticking out from the roof or tower to catch the wind (162).

In ancient Palestine we find "a fire on the (raised?) hearth" (eschara, âh, compare the Egyptian 'ḥ for firebowl (163)), the round wood-fire stove (medûrâ) (164), the cooking-fire (kîrájim) (probably a pottery stove on feet, Gr. kydropodes) (165). In towns they used a metal stove (matthékhet) (166) or a cubic pottery stove with two holes in the top suitable for heating and cooking (dâkhôn, Gr. docheion) (167). A brazier or charcoal fire (anthrakia, gumrîn) was also in general use in Hellenistic times, and the same holds true for Mesopotamia, where open fires are seldom reported (168). However, in the early strata, e.g. at Ur hearths were found, "a rough enclosure of broken burnt bricks of the flattened plano-convex type and one with a single fingerhole in the top". Such hearths were probable mainly used for cooking.

We find no special heating devices in ancient Crete or Mycenae and in classical times there were no special devices for heating the home except the usual small portable fires with charcoal, the braziers. Our modern stoves may claim descent from the ancient simple devices for heating a pan over a fire covered in by stones (169). The Greek word "kaminos" (Lat. caminus), originally meaning hearth, soon took the meaning "furnace", still it is at the base of some of our words for (heated) "room" like the German Kemenate and the Russian komnata. There was indeed much less need for heating devices in the Mediterranean region, where the brazier proved sufficient for the few cold days. The modern Italians are said to be more afraid of rain than of cold, and this tallies well with the "pluvius impeditis" in the annals of Caesar. In the north of Europe hearth and open fires were of course generally used, notwithstanding the gruesome pictures drawn by some classical authors, who in their horror of the cold, rainy climate tell us that the Germans had "no shelters against the lasting cold" (170) or "had the habit of hollowing out caves underground and heaping masses of refuse on the top" (171).

The most common means of heating was, therefore, the *brazier*. All open hearths in a town like Pompeii belonged to kitchens or industrial spaces. The same holds good for ancient Rome. The chimney in the Casa di Sallustio belongs to a bakery! Again wood was not smokeless unless specially pretreated and selected and the combustion gases and soot could in cases react with the pigments of the decorated walls and cause damage (172). Braziers were used even after hypocausts had been invented and the Romans of the Po valley and northern Italy had no other means of heating their homes. Winckelmann said (173) that "The rich amongst the ancients were better protected without a stove by means of a brazier than we". One need not follow Krell (174) in all his conclusions but certainly the heat contained in the combustion gases of the charcoal brazier is completely given off to the room. There was no soot or smoke and little danger to health. The ancients of course knew that newly painted or stuccoed houses and braziers could emit poisonous gases (175). We read this in the works of Galenus and other ancient physicians.

The emperor Julian in his Misopogon, a satire on the town of Antiochia, which he wrote in 363 A.D., tells us that at Lutetia (Paris) the rooms were heated with stoves. As he did not like them he slept there without a fire until it became too cold. Then he had a nearly extinguished brazier brought in but "the glowing coals extracted fumes from the walls" and he consulted a doctor who prescribed an emetic. Maybe he suffered of carbon monoxide poisoning, but Krell showed by experiment that if the height of the charcoal layer does not exceed 4"—6" there is little danger of this poisonous gas being formed and the combustion gases contain practically only carbon dioxide and water. We must also remember that the windows and doors of the ancient houses were seldom closed. The brazier was lighted outside, fans helped to make it glow properly before the brazier was brought in. The brazier found in situ in the tepidarium of the baths of the forum at Pompeii has a heating surface of 7'5" by 2'8" which "is evidently quite sufficient to heat even a small Romanesque church in winter time (Krell)". Such braziers could easily be transported from one room into another if need be. Several bronze braziers found at Pompeii have arrangements to combine the heating of the room with that of a kettle of water or other liquids. The regulation of the brazier was perfectly simple. It became dangerous only in small tightly closed spaces (176).

Now the brazier is hardly a classical invention, its story goes back many more centuries. The Egyptian language knew two forms of braziers, the low rectangular basin on a basis or on four feet (177) or the bowl on a high foot or a stand (178) sometimes made of pottery or of copper and silver (?). In ancient Palestine the brazier (mankal, mangal as it is now called) was as important. Charcoal "is material for glowing coals and dry sticks for fire" is the translation given by Sa'adja of a rather obscure passage in the Book of Proverbs (179). The charcoal fire (180) is more often mentioned in connection with the smith, who is therefore often called (pehâmî) after this charcoal (pehâm), but it also forms the fuel of the burning âh in front of which the king sits "in the ninth month in the winterhouse". The Jewish Law declares that "charcoal belongs to the smith like clay to the potter" (181). This brazier was either on a raised hearth or a portable bowl and the "winter house" mentioned above may have been a small, low room as still used in modern Istanbul (182). The charcoal fire (gumrîn) in the atrium of the palace of the High Priest shows that his attendants could not do without it even in the month of April. The Jewish Law speaks of a heated triclinum (183) without further details, but here a portable fire is probably meant and not the type of hearth still commonly seen in the middle of the floor of a peasant's hut in modern Jordan.

The qualities of a good fire were thoroughly appreciated (184). Speaking of the hewing of trees the prophet continues to say: "Then shall it be for a man to burn, for he will take thereof, and warm himself; yea, he kindleth it, and baketh bread; yea, he maketh it a graven image and falleth thereto. He burneth part thereof in the fire, with part thereof he eateth flesh; he roasteth roast, and is satisfied; yes, he warmeth himself, and saith, Aha, I am warm, I have seen the fire". However "the fire shall burn them, they shall not deliver themselves from the power of the flame, there shall not be a coal to warm at, nor fire to sit before it". In ancient Mesopotamia braziers are often mentioned in the texts of all periods (185).

Some of the classical braziers served more purposes than just heating

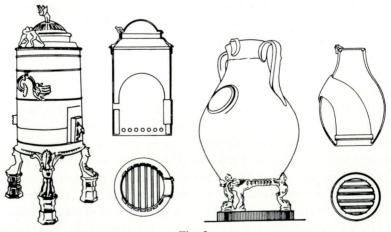

Fig. 3.
Roman vessels for heating liquids, found at Pompeii

the room. At Pompeii a stove was found consisting of a metal cylinder on three legs shaped like lion paws and a stove hole some way up from the bottom. About halfway two apertures masked with lion's heads admit the necessary air. The upper part of the cylinder contains a copper in which water could be heated. Another Pompeiian brazier fitted with a grate could also heat and boil water. The firebox was shaped like a vault and at the back there were small holes for the combustion gases to escape. The bars of the grate consisted of pipes throuh which circulated water to and from the surrounding boiler. The water or wine (calda) could be tapped without coals falling off the brazier. The ashes fell through the bars of the grate on to a tray supported by an artistic tripod.

The origin of our *stoves* is still in the dark (186). The Deutsches Museum at München shows a Greek heating device which looks like a cross between a brazier and a portable stove. In 1884 two Roman pottery furnaces were excavated in the remains of the ancient Nida. One of these, a round furnace had fourteen wide-mouthed pots built into its wall with their mouths giving into the furnace. In 1886 a second one was found and such stoves built up of pots seem the prototype of the later "Kachel" of Central and Eastern Europe.

In the Laws of Liutprand (713—144) the Longobard authorities lay down the wages of stove-builders. Stoves consisting of 250, 500 and 1000 pots are mentioned. The Old German "Khahala" was probably derived from the Latin "caculus, cacobolus", small pot. In older documents it is often translated as "hafan" or (anglosaxon) "cetil" but these words are also used for furnaces. Such were the humble beginnings of the stove, decorated with glazed tiles (the German word Kachel even came to mean glazed tile!) which, as a means of heating the home, came to dominate the Middle Ages in Central Europe, whereas the open fire grate was used more generally in the West. The eighteenth-century inventors and scientists, inspired by experiments on ventilation made by Christopher Wren, Desaguliers and Stephen Hales, had tried to build better stoves, the radiant heat of which was more efficiently spread throughout the space to be heated. Braziers were rather unsuited to the houses and buildings of Western Europe.

Still as late as 1791 the House of Commons was heated by charcoal braziers which rendered the air "pernicious in the extreme". Sir Humphrey Davy advocated a better heating and ventilating system but this was turned down and its execution did not start until 1846. In the meantime new systems of heating were being developed. As early as 1745 a colonel William Cook had used steam as a medium for the distribution of heat. However, John Hoyle of Halifax obtained the first patent for the use of steam to heat greenhouses, churches, etc. Steam was led to the top of the building and then gradually fell through a series of pipes to a tank near the boiler, to which the condensate was returned through a ball-cock. This system was favoured by gardeners. Even spinning factories tried it in 1790 and in 1800 it was definitely introduced in the spinning factory of Tord and Stevenson.

Benjamin Thompson, Count Rumford, was favourably impressed by the results obtained in greenhouses and installed a similar steam heating system in the Great Lecture Room of the Royal Institution in 1801. This was the beginning of the rise of steam-heating systems, of central heating. Rumford introduced it into Germany about 1815. A certain Dr. Alban is known to have heated his Plau (Mecklenburg) factory with low pressure steam about 1830, but houses equipped with central steam-heating systems are seldom found before 1870.

Hot-water heating systems were proposed by Bonnemaine to the Académie des Sciences in 1777, but such a system was not applied until 1819 in two houses in Burlington Arcade. The coppersmith Paalzow demonstrated it at the Industrial Exhibition of Berlin of 1844 and by 1860 the firm of Heckmann was building them for schools and public buildings.

Among the ancestors of modern central heating systems (187) we also count air-heating. The principles of air-heating were propagated by Prof. Meissner at Berlin and München in 1831. The warm-air furnace consisted of a fire-pot and an extended flue. Air passed through the casing, absorbing heat from the hot surface of the fire-pot and flue, and flowing through pipes to various rooms. The air supply could be taken from outside, but in order to save fuel it was usually partially or wholly recirculated from the rooms through a system of return ducts. This air-heating system is not only an ancestor of our modern air-conditioning systems but it was itself a descendant from the stove and from the ancient Roman heating system, the hypocaust.

5. *Roman Hypocausts*

Before comparing the more important theories about the Roman hypocausts (188), selected as representative of a host of publications of the past eighty years, we must survey the bare facts on which such theories were built. The Roman had grasped the principle that it is more efficient to heat the floor of a building than its ceiling and on this principle they based their hypocausts, heating a raised floor from below by means of the combustion gases of a furnace (Gr. hypocausis). (189) Hence Epiphanius (190) gives this definition: "A heating apparatus placed under the building it proposes to heat". As the hypocausts were built to heat a single room, a private house, a bath or public building or even several establishments (e.g. as much as three temples at Carnutum) they were not rigid systens. The Roman engineers, contrary to the belief of some earlier writers on this subject, used varying combinations of all or the majority of the following six elements:

1. The *furnace* (praefurnium, propnigeum) was a vaulted circular or rectangular room often preceded by an open space or depot chamber. It was usually lined with tiles or built with refractory (lava) bricks or even forged iron blocks and it had a stokehole. Often two such furnaces were used, and they sometimes no': only heated buildings but the hot water used there as well, for instance in the villa of Diomedes, the Stabian baths and the baths on the Forum (191).

2. The *flue* or channel, with a width about $^1/_3$ to $^1/_5$th of that of the furnace, led from the furnace (not necessarily from the wall opposite the fire-hole) to the heating chambers. The floor was often made of bricks placed vertically and carefully joined with clay. In cases where more spaces were heated by one furnace or more than one furnace was used we may expect to find two flues.

3. The *heating chambers* proper were built under the main appartments to be heated. The floor inclined slightly towards the centre and thence towards the furnace, probably for proper drainage of condensate. The floor was usually covered with large tiles or slabs, the height of this space varied from 40 to 60 cm.

4. The *pillars* (pilae) built in this space bear the floor of the room or bath to be heated. These pillars were built at intervals of about 30 30 cm. and consist of rectangular tiles or slabs, 15 cm. square and 4—5 cm. high. Vitruv advises joining them with clay mixed with fibrous materials, Palladius prefers horse-hair here. However, many exceptions to this average type have been found, the pillar may be circular, even small masonry vaults have been found (at Linz, Tyrol). Instead of slabs we also find rubble or lumps of granite set in mortar.

5. The actual *suspensura* was the floor built over these pillars. Its lower stratum consisted of large tiles resting on four pillars. On these tiles rested a layer of gravel-cement concrete, posed on a thin layer of cement or clay and covered with a layer of cement on which rested the final marble or mozaic floor. The construction was such, that the floor was impenetrable to gases, heat-proof and solid enough not to crack when properly heated. The name "suspensurae" is given by Seneca and Palladius (192), hence the term "balneae pensiles" for baths heated by hypocausts (193). From this "pensile" the French "poêle" (stove) and the Old High German pfiesal, Low German "Pesel" (heatable room) have been derived.

6. The *piping* varies considerably in the different hypocausts. The combustion gases after leaving the suspensura area must leave by a chimney of some kind. Unfortunately most of the upper structure of the buildings, in which hypocausts were built, has disappeared and many of the heated arguments on the arrangements and management of ancient hypocausts turn on the problem whether these flue gases were led into the open by a chimney or chimneys or whether the piping led them from the suspensura area into the chamber to be heated.

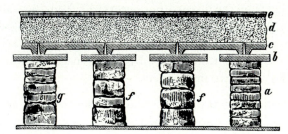

Fig. 4.
The "suspensurae", the pillars under the floor to be heated
(After Blümner)

Vitruv speaks only of a furnace heating the water of the boilers and sending its gases to heat the bath from below. As we shall see, after the turn of our era the Roman engineers were no longer satisfied with such a primitive arrangement and started to use to heat still remaining in the combusion gases after they left the heating chamber. By using large square, hollow bricks, with projections at the ends, called "tegulae mammatae", a hollow channel could be built against the inner wall or even a series of such channels communicating with the heating chamber. These "tegulae mammatae" were no new invention for they had already been used (194) to protect inner walls from humidity, but they had not yet been applied for heating purposes. Many examples of such jacketed walls or walls with projecting channels for hot flue gases have been found in Pompeii and other places. A later and more perfect system consisted in inserting pottery piping in a layer of cement between the rough wall and the lining. The ancient authors speak of "cuniculi" (195), "impressi parietibus tubi" (196) or "tubuli" (197). Seneca speaks of such an arrangement as a recent invention. The hollow-brick channels or the pipes were fastened to the body of the wall by iron clamps placed at intervals. This arrangement permitted a great development of Roman bathing from the simple Greek sweat-bath (laconium) to an elaborately graded system (198).

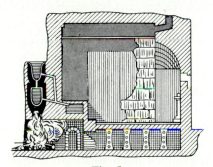

Fig. 5.
Hypocaust of the House of Diomed, Pompeii

However, hypocausts were certainly not confined to baths only nor was the system always as simple as described above. In the sacristy of the church of St. Caecilia, Rome we find a hypocaust containing horizontal pipes running through the heating chamber, the hot air of which seems to have flown into the chambers to be heated, and thus an indirect air-heating system was established. We also find a type of hypocaust, the channeled hypocaust, in which the combustion gases flow through the flue to a small central space from which channels radiate to all sides and heat the large mass of masonry on which the space to be heated rests. An example of such a channeled hypocaust was found at Silchester (199). Sometimes we even find the hypocaust on the first floor, e.g. in the house of the Vestals on the Forum of Rome.

Pliny (200) tells us of hypocausts in his country house at Laurentium and his Ostian villa. Seneca (201) mentions a dining room heated through floor and walls. Epiphanius mentions them in connection with a large meeting room. In fact many hypocausts were found in private and public buildings in northern provinces of the Roman Empire such as Gaul, Britain and the Rhine valley, where the colder climate forced the Romans to heat even living rooms ("diaetarum hypocaustarum") (202) properly.

In certain cases one furnace sent its gases through a series of heating chambers (each built to heat a special room or bath), the communicating channels containing one or more openings which could be closed to regulate the flow of heat. The "tubuli" in certain cases ended in the inner wall and hence the combustion gases finally mingled with the air of the room. In other cases they certainly gave into the open air. Again there are examples where the air used for ventilating the room was drawn in through the hypocaust system and thus this air had to be sucked in over the glowing embers of the fire through the flue and the heating chamber into the living quarters to use up the residual heat in these embers. In other hypocausts the "tubuli" or flue-system must have been inefficient for soot and tar were found in the heating chamber. On the other hand we know for certain that the fire was never in the heating chamber itself.

The fuel used for the hypocausts was either charcoal (or in some cases coal, as we have seen) or wood. In the furnace of the hypocaust of small thermae at Pompeii pitch was found, which certainly served to light the fire-wood. The system worked efficiently and it could be properly regulated at will. Pliny (203) says that the hypocaust of his villa could give up or retain heat at will and Statius (204) speaks of the hour "when the flame languishes and the hypocausts give no more than a feeble heat".

The classical authors agree in naming Sergius Orata, a native of Campania, as the inventor of the hypocaust or rather of the "balnaeae pensiles" (205). Sergius Orata was a wealthy businessman (206), a contemporary of Lucius Crassus the orator (who was consul in 95 B.C.), who lived in the neighbourhood of Baiae on or near the shore of the Lucrine Lake, a stretch of salt water separated from the the Bay of Puteoli by a narrow strip of sand. Here he raised fish in ponds and he seems to have been the first to undertake the artificial cultivation of oysters (207) on a commercial scale, probably in ponds connected with the lake. Primarily because of these experiments Lucrine oysters became famous and his interest in fish gave him his cognomen "gilt-head" (aurata or orata) (208) after the gold marking on the head of the

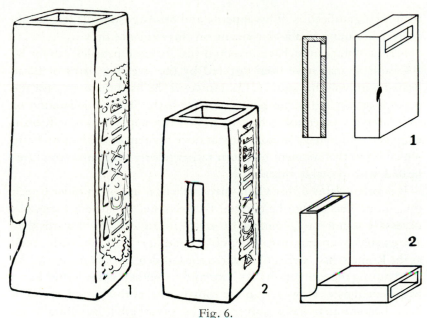

Fig. 6.
Hollow tiles used to build the hypocaust "chimney"
(Left from Saalburg, right from Basle).

(After Kretschmer)

chrysophrys aurata then a very popular fish food, the best variety of which, according to Martial (209) fed on Lucrine oysters.

Apart from his cultivation of fish and oysters Sergius Orata was also well known for his buying and selling of estates. By equipping them with "balneae pensiles" he was able to benefit himself through that invention. His wealth and luxurious way of life became proverbial. He seems to have combined a practical ingenuity, a shrewdness in business dealings and an elegant and luxurious taste. Valerius Maximus discusses him as his first example under the heading "De Luxuria et Libidine" and reports a remark made by Crassus in a case regarding public water rights to the effect that, if he kept away from the Lucrine Lake, Orata would probably find oysters on his roof (210). Cicero (211) mentions that in a certain case Orata was suing because the bill of sale of an estate he had bought had omitted mention of the fact that a third party of parties possessed certain rights in the property. As Orata had owned the land previously, and must have been well aware of this circumstance, he was presumably merely attempting to obtain a rebate. The outcome of this trial was successful for him. Orata's interest in oysters, therefore, stemmed from a desire for material profit rather than for a gratification of his appetite and St. Augustine (212) is hardly correct in calling him a bon-vivant on this evidence only.

Sergius Orata must have invented his "balneae pensiles" about 80 B.C. and he may have been inspired by the sweating baths of Baiae heated with volcanic steam (213). However, he used them only for the heating of fish and oyster ponds, not for baths. Then a generation or two later his invention seems to have been applied by the Roman engineers and to have led to the great development of the Roman bath, which up to that moment had been rather poorly ventilated structures heated with portable braziers.

It is often claimed that Orata made practical use of an older Greek invention. This cannot be correct. Baths existed in ancient Greece as necessary adjuncts to gymnasia. From the fourth century onwards they also existed as separate private or public buildings. Elaborate baths, such as the Romans had, were unknown in the Golden Age of Greece and indeed during the fifth century B.C. we find statements considering warm baths effeminate. However, in the fourth century this custom seems to have become practically universal. The sweatbath ("laconium") had come to stay. Baths (pyeloi) also existed in private houses, usually for the use of women. In the baths the vessel containing the water was usually a basin mounted on a stand; sometimes water is poured from a jug by an attendant over a crouching figure. This occurred even in a women's swimming bath. Douches were also obtained from the water flowing out of the lion's heads which discharged the water from a spring or aqueduct. Developments in Greece differed from those in Rome (214).

Hence both single (215) and collective (216) baths continued to exist but in the fourth century A.D. there is a definite change-over from collective baths to individual bathrooms. This is evident from thermae east of Delphi, Argos and north-east of Epidauros, where the change occurred between 319 A.D. and about 400 A.D. The reason may have been the advent of Christianity and a new sense of prudery and impropriety. The same happened in certain Roman baths fed by medicinal waters. In this case the change may have been a matter of greater ease and freedom, the kind of refinement which allowed a bath to be heated at a temperature which suited a particular client and gave him individual treatment. The hypocaust, not being confined to baths only, developed in other directions. In fact, when the problem was that of heating baths only the Romans sometimes resorted to different means of heating large masses of water. The ingenious heating system used in the caldarium of the Stabian thermae is described in detail by Jacobi:

"The horizontal boiler, made of bronze plates about 0,3″ thick, riveted together, is vaulted at the top and flat at the bottom, which is over the fire-room. Its height in the vertical section is 22″, its width 2′6″ and its length 5′10″. One end of the boiler is closed, the other opens into the front wall of the bath, which is nearly 16′ long, 6′5″ wide and just over 2″ deep. The flat bottom of the boiler lies 6″ below the bottom of the bath, causing the water to circulate freely between bath and boiler."

Together with Overbeck and Mau, Jacobi held that the hot fumes, produced by the furnace passed below the boiler and the stone bath to enter the hollow floor, walls and ceiling of the caldarium and the tepidarium to heat them. Krell violently attacked this opinion on the ground that such heating would destroy the basin and its white marble lining. He held that the boiler was heated by putting glowing charcoal in the fire-space below it, air being sucked from underneath the bath and between the walls into the fire-space in order to be dried and thence streamed into the adjacent fire of the main boiler which was probably heated with wood. This he could not prove but he held that in many cases the excavators destroyed the evidence of the heating and firing process by cleaning the heating chambers during excavation. As we shall see there is no need to believe in such intricate heating processes for the actual temperature in the heating chamber and other parts of the hypocaust were not as high as Krell wants us to believe.

6. *Speculations and Experiments on Hypocausts*

The earlier authors on hypocausts, even if they were engineers, were too much absorbed by the meagre literary evidence on the operation of hypocausts and paid little attention to actual conditions. They were also led astray, because they did not yet realize that a variety of combinations of certain elements were used by the Roman engineers who were masters in choosing the correct combination suitable for a particular case. Hence too much time was wasted in arguing about the universal hypocaust, which did not exist.

Though the texts on hypocausts had of course not been overlooked, interest in them was renewed when by the middle of the nineteenth century the theory of heat and thermodynamics was providing engineers with fundamental methods of comparing heating systems (217). In fact general Morin in a paper read to the Académie des Sciences in November 17, 1871, argued that the system of hypocausts would be very efficient for modern public buildings such as railway-stations. Describing three hypocausts excavated by M. de Roucy near Compiègne in the years 1862 to 1868 he enlarges on the passage in Vistruvius (218) running:

> "The same furnace and heating system will serve for both baths and for their fittings. Three bronze tanks are to be placed above the furnace: one for the cold bath (frigidarium), one for the tepid bath (tepidarium) and one for the hot bath (caldarium). They are so arranged that the hot water which flows from the tepid bath into the hot bath, may be replaced by a like amount of water flowing down from the cold into the tepid bath. The vaulted chambers which contain the basins, are to be heated from the common furnace. The suspensurae of the hot baths are to be made as follows: first the ground is paved with eighteen-inch tiles sloping towards the furnace, so that when a ball is thrown in it does not rest within, but comes back to the furnace room of itself. Thus the flame will more easily spread under the floor. (Now follows a description of the construction of the pilae and the vaulted chambers)."

Morin compared Vitruvius' description with the details of a hypocaust discovered at Uriage (near Grenoble) in 1844, where a bath was supplied with mineral water taken from a well. There was a furnace to heat this water and the only possible way in which the baths themselves could be heated was to lead the combustion gases of the furnace under the bath-tubs. Morin was not quite sure what part the "tubuli" played and he held that they served to recondition and replenish the air in the baths themselves, as he was not aware of their relation to the heating space below the suspensura. He based this reasoning on the passage in Seneca's letters (219) running: "Under the floor of the laconium there was a vault in which the fire was maintained. On all sides, or along the walls and up to the lower part of the vaulting (of the chamber of the laconium) channels built up from several pieces of pottery joined together, or pipes (tubuli) as Procolus calls them, transmit the heat given off by the flame and the vapours". He believed that these tubuli formed a kind of warm-air heating system and referred to the very peculiar system found in the laconium of the church of St. Caecilia at Rome (220) where horizontal pipes against the lower part of the suspensura were heated by the combustion gases. Their hot air was then conducted into vertical tubuli in the walls of the church.

He believed he had traced such pottery tubuli in the Compiègne museum.

Gradually good descriptions of different hypocausts were then published. Winckelmann, who was of the opinion that the Romans had used hypocausts long before the destruction of Pompeii and Herculaneum, described the system used in the Villa Tusculana (Herculaneum) Below the actual floor there was a space born by 24 pillars of bricks bound with clay and about 70 cm. high. This suspensura was executed in rough mozaicwork. Into the hypocaust led a narrow channel, on the other end of which was the praefurnium. The air of the first floor heated the second floor, or as Cato expressed it "in such a way the lower and upper floors are heated heterogeneously". Winckelmann noted that similar systems seemed to exist in baths in Germany (221).

Overbeck (222) gave detailed descriptions of several Pompeiian thermae, one of which we give here:

> "Immediately next to the caldarium is the heating apparatus, connected with a special entrance with the Strada delle Terme, the corridor of the Apodyterium and the dressing-room and a second corridor from the patio in which the fuel was stored. The entire furnace is enclosed by very strong masonry. The round furnace (fornax) (diam. 220) is slightly raised and a masonry channel takes the hot air below the floor of the caldarium and behind its hollow walls.
> The same furnace and stove which heats the caldarium of the men's baths also provided hot air and hot water to the women's bath. In front of the caldarium is the tepidarium, also with a hollow floor, under which the air of the suspensura of the caldarium could spread and this avoided the use of a brazier because of the small dimensions and distance from the furnace.
> The floor is made of mozaic and is carried by small clay pillars (suspensurae) which in turn bear the tiles which bear the mozaic. In the same way the channels in the walls were constructed. Different from other examples (they are perforated by a system of pottery tubes through which the hot air circulated) they form one large tube as 4″ in front of the wall a screen of tiles was built fixed to the wall with iron clamps, a construction which Vitruv calls camarae duplices".

Jacobi (223) gave a good description of the hypocausts of the civilian settlements in front of the Porta Decumana of the Saalburg, one of which we reproduce here:

"The praefurnium, at a distance of 5' from the building, was sunk some 2'8" in the ground, it was 4'8" long and 4'4" wide. Two steps 11" high led down to it. On the opposite side the stokehole bulges 14" high and 8" wide. Behind it are two elliptical bulges shaped like baking ovens. One is outside the building and covered with large lumps of basalt and earth. In this "snorehole" the charcoal was piled up and set afire. Thus the pillars (of the suspensura) were protected from direct contact with the fire, hot combustion gases alone being allowed to spread. The bottom of the fire-chamber ascends slowly from the stoke-hole to flues in the opposite wall. The hypocaust proper showed six rows of eight pillars 2'6" high. A group of nine at the north end were obviously made of pipes instead of bricks and filled with fragments of bricks and mortar. The pillars, standing some 10"—14" apart, were connected at the top by slabs 20"—24" square and 2" high. Their surface was generally grooved to offer a firm grip to the plaster of the floor above. A hole 20" square gave access to the hypocaust. It was closed with a slab of sandstone lifted by means of a stick and rope fastened in a hole in the centre.

A tube ran all the way round and showed a different cross-section from that of the spaces between the pillars. Seven pipes sheathed in tiles ascended from this tube. Five of these were $5^1/_2$" square, the two in the back corners measured $5^1/_2 \times 10$". These rose slightly above the level of the floor and admitted the hot combustion gases directly into the living room. A tongue divided the flue in the wall into two shafts. It seems to have continued as far as the roof and perhaps further up. Six convex tiles on the back wall formed the true flue, being opposite to the fire-hole. The double flue served especially for ventilation, removing foul and stale air from the room".

Jacobi believed that after the fire had gone out, the heat accumulated in the central hypocaust could be admitted directly into the appartment by means of slides in the pipes described above, cold air being sucked in through the fire-hole. This system would have a better heat transmission than radiation through the floor and walls only, though the pipes may have become very hot. Hypocausts seemed expensive but allowed more uniform heating of the floors and a better regulation of the temperature. In general he found his excavations to tally well with the description of hypocausts given by Vitruv.

Remains of hypocausts were found in many other countries such as Great Britain, where they had been described as early as 1733 (224) and in Africa (225). The archaeologists were rather confused by the variants they found, though they agreed that the space under the suspensura never carried a fire and that the tubuli were in some form of communication with the furnace and were an extension of the central heating system. By now specialists like Berger and Krell entered the fray. Krell (226) proposed a totally new theory of the hypocaust. He held that it was by no means certain that hypocausts were always meant to be heating systems. He admitted that there existed contrivances of this type but such hypocausts were used only for heating small spaces and one hypocaust was needed for each room to be heated, the floor of the suspensura transmitting no heat, which was conducted into the room through the system of tubuli. In such cases the fuances were fired with charcoal only.

His main thesis was that the pillars were built of limestone and plaster and were not fire-proof at all, the floor of such thickness that it was entirely impenetrable to a fire kindled underneath, which would crack and spoil it. Nor were traces of soot and ashes found in the heating spaces. Krell therefore held that the arrangements hitherto held to be hypocausts had served for drying the structure after it was built. The actual heating of the rooms was done with braziers, on which Krell collected many useful data, but the importance of which he overestimated. "The thermae of the Forum of Stabiae, as usually admitted, were heated exclusively with charcoal braziers for about one century until the introduction of the "floating floor" about 5 A.D.".

"If not with the frequency often assumed and certainly not in the Stabian baths, there were certain Roman hypocausts which fit the description given by Vitruv" and "the Pompeiian baths were never heated with hypocausts". His conclusion was that both rooms and baths were heated in Antiquity with braziers, which gave no soot, no smoke and were no danger to health. There was no hypocaust heating of floors and walls in the Pompeiian thermae. Nowhere were the channels in the walls or ceilings used to heat interior spaces, they served only in drying the walls as Vitruv informs us.

Krell's views were discussed and rejected by Anthes, Brauweiler and many others. Fusch (227) contributed many new arguments. He correctly concluded from the existing evidence that Sergius Orata had invented the "suspensura" but had only built hypocausts to heat stone bath tubs. Later the heating of the baths was extended to include the heating of entire rooms and buildings. It is wrong to base one's conclusions only on the thermae in the Forum of Pompeii, the Stabian baths and those of Caracalla which belong to the oldest types of hypocausts. Of course in certain cases hypocausts really served to dry buildings, but it is pointed out that Vitruv never mentions "suspensurae" in this connection and if the tubuli served as such, why was no direct connection between them and the furnace established? The Roman authors agree that there were different variants of hypocausts: heating floors, heating floors and walls together and warm-air heating systems.

Vitruv (238) giving details on the use of "tegulae mamatae" applies them to wet walls and such walls on which the condensation of water vapours might spoil the decoration. He does not refer to any application of such tubuli for heating systems. The argument used by Krell for such warm-air heating can be traced back to de Sicci's book on the installations in the thermae of Titus at Rome, but it is highly doubtful whether these were Roman. Such tubuli are first mentioned by Seneca in his letter to Lucilius, in which he seems to suggest that they had been only recently invented, to make an even more efficient use of the heat than by means of suspensurae alone.

Archaeology had by then proved that many private buildings were heated by hypocausts. In one of his letters (230) Pliny the Younger describes his new villa near Laurentum to his friend Gallus. Here he speaks of "passing into a bed-chamber through a passage, which, having a floating floor over a stove which runs underneath, and pipes in the walls, tempers the heat which it received and conveys it to the adjacent rooms". In the baths attached to this villa he has an "annointing room", the furnace adjoining, and the boiler room; and then come other little bathing-rooms, the frigidarium and a calidarium. He also had a small detached building erected with a "winter-room" and a bedchamber; "annexed, is a small stove-room, which, by opening a little window, warms the bedchamber to the degree of heat required".

In a letter to Domitius Apollinaris Pliny (231) speaks of his "dining-room" which is "extremely warm in winter, being much exposed to the sun, and in a cloudy day the hot air from an adjoining stove (hypocaust) very well supplies his absence".

In such private buildings the rooms seem to have had "fenestrae angustae" to admit hot air from the hypocaust into the room and also for admitting air into the hypocaust beyond the furnace. There is plenty evidence that such a system was more common than previously believed (231). Fusch agrees with Overbeck, Mau, Nissen and Jacobi that women's baths were heated and notes that the absence of soot in the hypocaust is a regular feature of Roman remains in the north too. Winckelmann made a mistake when he believed that there were separate entrances for combustion gases and fresh air in the bath of the villa of Diomedes, Roman ventilation methods were quite different. The tegulae mamatae are not always, indeed seldom, connected with the rooms, they are placed against the walls or built into the walls for insulation.

Vetter (232) agrees with Fusch: he too considers the tubuli or the channels, constructed of tegulae mamatae fixed with iron clamps to the walls, to be heating elements. In a few cases only hot air can be admitted directly into the room by means of stones, closing holes in the floor, which could be opened when the coals were no longer glowing.

Vetter agreed with Badermann (233) that some kind of chimney was needed as an exhaust for the combustion gases circulating in the suspensura. In the houses of the poor and the large appartment houses the piping in the wall could be used as such and even, if connected with the rooms, for ventilation too. In the houses of the rich, both in Italy and in other parts of the Roman Empire, this problem must have been solved properly. A system of pipe or channel heating, consisting of a series of channels between the furnace and the chimney, distributing the heat to walls and floors, must have been evolved from the hypocausts for cases where it was not necessary to heat the entire floor, especially in living rooms, where the excessive heat of the "caldarium" or "laconium" was not wanted. Such a system existed in the frontier tower at Saalburg. Here, as in other such installations, hot air could be directly admitted into the room.

It was gradually admitted that hypocausts could only be compared and discussed by giving comparative figures on different types. There were as yet no data on the relation between fuel consumption and the type of hypocaust. Nor was a solution given for the problem ot why they had spread all over the Roman Empire and continued in use until the ninth century but disappeared afterwards.

No less than six hypocausts were discovered in the excavations of Roman Bavai (234) only one of which can be said to have heated a bath-house; the others seem to have belonged to private establishments or houses. A Swiss hypocaust, found near Chur (235) heated a floor surface of 290×260 cm. and the gases were carried by a flue to a further space to be heated. The villa to which it belonged was proved by coins to have been destroyed together with the entire settlement during the reign of the emperor Valens (364—378 A.D.). In Germania very different types of hypocaust had been found. Hettner (236) had described in detail the thermae of St. Barbara and those of the Imperial Palace at Trier, dating from 286—388 A.D. In the latter building the praefurnium is a 2.50 m. high corridor running under the entire building, in which the slave stokers (fornicatores) worked. From this corridor the different furnaces were fired and tended, several of which provided combustion gases for circulation under suspensurae, which were found even under the 10 × 20 m. frigidarium. Further south on the Rhine the Roman thermae were gradually adopted by the native population and after 200 A.D. they formed part of the plan of new settlements (237). Here too in this rough northern climate the Romans introduced the thermae including the "apodyterium (undressing room), frigidarium and piscina (cold water baths), tepidarium (hot air bath) and caldarium with piscina and alveus (hot water baths with tubs and basins) to which a laconium or sudatorium (sweating room)" was sometimes added. At Cannstatt, Rottweil and other places the typical hypocaust with suspensurae were found, the pilae being the usual height of 45—70 cm. except at Rottweil where 122 cm. high sandstone pillars were used. The fuel used was charcoal or wood, in one case peat seems to have been used (Ummendorf). Tubuli placed along the inner walls reached into the heating chamber below. Some of these opened into the room, most did not reach the roof and can hardly have served as good chimneys. In certain cases, they had no contact with the lower heating chamber and must have served as insulation for the walls and not as chimneys.

However, the proof of the pudding is in the eating. Only recently have trials been conducted in a Roman hypocaust and proper measurements have been taken to furnish data on the operation of such hypocausts (238). Kretschmer showed beyond doubt, that we should forget such data on draught, fuel consumption, gas temperatures, etc. as are usually associated with modern central heating systems, because the Romans worked under quite different and more primitive conditions, which nevertheless proved very satisfactory. The experiments conducted during the years 1951 and 1952 were focussed on hypocausts with "pensiles" only, such as are typical in private houses, and on hypocausts with tubuli built into the walls, such as we find in baths with very few exceptions. These experiments were conducted in the hypocaust in the north-west corner of the principia of the Saalburg. The room to be heated measured 5 × 4 m., it was some 3 m. high; the floor, some 20 cm. thick, rested on pillars 60 cm., high. This part of the Saalburg had been carefully and correctly rebuilt. The walls contained ten vertical channels of tubuli leading up to the roof, but this was incorrect for the Roman "chimneys" probably gave into the outer air at ceiling height (Fig. 7).

The furnace was heated with charcoal or wood. Only 1 kgr. of charcoal per hour was needed to heat a room of 60 cubic m. As the furnace had no grate the fuel could be burned only with air impinging on the fuel, and only here were temperatures over 150° C ever measured and for this reason the Romans had used fire-proof tiles or bricks on the floors and walls of such furnaces. In the larger baths of Rome, where entire tree-trunks were burned, higher temperatures up to 800° C could be expected in parts. Many praefurniae were extended into the heating chambers by thin of walls or tongues, which promoted the penetration of these gases to the centre of the hypocaust and even distribution to the chimneys.

Vitruv's description is given of the "laterculi bessales" and "lateres bipedales" for the hypocausts in the larger Roman baths with their higher temperatures, which required fire-proof constructions. In other hypocausts with lower temperatures they were not needed; pillars of basalt, sandstone and limestone or even tufa from local quarries would do. Tubuli were very suitable for the purpose. The older construction with a series of tiles was then replaced by the one large top-slab, which had to absorb the relatively low temperature stresses. They also protected the suspensura from direct overheating and this "concrete" floor could easily take the stresses caused by heating without forming an appreciable amount of cracks.

The ancient chimneys were not only exists for smoke gases, they were also heating elements. No hypocaust would work with a single chimney, there would be at least four, one in each corner, all needed for proper heat transfer and convection. Most of these chimneys were built from tubuli, never against the outer surface of the wall but on its inner side, either built in or protruding into the room. No ancient houses have survived with complete chimneys, but none of the ancient pictures of houses show a chimney protruding from the roof and a watertight connection between this chimney and the roof tiles would have been difficult to achieve. As very little draught was

needed to make the hypocaust work, a simple side-opening in the
wall at ceiling height would be sufficient for the draught needed in
the chimney.

The necessary draught in the hypocaust system proved surprisingly

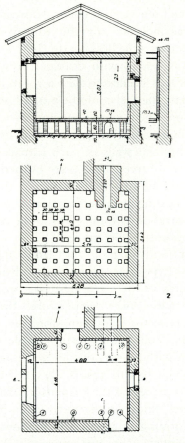

Fig. 7.
The Saalburg hypocaust used by Kretschmer in his experiments.

low. However, no draught was needed to force the air through a
grate bearing a layer of coal, very little was needed to force the combustion gases through the pillared heating chamber, a total of 0.2 mm
water pressure proving sufficient. With all due reserve and supposing
that the "chimneys" gave into the upper air at a maximum height of
6—8 m. above the floor, a pressure difference of $1^1/_2$ to 2 mm. water
pressure would be sufficient to work the system. This was easily

achieved. In Roman baths for the capital and its masses much higher temperatures prevailed. Seneca (239) complained that the water was hot enough to boil a criminal slave. Large tree-trunks burned like a funeral pyre (240) and Martial could exclaim "it is eleven o'clock, the hour of the bath, then the thermae of Nero send forth masses of smoke" (241). This stands in contrast with the statement of Statius (242) "ubi languidus ignis inerrat et tenuem volvunt hypocausta vaporum", which holds good for the Saalburg hypocaust. The heat content of most of the hypocausts is higher than would be needed for a room of equal floor space and a ceiling height of about 3 m.

Fire is an interplay between fuel and oxygen of the air, each per cent. of oxygen consumed giving one per cent. of carbon dioxide after combustion. In our modern central heating systems we usually give the double or triple amount of air needed for the oxidation of the carbon (coal or oil), which brings the carbon dioxide content up to 7—12%. This air surplus is directly related to the temperature attained and the heat efficiency for the surplus air has to be heated too. In our modern grate-fires the air is the primary fuel, its intimate contact with the coal makes it burn as much coal as possible for the oxygen available and temperatures rise to 1000° C. In the ancient open fires in which the air flowed over the fuel, the carbon burnt as far as it could by reaching for air with which the contact was none too good, hence the temperatures were seldom over 150° C in the combustion gases and the air surplus might be tenfold or more.

In Kretschmer's experiments the charcoal was fired and with an outdoor temperature of 0° C a room temperature of 22° C was reached within 36 hours and kept constant by burning about 25 kgr. of charcoal a day. The fire-hole was kept closed with a piece of sheet iron but even then the combustion gases in the praefurnium contained seldom more than 2—3% of carbon dioxide, which points to a tenfold air surplus and the temperatures between the pillars of the suspensura seldom rose over 80° C. The floor temperature was evenly 25—35° C. Along the chimneys the wall seldom attained a temperature of 30° C. but usually the walls were slightly below room temperature.

The fire also needed no more attention than four visits a day and could easily be kept burning all through the winter. Hence with an "ignis languidus" as described by Statius one could obtain a modestly heated room in which one could walk with bare feet without burning them. The Roman engineers must have learnt in practice to harmonize all factors of importance such as the heating area, velocities, draught and temperatures with the air surplus needed for a wood or charcoal fire and still they attained efficiency. The temperature in the heated room proved very homogeneous, there were few convection currents and no draught.

The suspensurae took up about 30% of the heat of the combustion gases by radiation and another 15% by convection, which lowered the temperature of the gases from 60 to 40° C. After the hypocaust the temperature fell to 20° C and therefore there was another 45% of the heat available if the chimney losses are taken to be 10%. This heat was made available by passing the gases through the tubuli which were covered only with a thin layer of stucco and transmitted an appreciable amount of heat. Hence the Roman architects made them protrude from the walls. If these "chimneys" were built into the walls, the radiation losses to the exterior would thus be compensated. Actually in the Saalburg the loss of heat through the exhaust gases was only 7% as compared with the usual 12% in modern systems. We know from Seneca's letters (243) that such tubuli came into use about 70—80 A.D.

Kretschmer then surveyed the history of the hypocaust and reached the following conclusions. About 80 B.C. Sergius Orata built the first hypocaust to heat the basins in which he cultivated fish and oysters. A few decades later the word "hypocaustum" appears in literature; it can hardly be a Greek invention, as some claim. In the first century A.D. hypocausts are applied to baths but not yet to houses and "tubuli" are not yet mentioned. Some 50 years after Vitruv's time really hot baths and sweating-baths are developed. This is the situation when Pompeii and Herculaneum were buried under lava, and it coincided with the introduction of window-panes mentioned by Seneca (244). Hypocausts then also begin to appear in private houses.

About the same time an extensive building of hypocausts starts north of the Alps. During the first century such baths have the arrangements mentioned by Vitruv, only suspensurae and no tubuli. Then the combination of suspensurae and tubuli begin to appear here too as well as living rooms heated by suspensurae only, for in the north heating rooms was much more imperative than in the south. There indeed even hot baths were a luxury and heating the rooms was mostly unnecessary. We can put this story in table-form:

80 B.C.	Sergius Orata invents hypocaust
0 A.D.	
50 A.D.	Baths with suspensurae but no tubuli
100 A.D.	
150 A.D.	Baths with suspensurae and tubuli
200 A.D.	
250 A.D.	Heated rooms without tubuli
300 A.D.	

Channeled hypocausts were found in the Limes areas only, mostly in cheap military buildings. They may represent progress in hypocaust heating but this can be decided by a practical test only. Such channeled hypocausts had a smaller heating surface and hence lower maintaining costs. Whether the residual heat was here efficiently used remains to be decided. This was certainly not the case in smaller buildings but it held true for large baths and public buildings. We should also remember that in the north the poor lived in their cellars in winter and only the rich could afford hypocausts probably built by local engineers. These hypocausts were of course adapted to the climate and tend to have certain elements in common only with the hypocausts of Republican times. The hypocaust tested in the Saalburg is a hundred years younger than the one Pliny mentions.

Sometimes we find hypocausts in series, which are not mentioned by the classical authors, but which are surely part of the evolution of the hypocaust. We have no idea how they were regulated and operated. Possibly the extra heat content of the combustion gases was led off and introduced into the rooms or sent into the open air through chimneys from the back of the hypocaust by means of slides, the "angusta fenestra" mentioned by Pliny. This too should be decided by proper experiments. Upto now we have no proof that any such system was ever used north of the Alps, it seems a refinement of the hypocausts in a few villas of the rich around Rome.

Another point that remained to be settled was whether tubuli had ever been used intentionally north of the Alps to heat private or public buildings in conjunction with the suspensura as they were in the unfinished thermae of Pompeii. It seems that there were definitely such wall-heating systems in Lauriacum and Carnutum in the Eastern Alps and another such an example was recently studied by Kretschmer (245). The Aula Palatina of Trier had a floor heating system but during reparation to the walls of this building, which is now a church, a tubuli-system was discovered connected with this hypocaust. This basilika is over 56 m. high but the tubuli do not reach above 8 m. and seem to have ended in chimneys conducted through the wall and probably protected against wind blowing back into the tubuli and creating a counter-pressure.

Here again we must remember that the ancient hypocausts worked with a "languishing fire" (246) and therefore under conditions very different from modern central heating systems. Taking into account his figures from the Saalburg hypocaust and his experimental data from measurements in this Aula Kretschmer arrives at the following conclusions: About 77% of the heat of the combustion gases is conducted into the Aula through the floor, 23% through the tubuli if we work with a sevenfold air surplus in the furnace, which yields about 2.5% of carbon dioxide in the combustion gases. Further calculations show that provided the space to be heated is not higher than 16 m., floor-heating alone would be quite sufficient. This is the case in most of the thermae. Here, however, in a very high building supplementary heating has to be installed, though the tubuli need not go to the very ceiling as in the case of the thermae where they help to prevent condensation of water vapours on the walls. In the case of the Aula the tubuli are real heating units which form part of the entire hypocaust system.

The fuel consumption for the five praefurniae of the Aula could be set at 130 kgr. of wood per hour, which means that a load of some 16 m³ of wood would have to be supplied to the Aula every two days. The draught in the entire system needed slightly over 1 mm. of water-pressure to work efficiently. The heating-chamber consisted of three divisions, and probably only part of it was used when the weather was mild. The existence of tubuli explains why the elegant light top-structure of the Aula does not reach down much further than one third of the height of the walls. Further down the structure had to be very solid to include the tubuli essential for heating this high hall. At Enns (Lauriacum) we even find tubuli heating by itself, the architects have here dispensed altogether with floor heating.

The few examples of this combined heating chamber/tubuli system, which have been properly described or studied, show that this form of heating was still used here and there up to the eleventh century. It was then forgotten for a long time until the Mechanics Magazine of 1825/26 published accounts of similar Chinese heating systems and it was then tried out in different places, and used fairly frequently, e.g. in Viennese hothouses during the early part of the nineteenth century.

We do not know why this ingenious system was discontinued in these regions. Perhaps the special tegulae for the tubuli had to be imported from Italy as they were not made locally. Perhaps the skilled masons and architects, specialized in building hypocausts were no longer available. It remains a fact that information about new installations built after the fall of the Roman Empire remain very scarce. In the biography of Thiadilde, abbess of Freckenhorst (247) we are told that: "Everword persevered until he had built a winter and a summer rectory near the oratorium, a hypocaust, etc.". The monastery of St. Gallen probably had a hypocaust for the oldest plan of 820 mentions a "caminus ad caleficiendum" and an "evaporatio fumis". Some, however, believe that this was the type of hot-air system which was introduced in the early Middle Ages and which achieved popularity under the name of "Steinofen-heizung" (lit. stone-heating-system).

The medieval heating system had a heating chamber in which the combustion gases of a furnace were led through a mass of stones, which were heated to a red heat to burn away all the soot and other contaminations deposited by gases. Then air was admitted into this heating chamber and drawn into the spaces to be heated by means of holes in the floor. Hence this was a hot-air system of heating of a type not favoured by the Romans. Only in the upper floor of a house at Herculaneum such holes have been found (248) and it is still doubtful whether here hot air was sucked in through the praefurnium and hypocaust after the fire was extinguished in order to profit from the heat of the glowing embers or whether this was an arrangement to make the upper floors profit from the hypocaust heating of the lower floors. Such a system has also been suggested by Jacobi (249) for the Kastell Marienfels hypocaust, but this contention is subject to grave doubts. It is certainly not needed in Italy, where one could even heat an open atrium with an open wood-fire on a winter's day (250) and where hypocausts only exist in private houses of the rich and in large public buildings or thermae.

In the light of our present evidence it seems that this medieval hot-air system was indeed derived from the Roman hypocaust, but that it was a Central European variant which was introduced for the heating of monasteries during the ninth to eleventh centuries and which was later also applied to larger public buildings and private

houses. Hence though we can now deny the legend that it was first
introduced by German knights returning from the Crusades we have
few details about its early history and we know little about its efficiency as compared with its ancestor, the Roman hypocaust. During
the later Middle Ages indirect air-heating systems were in use, which
the Romans did not apply and about which we should also like to
hear more.

7. *Fire and Food*

Apart from heating the body and the home the most important
part of fire in human life is its application to the preparation of food,
to cooking and all its variants. We hardly need to stress the fact, that
only through cooking did man become more independent from nature
and the natural products which are immediately digestible in a raw
stage. Through fire he enormously increased the range of foodstuffs,
he was able to vary his diet and subsist during those seasons in which
his principal foods were not too abundantly obtainable. It led him
to experiment with possible new foodstuffs and with new techniques
which might make promising foodstuffs more palatable. We need
not discuss such methods and their gradual development as this
subject belongs to the story of diet (251) rather than to the story of
heating devices with which we are concerned here.

Hough (252) has tabulated the "genesis of cooking devices" and
the "methods of cooking" in the following two tables:

> *Methods of cooking*
>
> Direct heat:
>   Roasting —
>   Open fire.
>   Broche and skewer.
>   Spit.
>   Gridiron.
>   Plank.
>   Reflector (direct and reflected heat).
>
> Indirect heat:
>   Frying —
>   Frying pan.
>   Deep fat.

Baking —
   Hot stones.
   Stone slabs.
   Burying in coals.
   Coating with clay.
   Oven and pit.
   Sand bath.
Boiling and stewing —
   Basket and hot stones.
   Pot.
   Stewpan.
   Chafing dish.
Steaming —
   Steamer.

Dessication in sun:
   By heat —
     Sunning —
       In hot sun.
   By air —
     Electrical.
     Chemical.

Genesis of cooking devices

Roasting and broiling:
   Camp fire.
   Broche and skewer (animal in skin).
   Spit.
   Gridiron.
   Grill.

Frying:
   Flat stone.
   Pan.
   Deep fat vessel.

Baking:
   Flat stone.
   Pottery, stone or iron griddle.
   Vessel with cover.
   Oven —

Hot stones on object.
Clay cover.
Pit oven.
Reflector.
Baker's oven.
Dutch oven.
Oven in range.
Electric oven.
Solar oven.

Boiling, stewing and chafing:
Cooking vessel.
Stones in basket.
Pot over fire.
Pot on range.

Steaming, sunning, electric and chemical:
In can or steaming.
Over boiling water.
Exposure to hot sun.
Above methods by lime and water.

Hough is of course correct in saying that such simple cooking devices as stones or pebbles heated in the hearth before being used to heat vegetable materials and water in leather bags or other "hot-water vessels", grills, sticks and gridirons must be very old, even though they have deluded the ingenuity of archaeologists. We can derive much proof for their existence from the observation of the food habits of primitive peoples all over the earth (253). From these inferences Hough deduces the following synoptic development:

Broiling sticks — gridiron — frying pan or stone — baking dishes — pit oven with alternate layers of food and hot stones — oven — boiling basket — pottery vessel for boiling.

However, it seems unjustified to attach too much importance to such a "logical" development seeing the great variety of food available in different regions of our earth. Generally speaking, the arctic zones yield predominantly animal, the tropical zones predominantly vege-table food and the temperate zones both types, but on the other hand one can never state that any tribe or people is strictly vegetarian, etc. as both types of food play a part of some importance everywhere and hence cooking devices suitable for both types of food have been developed by many peoples. The only thing we can say is that there has been a development in the use of different forms of heat for a variety of specialised ways of preparing food and that each operation entailed the development of certain cooking devices (254).

Therefore after man had learnt to use fire to prepare his food he travelled a long way to learn how to set aside and handle the required amount of fire to cook his food. He learnt to confine fire by a ring of

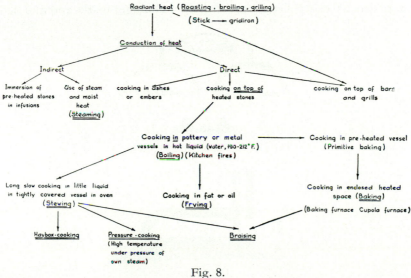

Fig. 8.
The evolution of cooking techniques.

stones, to regulate the draught, etc. using some of the devices which he had developed to warm his home and himself. The open fire in the middle of his dwelling could be shaped and made to heat vessels suspended over it. The Roman cooking-range was hardly more than a stone hearth about the height of our kitchen table and similar to our old-fashioned stone wash-boilers. A fire of charcoal was kept in a recess under the stove and then lit on the top, pans being placed on trivets over the flame (255) but the brazier also played its part in the Roman kitchen. Therefore, it will be better to confine ourselves to a discussion of the heating devices used by the ancient cooks, without trying to trace a genealogical sequence back into prehistoric times when evidence is so extremely poor, as this aspect of prehistoric life hardly ever has the attention of most archaeologists.

We must be prepared to acknowledge that various forms of furnaces and kilns have a much longer history than we are generally prepared to admit. Thus the mammoth hunters belonging to the Gravettian culture, who built a group of three huts at Vestonice (Czechoslovakia), had a hearth in one of the huts which was surrounded by the over-hanging edges of a vaulted structure of the same material as the walls and evidently the base of a beehive-shaped oven or kiln. The floor of this domed kiln was covered with a sooty layer and the inside of the kiln walls was burnt to a reddish colour. The layer of soot contained more dan 200 clay pellets, some of them with finger marks and mingled

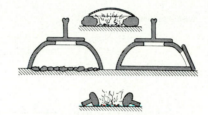

The sâg, the ṭâbûn and the zanṭu.

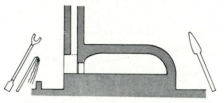

The furn.

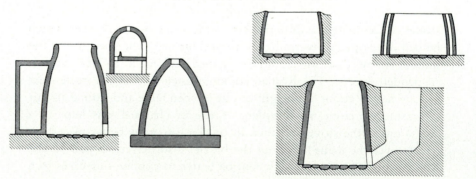

The 'arṣa and five types of the tannûr.

Fig. 9.
The different types of cooking and baking devices of ancient Palestine.

(After Dalman)

with them some fragments of the clay modeller's art. Some have supposed that this was the oldest potter's kiln, but it seems more reasonable
to suppose that it was used as a baking or drying kiln and that the clay
pellets are secondary phenomena.

Again grates appear in early Iron Age settlements in Europe.
Bodewig (256) and Dragendorff found at Oberlahnstein a furnace
of La Tène date which measured about 80 cm. at the bottom and
about 70 cm. in height. Its walls were made of burnt clay as hard as
brick. The vertical cylinder opens towards the top like a chalice.
In the middle there was a central pillar of loam about 60 cm. high
and 35 cm. in diameter with ten arms projecting to the walls of the
furnace. In the wall there was an opening leading to a small fire-
place like the praefurnium of a Roman hypocaust, the combustion
gases of which circulated through the furnace and escaped through
the grate. The large circular surface of this grate could hold several
vessels simultaneously. It cannot have been used for pottery making
but clearly was a cooking range, which was a decided improvement
on the earlier fireplaces and crudely built stone hearths. It belonged
to a larger establishment dating back to the last century B.C. when
Roman influence was penetrating the Nassau district.

Our most complete picture of preclassical baking and cooking devices
comes from ancient Palestine (257) where so many ancient forms
have survived up to the present day (Fig. 9). There are two forms of
"hot-plate", the ṣâǧ and the zantû', both variants of the old device
of cooking or baking by putting the food immediately on a flat stone
supported by three upright stones in or round the fire. The ṣâǧ is a
flat convex round dish about 34 to 50 cm. in diameter and 7 to 8 cm.
high, which is now made of wrought iron, but the form of which
certainly goes back to a pottery ancestor. In the Jewish Law it is
called "maḥabat", which word is usually translated as "pan" or
"frying-pan" in the authorized version (258). It is, however, described
as a flat metal plate in contrast to the later shallow pan-shaped "mar-
ḥešet" used to fry dough in oil. The ancestor of this pan is represented
by the zantû' which is a kind of mushroom-shaped clay disc about
16 cm. in diameter, which is placed above the fire on three stones and
on the surface of which the dough or foodstuff is exposed to the
heat. Pottery ancestors of the present iron forms have been found
in several excavations in Palestine (259). This is the "pan on which
the cake shall be turned" (260). It is also sometimes provided with a
grip and pre-heated in the fire before use.

The third type in use in modern Palestine is the ṭâbûn, a word related to the Arabic taban, Hebrew ṭâman, to hide, as the bread is baked inside the oven but not in contact with ashes. The simplest form is an inverted open dish, some 80 cm. in diameter, about 26 cm. high and with a wall diameter of 3 cm. At the top there is an opening, some 26 cm. in diamter with an 8 cm. flat rim to hold a pottery lid. It is heated from the outside by covering it with dung or other fuel which is set alight. There is also a ṭâbûn with a bottom, which is called "furn". Here the fire is lighted in the inside of the furn and subsequently raked out. Then the cakes of dough are placed against the walls through the top opening and baked either after closing the lid or, when the fire is raked to one side, by leaving the combustion gases to escape through it. This ṭâbûn seems to have come to Palestine after the Arab conquest and in Jewish literature there is nothing comparable to it except the kuppaḥ (261) which like the tâbûn has an "eye" ('ajin) and a "mouth" (pe). This kuppaḥ was probably very much like the small pottery or metal baking furnace which the ancients called klibanos or clibanus (262). However, the klibanos of the New Testament was certainly of the type to be discussed next, it was a tannûr and not a kuppaḥ (263).

The tannûr is the most common form of baking furnace. One type is cylindrical or slightly conical, about 70 to 100 cm. high and 50 to 60 cm. in diameter, partly sunk into the earth. It is the form now common in the Lebanon, Iraq and northern Galilei. The other form is cylindrical or eggshaped, sometimes even pointed or vaulted and in certain cases a large, inverted water-jar is used as a substitute. This tânnûr is the only form of furnace mentioned in the Old Testament (264). The fire is lighted inside the furnace (265) smoke and fire are emitted and make it look like a torch (266); it burns and glows (267).

More precise information about the tannûr is given in the Jewish Law which sets down that its rim shall be a hand's breadth smaller than its largest diameter (268). It shall be above ground (269) and have a "mouth" (270) and an "eye" (271). Its fuel is generally wood (272) or eventually straw, twigs and shrubs or the dregs of pressed olives. The ashes are scraped out with a kind of rake (magrêphâ). The tannûr stood either in the house or in the courtyard. Many such furnaces have been found in excavations in Palestine (273). It was pre-heated before inserting the cakes of dough, but it could also be operated for real baking of bread and for the preparation of other food.

According to Sir Mortimer Wheeler a circular breadoven, 3′8″ in diameter and 3½′ high, was found at Mohenjo-Daro (Indus Valley).

A real baking furnace of the modern type was represented by the 'arṣa or furn which like the classical phournos or furnus was a horizontal cylindrical or round space, upto 300 cm. in diameter and about 50 cm. high. In Jewish Law it is mentioned as purnâ (274) or purnê (275) and its product is pure only when the furn is not transportable but firmly planted on the soil. It was probably introduced in Roman times.

The Egyptian reliefs of the Old Kingdom period (276) show baking and cooking on hot embers, on a straw fire and on flat heated stones- Flat pans of the ṣâǧ type are placed on the glowing embers or supported on stones over the fire. We also find a pottery brazier in use with holes in the bottom to supply the necessary draught air. In Middle Kingdom times (277) we find very often flat braziers and also shallow or deep cooking pans on stone supports. Certain types of cakes are baked in pots heated in a fire and then placed on top of each other with the dough inside. Furnaces of stone slabs are used to support the pots used for cooking, they are a primitive form of the cooking range. The flat pans are denoted by a foreign loan-word (278).

In New Kingdom times (279) we find the tannûr in use for different types of cooking ranges, which vary from a pot on a pottery or masonry support to different forms of braziers. The latter seem most popular for preparing the innumerable forms of bread which the ancient Egyptians knew, for both the baker's furnace (280) and the baker who tends the fire (281) are written with ideograms connected with the brazier or firepot.

Our information on the cooking devices of ancient Mesopotamia (282) is none too detailed. From the texts and the results of excavations we know (282) that kettles or pans were supported on three upright stones in the hearth and that closed roasting furnaces, sometimes equipped with a spit, were available of old. Bread and other foodstuffs were baked in ashes (284) but also in baking furnaces, ancestors of the present tannûr. The most primitive form was a bowl-shaped hole lined with clay or lumps of clay sunk in the centre of the kitchen and containing the fire which was removed from this bowl when one wanted to bake flans or cakes of dough (285). This tinûru, tunûra (Sum. BE, dili-na, im-šu-nigin₂-na, ti-nu-ur, u₂-lal) was definitely the central kitchen stove used for cooking the meat, broiling dates and other kitchen activities. Gradually they developed into the beehive-shaped ovens, already found at Tall-Halâf and Tepe Gawra (periods IX and X) and quite common in later excavations such as that of the palace of Sargon. The modern tannûr of Iraq is some 70 cm. high and 60—70 cm. in diameter. Transportable forms, then called "tinûru mutalliku (Sum. im-šu-nigin₂-na-DUDU), are still in use too.

The second form, the grill, is called laptu (Sum. udun-še-sa-a), of which the texts mention more specialized forms such as the maqlû, maqlûtû (Sum. udun-še-sa-a), the "furnace for roasting corn", the qal-qallu (Sum. nig₂-sa-sa), the grill proper and the kannu (Sum. udun-gub-ba), the furnace to "burn (sesam) oil", the sesam seeds being roasted and then ground to pulp which was subsequently boiled with water to extract the oil.

The open brazier, the "aṣur pênti" (bowl of (glowing) coals" and the smaller variant sometimes called huluppaqqu (Sum. nig₂-tab-tur-ra) was often made of bronze. The more general term is kinûnu (286) and it was used for cooking, broiling and heating, being fired with charcoal (pentû) in contrast to the tannûr which consumed twigs and shrubs from the desert (287) or dung. The brazier was also a transportable fireplace, its fuel being fanned into glowing, its ashed being wiped out. It was mostly a bowl of bronze and later made of iron too. Its weight ran upto 35 kgrs. and some forms stood on a tripod, such as the small brazier, the "ša išâti" which was used to keep the dishes hot on the dinner table. The texts also mentions such tools as pokers, tongs, etc. and specify that it was not only used in cooking, but also to heat the living room and the bathroom if needed. The brazier was indeed in such general use that the term "dead brazier" (288) was used to denote the end of a firm or a family.

Such charcoal braziers continued to be in general use in Mesopotamia and Persia (289) though charcoal became more scarce by the fourteenth century. But even in tenth-century Nishapur the houses had no fire-place but a central hearth enclosed by a rectangular plaster frame about 2¹/₂ feet long and two feet wide raised slightly above the level of the floor. A jar or stone pot is sunk into the centre of the hearth as a brazier to hold the coals. About two feet away an orifice connected with the bottom of the pot by an earthenware pipe supplies the necessary air for the fire to burn properly. Kitchens contained crude stoves or ranges for wood or charcoal consisting merely of two low brick walls between which the open fire was laid and they usually had a well and a drain. Later the krusî or portable brazier came into general use for cooking and heating.

Such primitive devices are still in use in the Near East and in fact in the entire Orient but they do not prevent skilled cooks from preparing the most delicate foods on them. The Greeks and Romans used similar devices and only in a few cases did they devise anything more elaborate. In order to prepare the very popular "caldum", a mixture of honey, wine and water or to heat water or wine they invented more sophisticated combinations of braziers and kettles than the simple kettle suspended over the fire (arenum) or placed on a tripod over the fire (cacabus). These vessels are based on an outer heating mantle or on a circulation of the liquid to be heated through copper tubes which form the grate of a brazier (Fig. 3). Pollux (290) gives us a host of terms for the first type of vessel and Seneca described the heating "serpentes" (291). We have several detailed descriptions of the vessels of this kind excavated at Pompeii and other sites (292).

In the words of Overbeck:

"Like other kinds of coal-pans they consist of a fire-grate or place bordered by a rim, but this rim is double, closed at the top and formed into a groove around which water could run. It is obvious that the water in it was quickly warmed when the brazier was filled with glowing coals and the food placed in dishes on the heated rim was thus kept warm. The heat rising from the brazier may have contributed to the same purpose. At the same time the water could be boiling. This contrivance is shown in all its simplicity in the two drawings. The latter ressembles a little fortress crowned with battlements, a form which was particularly popular as an ornament for chafing dishes. In each of the four corners a crenellated turret rises up covered with a hinged lid. If a lid was opened as seen on one of the turrets on the figure, a vessel with gravy could be placed directly on the hot water, or the water could be drawn from the tap seen to the left".

A combination of brazier and hearth, a semic-circular pan with double walls containing hot water, was also found on which a kettle could be placed for boiling water. The semicircular container is emptied through a tap, and communicates with a barrel-shaped container provided with a hinged lid and a spout in the form of a mask near the brim. There was a spout near the rim for the evacuation of vapour.

8. *Industrial Furnaces*

Turning our attention to the furnaces built especially for technical processes and operation we must prepare for even greater uncertainty. In most cases such furnaces have been loosely identified and described, proper detailed drawings and dimensions are seldom available and only in rare cases have experiments been carried on in such excavated furnaces or models of them and temperatures and other conditions properly measured. But this is a conditio sine qua non if we wish to trace their evolution and obtain a proper standard to judge the skill of ancient craftsmen. For in knowing the tools and apparatus they disposed of and the optimum results they could achieve with them

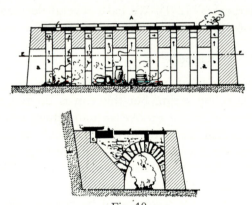

Fig. 10.
Ancient Mesopotamian pottery kiln (Nippur, around 2000 B.C.).

we would be able to judge the efficiency with which they worked and their skill in exploiting all the possibilities of the tools they handled.

There is no doubt that the kitchen was the mother of all technical furnaces. As far as we know man's skill in cooking and preparing food was later applied to the transformation of such natural materials as clays and ores which his ingenuity or accidental discoveries had proved to yield even better materials and objects for his use. There is no doubt that the hearths, braziers and baking furnaces we have discussed have, at a later stage in man's history, been applied to the drying of cereals, etc. and to the manufacture of bricks, pottery, lime, glass and metals, to name but a few products.

No thorough study has been made of the development of the potter's kiln, but its early stages seem to run parallel with the development of cooking devices (293). Unfortunately the archaeological material is too meagre to allow us to classify and specify such furnaces or to describe details. The cuneiform texts designate the utûnu, atûnu (Sum. alum: $NA_4.KU$; alum, udun) as the furnace, which originally used in the kitchen is soon applied by the artisans to roast malt (udun-bappir = furnace to prepare malt-cakes), for the smelting and melting of metals, the baking of tiles and bricks and other industrial purposes. Apart from this general term find find the word kîru, kûru (Sum. di-di.izi; gir_4; KI.NE) used as a furnace by bitumen-workers, glas-workers and smelters of metals. It seems to have been a furnace with two compartiments, the firing chamber and the hearth, the "hot" and the "cold" space of the texts. Later Assyrian forms, notably those for the manufacture of glass and metals have an "eye" from which "the fire issues" and which maintains the proper draft, as well as "holes to insert the bellows". Larger forms bear the name girmahhu (Sum. gir_4-mah). The texts also mention a special smelting furnace, the "kiškittu, kiškattu" and the "naṣrapu, našrapu" (Sum. nig_2-tab), the former probably being the brick-burning furnace and the latter a metallurgical smelter, but unfortunately the texts give too few details to describe them in detail, though various parts are mentioned.

At Sialk (Persia) abundant material was excavated to obtain a clear picture of these stages which could be correlated with those of the pottery found on the spot. There is no doubt that the most primitive form of firing pottery took place in unenclosed fires, that is in the domestic hearth, in stacks of fuel and dried materials piled on the ground or in hollows dug in the soil, similar to the way in which charcoal was obtained. The fuel used was brushwood, grass, straw, reeds or dung and these methods of firing can still be observed with primitive peoples and tribes.

Improvement was only possible by building real kilns or furnaces, enclosed domed spaces (294). In such kilns hearth and firing chamber were separated, the dried wares were subjected to the heat of the combustion gases from the lower chamber and in later models ope-nings in the sides of the firing chamber allowed some regulation of the passage of these gases. Ghirshman found at Sialk that the con-struction of such more permanent kilns modelled on the charcoal burner's "coalpits" or "piles" resulted in a marked improvement of the wares and with the introduction of the true kiln (fig. 10) the baking of small pots became perfect at the turn of "period III". Then, at the beginning of the Sialk "period IV" the true vertical reverberatory furnace is introduced, examples of which have also been found at Susa and Khafaje (Iraq) (fig. 11).

A ceramic factory with at least fourteen potter's kilns, dating from the Uruk and Jemdet Nasr period was found at Ur. Below these circular kilns was a "circular pit 0.90½ m. in diameter and 0.35 m. deep, lined with fire-clay and originally roofed with bricks; holes 0.10 m. in diameter and 0.45 m. apart with a larger one in the centre led the heat from the furnace to the kiln above; channels cut in the soil sloped down to holes in the sides of the furnace to supply the draught. The kiln proper was some 1.30 m. in diameter".

Fig. 11.
Greek potter's kiln.

In Egypt the Old Kingdom pictures show only the first stage, which is called the "burning of the pots", but few details are available from these sources (295). We have an expression in the ancient Egyptian language which may denote this primitive baking of pottery (296). At a later period, during the Middle Kingdom, pictures appear which show a vertical furnace, akin to the tannûr, piled up with fuel from which flames rise (297). This is the t3-furnace mentioned in the texts (298), and which is built of clay or bricks as far as we can see.

The open hearth and camp-fire of the earliest stages hardly allowed the potter to reach a temperature over 700—800° C, but the potter's kiln gave temperatures of 1050—1150° C and Sialk pottery has been shown to have been burnt at such temperatures, whereas Susan pottery must have been burned at about 900—1000° C, probably in the very early and tentative kilns as shown in fig. 10.

As far as we know the Near Eastern kilns remained of a very simple pattern and in the West too the vertical kiln remained dominant until very recent times. However, its proper draught-control, the capital expenditure involved, its restricted capacity and the need for high quality fuel such as billets of wood or charcoal must have exerted an influence on its spread and on the centralisation of the potter's trade. As the standards for pottery rose with the craftsman's skill the essential weakness of the vertical kiln, the limited means of regulating the circulation of the combustion gases must have become. apparent. The horizontal kiln became predominant because here the

Fig. 12.
Glass furnace of the tenth century A.D.
(Reconstruction of furnace described by Theophilus).

hot gases could be directed thus equalizing the temperatures in the kiln.

In Greece as in prehistoric Europe much pottery ware must still have been fired in shallows holes as one finds on the site of many kilns and these methods continued to survive for many centuries, especially when pottery was manufactured for private and local use only. In Greece, however, vertical kilns with permanent domes and side doors for ventilation were in common use. These were the kaminoi (299) and the fornaces (300) of the ancients. Usually only the perforated floor of the firing chamber survived. Sometimes we find that better combustion-gas circulation has been achieved by dividing the fire chamber up into a series of air ducts and in many cases the kiln had a conical form concentrating the circulation of the gases to a top hole, possibly to chimneys of wood which have seldom survived. An interesting find of a potter's workshop with kilns, dating from the Carthaginian period and probably going back to Phoenician examples, has been made in Utica (Tunis).

The majority of these classical pottery furnaces have been found in southern and western Germany, France, England and a few in Italy. They were built of burned or unburnt bricks and sometimes red with cement. A praefurnium gives into the heating space which is usually round and provided with a central pillar or ribs, the ceiling being pierced with a series of holes. On top of this, separated by the floor pierced with holes, is the firing chamber which contains the pottery to be burnt and which bears a few vents which are extended into small chimneys in som cases. The kilns for tiles and bricks are mostly developed from the original stacks of the earliest pottery fires.

In prehistoric Western Europe we also find the earliest horizontal kilns built about 1500 B.C. of stone blocks packed with turf to make them gas-tight. The gases are drawn from a flat hearth into a low, broad baking chamber with a central stone block to support the roof, built of slabs. Baffle-slabs are used in the chamber to regulate the gas currents and to protect the pots from direct contact with the flames. Wooden chimneys have probably been used, but these have not survived. These horizontal kilns were only used during a short period, then they disappear to re-appear again in Roman times, together with the corn-drying kilns, which look very much like the vertical potter's kiln and may have a common ancestry. Horizontal kilns continue to be built during the century, but their superiority to the vertical kiln was only properly realised during the nineteenth century.

Strangely enough, we know little about the evolution of the brick-maker's kiln (300a). Woolley found an unquestionable example of a kiln-fired brick at Ur in an al-Ubaid layer and they were fairly frequently used in later period but no brickmaker's kiln is described in any of the excavation reports. Neither have they been found in the Indus Valley civilisation and Mackay supposes that the bricks were stacked for firing in large heaps with flues in between. The outside of the pile would then be plastered with mud and the fire lighted, e.g. the method used in medieval Europe. In Roman times brick-kilns were frequently built in various places in the Empire.

If we now turn to the *metallurgical furnace* as a representative of another important class of industrial furnaces we find our difficulties multiplied. Not only are data on such furnaces practically absent for many regions in the Ancient Near East, but the abundant if incomplete data from other regions such as prehistoric Europe or present-day Africa show such a welter of types and such a lack of exact description and observation, that there is only one solution. The archaeologist should always call in an expert to identify and measure any type of furnace and no loose identification should be left to trail through excavation reports and publications. Proper identification may mean a total change of interpretation. We need only remind our reader of the fact that an expert like Wyndham Hulme showed that Sir W. Flinders Petrie had not found "smelting furnaces" at Gerar but "military forges", where bar iron was worked and no piece of ore ever smelted.

We get little help from the ancient texts as the various types of furnaces were not yet clearly differentiated in the minds of the craftsmen, who applied the well-known pottery furnace to the melting of metals or to the manufacture of glass as required without modifying and adapting it as much as a modern specialist would tend to do. In metallurgy a period of mould-casting followed the earlier period of working (hammering, etc.) native metal. Hence during an early stage of metallurgy the metalworkers used furnaces which obtained a sufficiently high temperature to *melt* native metals, but they had not yet learnt the art of *smelting* ores! Furnaces such as Speiser found at Tepe Gawra (302) could have melted metals placed in crucibles and thus liquify them for use in mould-casting. Kilns adapted for the smelting of metals of the type found at Uruk (303) came later.

This simple fact that the melting of metals came before the smelting of ores accounts for the fact that so many hearths and brazier-type fires are mentioned in ancient literature in connection with metallurgy. Indeed charcoal fires were used to heat the crucibles in which the metals or alloys were melted. Wainwright (304) has stressed the fact that the Egyptians always depict their smiths as working with crucibles on charcoal fires or hearths and that their reliefs never depict a smelting furnace. Their texts mostly mention a charcoal fire ('ḫ, Coptic "ash") and this word is later loosely identified with the Greek "kaminos" (furnace). Only during the later period of their history do the Egyptians use a special word for the "furnace of the metal-workers" (305), which word is related to a verb meaning "to conquer, subdue". In later Coptic literature different words are used for metallurgical furnaces, some of which are the old baker's or potter's furnaces we have already discussed, others are less specific and mean a bowl-furnace or hearth in a general sense (306).

The ancient Mesopotamian texts show the same picture. Here too we find both the charcoal fire and real furnace in use in metallurgy. The ancient Sumerian sign for smith is simply the "brazier" (SIMUG), which is identical with the "manqal" of modern Iraq. This signifies that at an early stage in Sumerian metallurgy the charcoal fire and crucible melting or smelting was predominant. Later texts mention a smelting furnace called "kîru, kûru" in Accadian (Sumerian KI-NE) though sometimes the more general term "utûnu" is used.

The latter word seems related to the "attûn", the kiln for burning lime and bricks mentioned in the Old Testament (307). The "kûr" mentioned in several passages (308) seems to indicate the "refining furnace" as contrasted to the "kibšan" or smelting furnace (309). A certain amount of specialisation in furnaces has already occurred

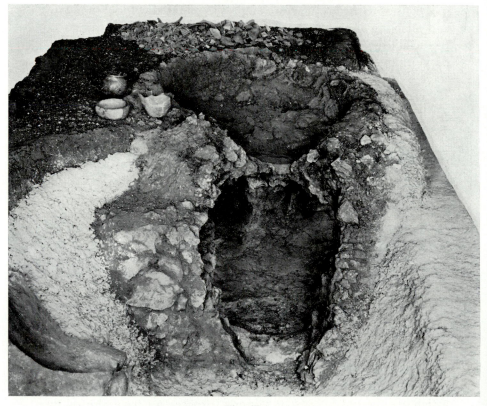

Fig. 13.
Roman pottery kiln.
(Photo Science Museum, London).

in Old Testament times for the Bible also mentions the "tannûr" or baking furnace (310), the potter's furnace (311) and the blacksmith's forge (312).

Hence crucible processes played a dominating role in early metallurgy. The Egyptian sign for "copper" (313) depicts such a crucible, examples of which have been found in the Sinai district and elsewhere and picture of which are shown on several reliefs and mural paintings. These crucibles would seem to have measured about 5″ in diameter and 5″ in height. Sayce found such clay crucibles at Kerma (Sudan) which had been used in iron smelting. Crucibles of the same type have turned up in several excavations in Mesopotamia and in Troy. A lump of stamped silver (dating back to about 700 B.C.) found at Zenjirli still retained the form of the bottom of a crucible. Herodotus tells us that the Persian treasury melted down their silver and gold in crucibles (pithoi) (313). In Palestine such crucibles (âlîl) have been found at Gezer, they are the "fining pots" mentioned in the Bible (314).

There is no doubt that this use of crucibles (or cupels, the special type used in the refining of precious metals) was the result of the evolution of the potter's art and they gave rise to a specific type of metallurgical furnace. Crucibles could be and were used in charcoal fires or open hearths, but as smelting processes were developed crucibles were mainly used for refining operations. The *crucible furnaces* which came into use in later stages of metallurgy were derived from the potter's furnaces. Working in crucibles enabled the metallurgist to carry out processes under conditions which protected the contents of the crucible from direct contact with the combustion gases of the fire and from other impurities which might affect the reactions. As far as we know even the Romans had not yet invented the *muffle furnace* with its fixed heating chamber admitting the introduction of one or more crucibles during the heating. Such furnaces were known to the metallurgists in the days of Agricola and widely used for assaying.

Still the correct method of manufacturing such crucibles was common knowledge in classical times. Pliny (315) informs us that "tasconium (from the Spanish tasco; crucible or cupel) is a white earth like potter's clay, which is the only substance which can endure the combined efforts of the blast, the heat of the fire and the glowing charge of the crucible". The term "kálathos" (316) seems to denote the melting crucible. Some authors claim that the term "periodos" occurs for the smelting crucible of steel manufacturers, but we have found no reference to this word.

We have a certain number of precise data on early and primitive furnaces and metallurgical processes (317), some of which (318) refer to iron manufacture only. Unfortunately they are still too few to enable us to draw up a morphological table of the types of furnace evolved since the beginnings of metallurgy. The attempts made in this direction by Klosemann, Weiershausen and Deichmüller were doomed to failure or they can only be appreciated as a picture of local developments which is liable to be drastically changed when further data from other regions become available. There are, however, certain basic facts which should be kept in mind when describing early furnaces and judging their merits.

A metallurgical furnace always consists of two essential parts: a) the fire-box or furnace in which the fuel is burnt, and b) the hearth in which the actual operation is carried out. In many primive furnaces these two parts are actually one. The main difficulty in the early days consisted in attaining the required temperature. High temperature processes could be achieved only on a small scale as proper materials such as cast-iron bars were not available for grates and fire-bricks of high resistance were unknown. In most processes blast air was used to produce high temperatures, the ancients possessed several means of producing such an artificial draught. We shall deal with these in the next section.

The typology of metallurgical furnaces can be based on the contact between fuel and the mass to be heated. Some furnaces have an intimate contact between the fuel and the ores, slagging compounds, etc. In others the ores are heated by the products of combustion. In the crucibles and crucible furnace processes, which we have just described there is no contact between fuel or combustion gases and the substances to be heated.

When both the fuel and the ores, etc. in are in contact we speak of hearth or shaft furnaces. In the case of shaft furnaces the height is considerably more than the diameter. There are two types. The *shaft furnaces* worked with natural draught usually do not yield very high temperatures, but they can be used for calcining ores, burning lime, etc. They can also be adapted to continuous operation, being fed at the top as the end-product is withdrawn at the other end. Such shaft furnaces are often called *kilns*. If forced draught or blast air is applied to a shaft furnace, we call it a *blast furnace*. Such blast furnaces are used for the smelting of iron, copper and lead. The oldest types had a square section, now they are cylindrical. There is usually a conical bottom forming a well in which the metal collects. At present there are a series of special blast furnaces, each of which is peculiar to a special metallurgical process and each of which bears a special name such as "rapid cupola", "fire-hearth furnace", etc.

In *hearth furnaces* the height is either equal to or less than the diameter. These too can be worked with a forced draught and they are used both for oxidising or reduction processes. Among this type of shaft furnace we find the "liquation hearths", "finery fires" and furnaces for producing lead from galena, wrought iron (by the direct process from ore) or used as smith's hearths.

Furnaces using the combustion gases to heat the ore or metal are called *reverberatory furnaces*. They were quite unknown in ancient times, but now they are very important in roasting, calcining and refining processes.

The crucible processes used in the "melting stage" of metallurgy led up to the use of furnaces (akin to potter's kilns and baking ovens) for heating crucibles with their valuable contents not to be contaminated by gases or soot and grit. The ancients used such furnaces for the refining of gold, for the production of crucible "wootz" steel, etc. They did not yet possess the *muffle furnaces* so dear to the Renaissance assayist and alchemist, nor did they have the modern *retort furnaces* as used in zinc manufacture.

The formation of certain corrosive compounds during the interaction of carbon, ore and slagging compound and the high temperatures reigning in the reaction zone are important factors in the life of a furnace. The ancient smiths had not yet understood this or they were unable to cope with such factors and hence ancient smelting sites show the remains of primitive hearths and kilns by the hundred. Gradually experience showed them how to line the walls of their furnaces with certain stones to combat this corrosion, or even to build the entire furnace with such materials. *Acid* materials such as flint, ganister, sand and fire-clays, *neutral* fire-proof materials such as graphite and chromite or *basic* materials such as limestone, dolomite, magnesite and bauxite can be chosen. The choice depends on the nature of the gangue (mineral impurities) of the ore and should aid the flux to destroy this corrosive factor. Thus an acid, siliceous gangue requires a basic lining of the furnace, which has to be renewed from time to time. In ancient metallurgy this principle was realised fairly early where large quantities of an ore of constant composition were worked. Thus certain types of furnaces smelting iron ores of the type found in Carinthia were developed by the Illyrians and Celts and taken over by the Romans, whose "lip-fires" survived until the puddling process was invented in the eighteenth century. The same good choice of lining materials is found in the bloomery fires of the early Celtic iron-smiths and the Roman shaft furnaces which remained in use even after the development of the Stückofen and the real blast-furnace.

Another complication is the fairly early development of furnaces adapted to special processes. The *"roasting furnace"* is a typical example.

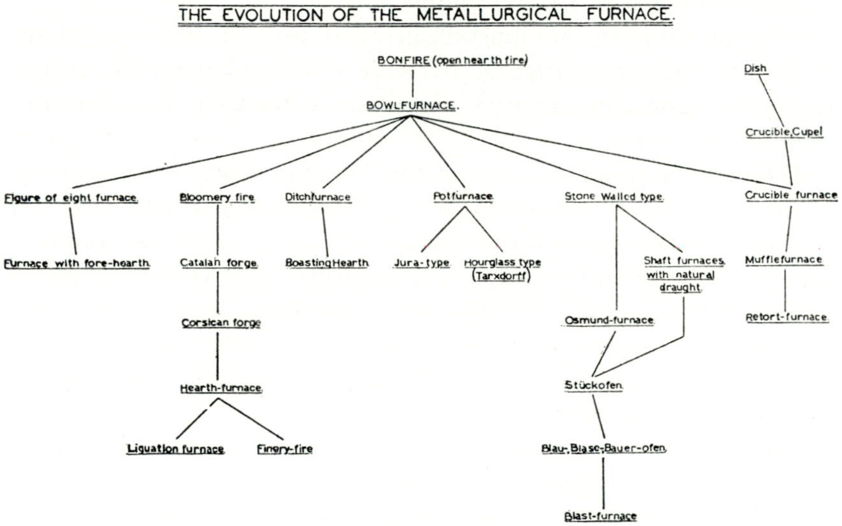

THE EVOLUTION OF THE METALLURGICAL FURNACE.

Fig. 14.
Evolution of the Metallurgical Furnace.

It was used to drive off water and to make the ore more porous for smelting in the case of iron ores. Copper or lead ores were treated in such furnaces to expel the larger part of the sulphur and the arsenic from the ore before smelting. The most primitive roasting or calcining furnaces were simply heaps of ore in fire-wood. Still in prehistoric Mitterberg we find long narrow buildings used for the roasting of the copper ore, in which a bed of slag carried the charcoal on which the ore was heaped. The Romans used either large bowl-shaped hearths (sometimes equipped with tapping channels) or round open-hearths. In Hüttenberg each smelting furnace is equipped with its own roasting furnace.

Notwithstanding this evidence which is sometimes only vague

and in other cases confusing at first sight, we now know that metallurgy was certainly of Near Eastern origin but spread fairly quickly to Europe and Africa. Tentatively we can give the following outline:

The most primitive type of smelting furnace seems to have been the simple *bowl furnace*, well-known to the copper and bronze smiths and further developed by the early iron smiths. It was developed from the bonfire or open-hearth fire, which, however, as Coghlan showed by experiments, does not produce any temperatures over 750° C and hence is unsuited for melting copper for which a temperature of 1085° C is requires. Though the simple reduction of copper ores such as oxides and carbonates requires temperatures of 750—800° C only hearths heating crucibles or bowl furnaces smelting ore were worked with the help of blast air. The bowl furnace is essentially a clay-lined hole in the ground, provided with a tuyère blowing the blast air over the rim on to the contents such as the primitive smiths of Africa still use. They served at Hüttenberg for the smelting of ores which had been roasted in smaller bowl furnaces. In the Ancient Near East it was very common; Hesiod (319) knows it and the Romans used it side by side with more sophisticated types. The Germans smelted their bog-iron in such furnaces for centuries.

This type of furnace wasted all the heat escaping from the zone of combustion and much of the metal formed was lost in the slag. Hence arose the domed or *pot furnace* type, probably inspired by the baker's and potter's ovens. As the neck of the furnace is contracted, it looks like a dug-in pot, blast and tapping holes being provided at the base, but the walls did not yet rise above the ground. In prehistoric Europe we find such furnaces at Lausitz and Silesia. In Tarxdorff a special "hour-glass" type was in use, consiting of two chambers the lower chamber collecting the slag. All over the Roman Empire such pot furnaces were in use.

A more developed type of pot furnace was the *Jura-type* built into the hill-side and already using some of the features of the shaft furnace. It was not only found in eastern France but also in Carinthia. Such furnaces are mostly vertical holes in the hills close to the face of a steep bank, with lateral apertures near the base, to which the wind is admitted through a horizontal channel lined with stone. They were worked with natural draught, even though free-standing furnaces of this type would have been more efficient. Here again we can quote a clear proof, that the evolution of the furnace is a complicated story and hardly bound to any one region. When Cieza de Leon visited

the silver-mining district of Potosi in 1549, two years after the discovery of the silver lode, he found that the Indians

> "therefore, made certain moulds of clay, in the shape of a flower-
> pot in Spain, with many air-holes in all parts. Charcoal was put
> into these moulds, with the metal on top, and they were then
> placed on the part of the hill where the wind blew strongest,
> and thus the metal was extracted, which was then purified and
> refined with a small bellows. In this manner all the metal that
> has been taken from the hill is extracted. The Indians go to the
> heights with the ores to extract the silver, and they call the
> moulds Guayras (huayras). In the night there are so many of them
> on all parts of the hill that it looks like an illumination."

Another type of bowl furnace is the *ditch furnace* mostly used for
roasting and the ancestor of the *roasting hearth*. Further types of bowl
furnace take over characteristics from the baking furnaces. Stone
lining is introduced and part of the furnace is raised overground.
Some of these stone-walled bowl furnaces were covered up after
filling them with ore and fuel. Such furnaces are still in use in Madagascar and they are probably the ancestors of the cupola furnaces
of later date, which look very much like the ancient tannûr of the
Near East.

The stone-lined bowl leads to forms like the *bloomery hearth*, the
ancestor of the later *Catalan forge* and the *Corsican forge* and of the *hearth
furnace* including the liquation hearth and the finery fires.

The raising of the walls over the bowl and adoption of the characteristics of the older pottery furnaces leads to the *shaft-furnace* type
and to the establishment of the fire as distinct from the hearth, which
involves a gradual improvement of the draught and its regulation,
that is a proper manipulation of the smelting process. Primitive forms
of shaft furnaces are the *Osmund furnace* and the "high" and "low" type
of Jura furnace, which we discussed above, both of which could be
worked with natural draught or with bellows.

Doubling the size of the Osmund furnace we get the typical medieval
Stückofen and its varieties, the "Bauer-ofen", "Blau-ofen" and "Blase-
ofen" from which the blast-furnace was evolved. In Antiquity we find
all kinds of shaft furnaces up to primitive types of Stückofen. They are
typical for the coming of iron and many early forms are still employed
by primitive iron-smiths such as the Agaria of Central India which
Elwin described (320):

"The furnace is a cylindrical clay kiln, called kothi or bhatti, $2^1/_2$ feet high, with a circumference of eight feet at the base and five feet at the top. In Mandla it does not stand upright but is tilted backwards on a large stone. At the top there is a mouth 6″ by 6″ to receive the charcoal and ore, and at the base there is another mouth 10 inches high and 9 inches broad, to take the blast and to allow the iron to be removed. On the right-hand side towards the back is a flue for the slag called appropriately the hagân or—in Bilaspur—lohâ hagôra (aperture for excretion) From the top of the tilted kiln there runs backward a bamboo platform $2^1/_2$ by 4 feet long and $1^1/_4$ to $1^1/_2$ feet broad, inclining upwards, supported by light poles. This is the machân, the slide down which ore and charcoal are poured into the furnace. It is plastered with mud, and provided with little walls 3 inches high."

Fig. 15.
The forge of Hephaistus as depicted on a black-figured Attic vase.
(Sixth century B.C.).

Transitional types from the bowl furnace to the shaft furnace were found in large numbers in the Jura and in Carinthia. The shaft furnaces of Eisenberg were only partly detached from the hill-side and look as if they were built around the charge. The walls consist of stones lined and smeared with refractory clay. More developed types were found in very early remains at Mitterberg and Velem St. Vid, though the more primitive bowl furnaces persisted in the Eastern Alps. It seems that the more developed type of shaft furnace was imported from the Near East where (321) "the Chalybes cleave to their hard iron-bearing land and exchange their wages for daily sustenance; never does the morn rise for them without toil, but amid black sooty flames they endure heavy labour".

Shaft furnaces worked with artificial blast were used quite early at Hüttenberg and Lölling, but as old furnaces were often torn down and rebuilt the dating of these remains is exceedingly difficult. At Laurion near Athens shaft furnaces were used in the silver mines and the type was common in Siphnos in the sixth century B.C. Comparing the Hallstatt furnaces of Neuwied with the La Tène furnaces of the Siegen region one sees how the Stückofen furnace is gradually evolved. The Celts developed a type with a chimney and a tapping

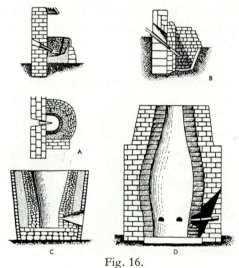

Fig. 16.
The iron-smelting furnaces: A. Corsican furnace; B. Catalan furnace; C. The Osmund furnace; D. Stückofen.

hole and in Sardinia high chimneys were used in roasting furnaces working sulphurous ores. The Roman shaft furnaces, as found at Bibracte, Carthagena and in Etruria are usually small cylindrical shafts, some 3'—4' high and working with blast air introduced through tuyères, In Populonia both natural and artificial blast are used and some furnaces have up to six blast-holes. Such furnaces were used in Moravia from Hallstatt times up to the tenth century A.D.

The most important developments of the metallurgical furnace consisted in mechanizing the production of blast air (which allowed the temperatures to be raised, larger masses to be treated and cast-iron to be produced), the development of the true reverberatory furnace (which allowed regulation of temperature and easy handling of masses of metal at temperatures between 1000 and 1200° C) and the use of electric current and magnetic phenomena (which allowed the production of very pure metals).

9. *Fan, Blowpipe and Bellows*

No discussion of ancient furnaces would be complete without a survey of the ancient method of producing blast air. We have seen that in most furnaces draught air is essential to circulate the heat produced by the combustion of the fuel to the mass to be heated. In the case of metallurgical furnaces this need for a draught is even more pressing. In such furnaces there is first of all a need for higher temperatures than used in baking bread or melting glass. Hence in order to achieve this more fuel should be oxidised per hour, that is more air containing the oxygen to burn this fuel should be introduced into the furnace. Secondly the air plays an important part in such chemical reactions as the reduction of ores and therefore over and above the air needed for the burning of the fuel sufficient air should be introduced to supply this oxygen which takes part in the chemical reaction. Only a few metallurgical processes like some of the crucible processes can derive their oxygen from the ores and ingredients used.

We have a fairly clear picture of the development of the means of supplying blast air to the furnace, the evolution from fan to blowpipe and bellows (322). The simplest form of blast air production is the *fan* with which the ancient Egyptian cook made his charcoal glow, and which we see depicted in so many a wall-painting. In fact the Egyptian language used the expression "rowing the arm" for "fanning the fire" (323). The Egyptian word more commonly used for fanning a fire is related to the Greek "anthrakia" for coal fire (324). This simple fan (325) was better suited for air-conditioning and hence it is the ancestor of such machinery used in houses and mines.

The *blowpipe* was, however, well-suited for the work of the smith. It gave a much stronger air-blast and could be directed to the exact point of the fire where it was wanted. It raised the temperature of the charcoal fire much higher and it was eminently suited for the work of the jeweller and the goldsmith for whose granulation work it was used quite early as Egyptian murals show. Bergsøe's studies have shown what primitive South-American Indians were able to

do with this simple instrument (326). From the Old Kingdom onwards the blowpipe was in common use in ancient Egypt (327).
These blowpipes were probably reeds or metal tubes with clay tipes,
such as also used by the Sumerians and Babylonians. In Mesopotamia
it was quite old, for it is depicted on a seal of the Uruk period (328).
In fact the two words used for "blowpipe", uppu (MUD) and nap-
pâchu (BÚN) go back to a verb meaning "blowing", the latter term
being more often used to denote the bellows. A Sumerian ideogram
for "blowpipe" (329) contains an element meaning "a reed" which
shows that at least as late as the seventeenth century B.C. the blowpipe
was still a reed tipped with clay (330). In the Bible we do not hear of
the blowpipe, a Coptic word for skin or bellows being used for the
vent mentioned in the Book of Job (331) where the Greek text uses
the word "physeter" (blowpipe). The Jewish Law (332), however,
mentions the blowpipe or šephophéret.

The clay nozzle or *tuyère* is the essential part of the bellows, the
other part of the *bellows* taking different forms in order to send as
much air as possible through these tuyères. They have often been
found near ancient smelting furnaces or on smelting sites; they have,
however, often been disregarded even though they form clear proofs
for the use of blast air in metallurgy.

Most authors agree that the oldest form of bellows was the *skin
bellows* (Schlauchgebläse) made by sewing together the skin of an
animal (often a goat's skin), attaching the pipe and tuyère to one of
the legs and using a slit with two wooden rims as the opening for
introducing fresh air into the bag. Most authors hold that this is a
very old form in the Near East but that it was probably evolved in
Western or Central Asia. It is the typical form of bellows of classical
civilisation (333) and even though Cline believes that it admits of
little variation it is certainly the parent of all modern forms of bellows.
Frobenius held that two categories of bellows sprang from this
primitive form, viz. the wooden forms current in Asia (pump bellows,
box bellows and drum bellows) and the typical drum bellows of
Africa, which country did not allow a long span of life to leather or
skin forms. Though there is much truth in his remarks, his conclusions
are rather sketchy and less well founded than those of Foy who
studied this problem very thoroughly.

As practice demanded a constant supply of air in the furnace two
or more pairs of bellows were commonly used, each smith working
one pair. Are we not told that in Hephaistos' forge "through twenty

pipes at once forthwith they poured their diverse-tempered blasts"
(334)? And again the Pythian priestess describes the smithy at Tegea
with these lines:

"There is a place, Tegea in the level plain of Arcadia,
Where by stark stress driven twin winds are ever a-blowing
Shock makes answer to shock and anguish is laid upon anguish"
(335).

Contrary to the belief of von Luschan such bellows did not originate
in Africa but they came thence as they came to Europe from the Near
East and they are still in use amongst primitive tribes of Africa and
Asia. They are also still the typical bellows of the Gypsies.

A second type of bellows, the *pump bellows* (Stempelgebläse) was
probably invented in Southern or Eastern Asia. The blast air is forced
into the tuyère from a wooden or bamboo cylinder in which a piston
is moved up and down. Here again, two cylinders are worked alternately to maintain a constant stream of air. It is a typical wooden form of
the old skin bellows, peculiar to those regions where leather does not
keep well and where natural (bamboo) cylinders are easily available, it
is found in the Far East, Farther India, Malaya, Indonesia and East
Africa. In the latter region it penetrated together with Islam from the
coast, for instance up the Zambesi river. One form with horizontal
pistons is typical for the Far East, it was elaborated and mechanised
to form the "tatara" or *box bellows* of the Japanese and Chinese metal-
workers. The type with vertical pistons is still characteristic of Farther
India and Indonesia but it also occurs in such regions as Burma, India
and Madagascar where Malayan influence made itself felt.

Chinese documents carry back the history of such an application of a
double-acting force and suction pump to the beginning of our era like
that of the (hinged-fan) box bellows. May be references to the use of
bellows in sending toxic smokes towards a besieged city, as mentioned
in documents of the fourth century B.C. are signs that their practical
application is even earlier. (335a)

The *dish* or *drum bellows* (Gefäszblasebalg) are an intermediate form
between the bag and the piston bellows. They were probably developed
in Central Asia or India on the border of the regions covered by the
two primary types. Then they spread over the Near East into Africa
where they still predominate in Southern and Central Africa below a
line running from Liberia to the Upper Nile. They consist of a loose
diaphragm fitted over a solid chamber made of wood or pottery. The

air is sucked in either through a slit in the diaphragm which is closed when the diaphragm is depressed or else through a flue leading into the air chamber. In the latter case the spout of the bellows is inserted far enough into the broad end of the tuyère to direct the blast straight into the fire, but not far enough to prevent the intake of fresh air when the diaphragm is raised. The dish bellows are moved by a set of sticks (Africa) or with a pair of strings (Near East, India and Malaya). In the latter case the operator usually stands on them and keeps the strings in his hands, depressing the diaphragm with his heels and pulling it up with the strings, whereas in Africa the sticks and the diaphragm are worked by hand only though proverbs like "Death treads the bellows (against me)" still keep the memories of the older method of operation alive (336).

A hybrid form, invented in Eastern Asia (as parallels are found in Siberia), the *concertina bellows*, is a cross between the piston and the dish bellows. They resemble the double-bodied dish bellows except for the larger size of the body and the voluminous skin, which encloses a large stack of rings which are drawn apart by short pistons and allowed to fall as the bellows are raised and lowered. They are still in use in Africa where they came from the Mediterranean. In Europe they were introduced from Asia and crossed with the skin bellows to give our leather *house bellows* with an accordion-like bag expanded and collapsed between two woorden boards. Others have suggested that the house bellows were evolved in Europe from certain forms of dish or drum bellows. The earliest reference to such bellows can be found in Ausonius' poem on the river Moselle, dating back to the fourth century A.D., which runs (337): "when the blast fans a smithy fire, the valve of wool which plays in the hollow of the beechen bellows alternately sucks in and confines the winds now by this hole, now by that". In the tenth century Theophilus (338) gives an adequate description of their construction and manufacture.

The house bellows grew larger as the volume of air needed for smelting the ores increased with the size of the furnaces. When water power was harnessed and turned to use to move the bellows we find a growing number of more and more intricate forms of the typical *smith's bellows*, of which we find no trace in Antiquity.

The dish bellows with their wooden and pottery chambers are now more or less African forms, showing the great ingenuity of the native smith, but they have disappeared from the European scene. They survived more particularly in those countries where leather was less common or where the climate was too harsh and hot for this material. For the same reason the piston bellows remained in use in Malaya.

Dish bellows are not shown in Egyptian mural paintings until the middle of the eighteenth dynasty, e.g. about 1500 B.C. (339). They are pottery dishes covered with a piece of skin moved by strings. They resemble those still in use with the Agaria (340) of India who have dish-shaped bellows covered with cow or buffalo hide. There seems to be no term for bellows though Coptic literature knows a word used for "skin (container)" and "bellows" (341). At any rate they do not seem to have been invented in Egypt and indeed we have proofs that such bellows were used at a far earlier date in northern lands such as Mesopotamia.

In the Land of the Two Rivers the dish bellows were known as far back as the middle of the third millenium B.C., for a pottery fire pan with two nozzles for bellows has been found at Telloh (342). Indeed the smith (nappâhu) is in fact called the "user of bellows (nappahu) (or the blowpipe)" as in Hebrew literature. No picture of such dish bellows was found and archaeologists should be on the lookout for further remains of dish bellows which are certain to crop up in the pottery excavated in Mesopotamia.

Such expressions as "blowing the coals in the fire", "blow upon you in the fire of my wrath" and "his breath kindleth coals" refer to the use of bellows (nâphah) in the Old Testament (343) where the smith is also the nappah or "user of bellows". The passage in Jeremiah refers to the smelting of lead ores and though some lead or copper ores could have been smelted without bellows, they were certainly needed for most ores and the clay nozzles, being the most stable part of the bellows, have been found on several ancient smelting sites in the Near East. A diligent search for such tuyères (properly dated) will possible reveal interesting data on the introduction of the dish bellows in this region.

Though Vitruv describes the use of a piston moving in a cylinder to produce air for a water-organ (344), we do not know whether piston bellows were ever used by the classical smiths. Their oldest type of bellows were the skin bellows possibly mentioned by Homer: "Aeolus gave me (Odysseus) a skin bag (askos) flayed from an ox of nine years, and therein bound the paths of the blustering winds" (345).

Wainwright suggested that the idea of using skins as bellows may have arisen from the fact that inflated skins have of old been used to help swimmers across rivers and to float rafts and goods. We find skin bellows depicted on many Greek vases (346). If therefore the Greek word "askos" is sometimes used for bellows, Homer (347) already refers to the "physa" in Vulcan's shop. Herodotus employs the same word (348) when he describes the two bellows in the smithy of Tegea where the bones of Orestes are discovered, and Thucydides mentions such a "physa" in the story of the successful attempt of the Boeotians to construct a primitive kind of flame-thrower (349). Still the modern Greeks call the bellows "physeter", that is "blow-pipe!" On Roman smelting sites there is ample evidence of the use of bellows (35), the invention of which is sometimes ascribed to Anarchasis, a Thracian prince who lived about 600 B.C. (351). In Latin bellows are called "follis" or occasionally "fabrilis". They are not often depicted but a few pictures of the early Middle Ages (352) show that the shape changed little in the course of the centuries.

BIBLIOGRAPHY

1. PLINY, *Nat. Hist.* XXXVI, pp. 200—203
2. TYLOR, E. B., *Primitive Culture* (London, 1874)
   PAUSCHMANN, J. A. G., *Das Feuer und die Menschheit* (Erlangen, 1908)
   HOUGH, W., *Fire as an agent in Human Culture* (*U.S. National Museum Bulletin* No. 139, 1926)
   LANGHANS, H., *Feuer, eine kulturhistorische Studie in 30 Streiflichter* (*Sonder-Beilage Z. f. d. Gesamte Schiess- und Sprengstoffwesen* vol. 32, 1937, No. 1)
   DARYLL FORDE, C., *Habitat, Economy and Society* (London, 1934)
   LIPS, J. E., *The Origin of Things* (London, 1949)
   EISELEY, L. C., *Man the Fire-Maker* (*Scient. American* vol 191, 1954, pp. 52—57)
   OAKLEY, K., *The earliest fire-makers* (*Antiquity* vol. 30, 1956, pp. 102—107)
3. WERNERT, P., *Le rôle du feu dans les rites funéraires des hommes* (*Revue Gén. des Sciences* vols. 48/49, 1937/38, pp. 211—217)
   BURKISS, E. E., *The Use and Worship of Fire among the Romans* (*Class. Weekly* vol. XXIV, 1930/31, pp. 43—45)
   NILSSON, M. P., *Geschichte der Griechischen Religion* (München, 2 vols., 1941/50)
   COUTANT, V., *Theophrastus and the firewalk* (*Isis* vol. 45, 1954, pp. 95—97)
4. The common Egyptian terms for fire were h.t (III. 217.10) (These figures indicate the volume and page of ERMAN-GRAPOW's *Wörterbuch der Aegyptischen Sprache*), śd̩. t (IV.3 75.12), Coptic ⲥⲁⲧⲉ, ⲥⲉⲧⲉ and the late word śt3 (IV.333.12). However there were many other expressions denoting fire such as ḥb.t (III. 252.16) "the executioner", dśr.t (V. 494.4) "the red one"; dndn. t (V. 580.1) "the angry one"; 3ḫ. t (I. 17.6) "the useful one"; 'nḫ. t (I. 205.15) "the living one"; w3. w3. t (I. 250.4) "the planned"; wnmj. t (I. 321.21) "the devouring one"; wśr. t (I. 363.16) "the mighty"; wśḥ (I. 364.9) "the burning"; nfr (II. 262.1) "the beautiful"; nśw. t (II. 324.14) "the withering one"; hw. t (II. 485.4) "the scorching"
5. snsn. t (III. 461.9), fire, disaster
6. FESTUS, s. v. ignis 106 M
7. HOMER, *Odyssey* V, 488—491
8. PLAUTUS, *Trinummus* III. 2.53
9. LEOPOLD, H. M. R., *Vuurmaken in de Oudheid* (In: *Leerschool der Spade* vol. IV, 1929, pp. 240—254)
10. XENOPHON, *Hell.* IV. 5.4
11. XENOPHON, *Cyr.* VIII. 3.12; AMMIAN. MARC. XXIII. 6.34; CURTIUS RUFUS III. 3.7; DIO CASSIUS 71.35.5; HERODIANUS I. 8.4; I. 16.4; II. 3.2; VII. 1.9; VII. 6.2
12. XENOPHON resp. LACED. XII. 2; NICOLAUS DAMASCENUS in STOBAEUS XLIV. 41; HESYCHIUS s. v. pyrosphoros

13. Curtius Rufus V. 2.7
14. Herodotus IV. 68
15. Servius on Virgil, *Aen.* X. 228
16. Plutarch, *de fort. Roman.* 10. Dionysius Halic. IV. 1; Ovid, *Fastes* VI. 627; Plutarch, *Rom.* 2; Servius on Virgil *Aen.* VII. 678
17. Plutarch, *de def. orac.* cap. 2; Paus. I. 26.7; Strabo IX. 1; Paus. II. 19.5; VIII. 9.2; VIII. 15; V. 15.9; VIII. 37.11; Xenophon, *Cvr.* VIII. 3.12; Diodor Sic. XXIV, frag. 1
18. Böhm, C. Richard, *Die Entwicklung der Feuerzeuge (Z. Ver. Gas- und Wasserfachmänner in Oesterreich-Ungarn,* vol. LI, 1911, pp. 15—20, 40—47)
    Frazer, J. G., *Myths of the Origin of Fire* (London, 1930)
19. Diodor I. 13.3
20. Lucretius V. 1091—1101; Vitruv. II. 1.1; Thucydides II. 77; Suidas s. v. drymos
21. Pliny, *Nat. Hist. II.* 239
22. Kuhn, A., *Die Herabkunft des Feuers* (Berlin, 1859)
    Mausch, B., *Das Feuerzeug (Welt der Technik* 1906, pp. 386 ff)
    Böhm, C. R., *Die Entwicklung der Feuerzeuge (Z. d. V. Gas- und Wasserfachmänner in Oesterreich-Ungarn* vol. LI, 1911, pp. 15—20, 40—47)
    O'Dea, W. T., *Making Fire (Science Museum* illustrated booklet, H.M.S.O., London, 1964)
    Niemann W. B. & du Bois, H., *Feuerfindung und Feuererzeugung (Der Mensch und die Erde,* vol. 7, 1911, pp. 28 ff)
    Hough, W., *Fire as an agent in human culture* (Washington, 1926)
    Hough, W., *Collection of Heating and Lighting Utensils in the United States National Museum* (Washington, 1928, *U.S. Nat. Museum Bull.* No. 141)
    Harrison, H. S., *The Evolution of Domestic Arts* (London, 1925, vol. I, pp. 32—40)
    Harrison, H. S., *Fire-making, Fuel and Lighting* (In: Singer, Holmyard and Hall, *History of Technology,* vol. I, pp. 216—237)
23. Watson, Warren, N., *Methods of Fire Making used by Early Man (J. Chem. Educ.* vol. 16, 1939, pp. 36—45)
24. Christy, *The Bryant and May Museum of Fire-making Appliances* (Bryant and May Ltd., 1926, London)
    Crass, M. F., *History of the match industry (J. Chem. Educ.* vol. 18, 1941)
25. Fustel de Coulanges, *La cité antique* (Paris, 1874, vol. III. iv, p. 171)
    Cook, A. B., *Zeus* (London, 1914, pp. 325 ff, vol. I)
    Jacob, A., *Igniaria* (Daremberg-Saglio vol. II, pp. 371—372)
    Miller, J. M., *Die Beleuchtung im Altertum* (Würzberg, 1885)
    Planck, M., *Die Feuerzeuge der Griechen und Römer und ihre Verwendung zu profanen und sacralen Zwecken* (Stuttgart, 1884)
26. *Genesis* 22.6
27. *Isaiah* 30.14
28. *Isaiah* 6.6
29. *Leviticus* 6.12—13; *Jom.* IV. 6; *b. Jom.* 45a; *Siphra* 30c; *Tos. Sot.* XIII. 7; *Ab.* V. 5
30. 2 *Chron.* 7.1

31. *Leviticus* 9.24
32. II. *Maccab.* 1.19
33. II. *Maccab.* 10.3
34. *Num.* 3.4; *Lev.* 10.1; *Num.* 26.21; *Siphra* 45c
35. j. *Ber.* 12b; *Ber.* R. 11(21b), 12(25a), 82(177a); b. *Pes.* 54b
36. H. *Jom. Tob.* IV. 1
37. *Genesis* 19.24; *Job* 18.15
38. SOPHOCLES, *Phil.* 36; PLATO, *civit.* 435 A; LUCIAN, *vera hist.* I. 32; APOLL. RHOD., *Argon.* I. 1182—1184; THEOPHRASTUS *de Igne I.* 29 & 64; GALEN, *de causis morb. c.* 2; SENECA, *Quaest. natur.* II. 22; PLINY, *Nat. Hist.* II. 239; XVI. 208
39. LUCRETIUS, *de rer. nat. V.* 1094; I. 897; SERVIUS, ad *Aen.* I. 743
40. THEOPHRASTUS, *de Igne* 63; *Etym. magn.* 697,42
41. GALEN, *de temperam.* 3.2; *Eutocius*, ARCHIMEDES
42. PLINY, *Nat. Hist.* XVI. 208
43. HOMER, *Odyssey* V. 488; THEOCRIT XI. 51; XXIV. 86; VIRGIL, *Aen.* VIII. 410; MORET. 8; OVID, *Metam.* VIII. 641; *Fast.* V. 506; LUCAN, *Phars.* V. 523
44. XENOPHON, *Hell.* IV. 5.4
45. PLINY, *Nat. Hist.* XXXVI. 139; VII. 198
46. dś (V. 485.16) and bšw (I. 478.9)
47. PLINY, *Nat. Hist.* XXXVI. 139; DIOSCORIDES, V. 143
48. MARCELL, *Empiric.* 33; *Etym. magn.* 697.42; ARISTOTLE, *Hist. anim.* 3.7; THEOPHR. *de Igne* 1 & 63; GALEN, *de temp.* 3.2; PHILOSTRATUS, *Imag.* p. 849; VIRGIL, *Georg.* I. 139; *Aen.* I. 174; VI. 6; OVID. *fast.* IV. 795; *metam.* XV. 347; CICERO, *nat. deor.* II. 9.55
49. VIRGIL, *Aen.* VI. 6
50. LUCRETIUS VI. 162 & 314
51. LUCRETIUS, *de rer. nat.* VI. 162; PLINY, *Nat. Hist.* XXXVI. 138
52. COLUMELLA XII. 19.3
53. OVID. *Metam.* VIII. 614
54. BIL, baḫrû, hot, hence ᵈBIL-GI (fire + reed), ᵈGibil (ᵈGIŠ-BAR) the god of the fire, whence ᵍⁱˢGIBIL, qilûtu, grill, brazier, charcoal fire
55. d3 (V. 511.10), fire-drill
56. DIODOR V. 67
57. HOM. *Hymns ad Hermes* V. 108—114 (edit. SIKES and ALLEN)
58. THEOCRITUS XXII. 33
59. APOLLODORUS, *Argon.* I. 1184
60. VALERIUS FLACCUS, *Argon.* II. 448; NONNUS, *Dionys.* XXXVII. 62
61. LUCIAN, *ver. hist.* I. 32; SOPHOCLES, *Philoct.* 36
62. LYCOPHRON, *Alex.* 537
63. FULGENTIUS 2.9; HESYCHIUS s. v. Ithax
64. HOMER, *Odys.* XIX. 183; STEPHANUS BYZANTINUS s. v. Ithakè; EUSTATHIUS on HOMER, *Iliad* 307,9; EURIPIDES, *Cycl.* 103
65. THEOPHRASTUS, *hist. plant.* V. 9.7, *de Igne* 64
66. or orignitabulum, MACROBIUS 2.8.4
67. PLINY, *Nat. Hist.* XVI. 208; THEOPHRASTUS, *de igne* 73, SOPHOCLES, *frag.* 732

68. THEOPHRASTUS, *de igne* 29, APOLL. RHOD., *Argon.* I. 1182—1184
69. THEOPHRASTUS, *hist. plant.* V. 3.4
70. THEOPHRASTUS, *hist. plant.* V. 9.6—7
71. THEOPHRASTUS, *de caus. plant.* I. 21.7
72. THEOPHRASTUS, *de igne* 63—64
73. LUCRETIUS, *de rer. nat.* I. 871—872, 901—905
74. PLINY, *Nat. Hist.* XXXVI. 199; XXXVII. 28
75. FORBES, R. J., *Studies in Ancient Technology* (Leiden, 1965, vol. V, pp. 189—191)
76. THEOPHRASTUS, *de igne* 73; EUCLID, *Catoptr.* 31; PLUTARCH, *Numa c.* 9; *Apuleius apol. cap.* 16
77. EUCLID, *Catoptr.* 31
78. CHILDE, V. G., *Skara Brae, a Pictish Village in Orkney* (London, 1931, p. 48)
79. RAYMENT, CH. S., *A curious sidelight on Roman history* (*Class. J.* vol. 40, 1944, pp. 292—295)
80. *Nahum* 1.10; *Koh. R.* 7.6(102b); *Jalk. Schim.* II. 973
81. *Schebi* VIII. 1; *Psalms* 120.4; *Midr. Teh.* 120.4
82. *Exodus* 15.7; *Isa.* 5.14; 47.14; *Job.* 2.5; *Obad.* 18; *Mal.* 3.19
83. *Exodus* 5.7—10; *Tos. Schebi* V. 19; *Schebi* VIII. 11; *Schabb.* III. 2; *j. Schabb.* 5c
84. *Schabb.* III. 1—2; *Tos. Kel. Bab. k.* VI. 18; *Tos. Schabb.* III. 1
85. *j. Schabb.* 4b & 5c
86. *Ezek.* XXIV. 5—10
78. STRABO XVI. 1.14
88 .MACROBIUS *Sat.* VII. 16.22
89. ḫt n śḏ. t (IV. 377.5) and ḫt n šmw (IV. 469.10)
90. THEOPHRASTUS, *Hist. Plant.* IV. 8.4
91. DALMAN, G., *Arbeit und Sitte in Palästina* (Gütersloh, vol. IV, 1935, pp. 4—140)
92. *Gen.* 22.3; *Levit.* 1.7; *Judges* 6.26; 1. *Sam.* 6.14; 2. *Sam.* 24.22; *Isa.* 30.33
93. 1. *Ki.* 17.10; *Isa.* 44.15.19
94. *Prov.* 26.20
95. *Sirach* 39.36
96. *Sirach* 28.10; *James* 3.5; *Zach.* 12.36
97. *Ezech.* 24.9
98. *Isaiah* 30.30
99. *Wisdom of Solomon* 13.12
100. *Deut.* 19.5; 20.19; *Isaiah* 10.15
101. *Num.* 15.32; 1 *Ki.* 17.10—12
102. *Siphre, Nu.* 113(33b); *j. Sanh.* 22d; *Targ. Jer.* I *Num.* 15.32; *b. Schabb.* 96b
103. *'eduj.* VIII. 5; *b. Schabb.* 143a; *Bez.* 33a; *Bez.* IV. 2
104. *Midd.* V. 4; *Tos. Schek.* II. 14; *Midd.* II. 5; *Schek.* V. I
105. *Par.* III. 8
106. *Tam.* II. 3
107. *Ekha R. Peth* 15 b; *j. Ta'an* 69c; *Midd.* II. 6
108. *Keth.* VIII. 5; *Bab.* m. VIII. 5

109. b. *Bab.* b. 81a; *'Er* 17a; *Deut.* 20.19

110. *Deut.* 20.19

111. *Bab. k.* X. 10.119b; *'Arakh.* VI. 3; *Bez.* IV. 3; *j. Bez.* 62c

112. *Sanh.* IX. 6

113. *Sirach* 28.11

113a. SALONEN, ARMAS, *Bemerkungen zur Sumerisch-Akkadischen Brennholz-Terminologie* (*J.E.O.L.* vol. XVIII, 1965 pp. 331—333)

114. UNGNAD, A., *Babylonische Briefe der Hammurapi Dynastie* (Leipzig, 1914, VAB vol. VI, No. 52, p. 49)

115. SCHULHOF & HUVEL, (*Bull. Corr. Hell.* 1907, pp. 46—93) and JARDÉ (*Bull. Corr. Hell.* 1923, pp. 301—306)

116. STRABO XIV. 6.5

117. PLINY, *Nat. Hist.* XXXIV. 96

118. PLINY, *Nat. Hist.* XXXIV. 67—

119. PETRIE, W. F., *El-Amarnah* (London, 1894, p. 26)

120. d'b, d'b. t (V. 536.8), Coptic ϫⲉⲃⲥ, ⲣⲃⲃⲥ

121. 'ḥm (I. 225.1), Coptic ⲁⲩϫⲓ from a verb meaning quenching!

122. PLINY, *Nat. Hist.* XXXVI. 201

123. gśr (V. 206.13)

124. THEOPHRASTUS, *Hist. Plant.* IV. 8.5

125. STRABO III. 2.8, cap. 146

126. *Isaiah* 44.12; 54.16

127. *Prov.* 26.21; *Sirach* 11.32; *Prov.* 25.22; *Romans* 12.20; *Isaiah* 47.14; KLASSEN, W., *Coals of fire, sign of repentance or revenge* (*New Test. Studies* vol. IX, 1962—1963, pp. 337—350)

128. *Jerem.* 36.22

129. *John* 18.18; *Mark* 14.54; *Luke* 22.35; *John* 21.9

130. *Schabb.* XIX.1

131. *j. Ter.* 45d, *'Ab.* z. 41a; *Schem. R.* 42(99a)

132. HOMER, *Iliad* IX. 212

133. NIELSEN, N., *La production du fer en Jutlande septentrionale dans les temps préhistoriques et au moyen-âge* (*Mém. Antiq. du Nord* 1920/1925, pp. 337—440)

134. PLINY, *Nat. Hist.* XVI. 32

135. THEOPHRASTUS, *Hist. Plant.* V. 9. 1—6

136. THEOPHRASTUS, *de igne* 67; PLINY, *Nat. Hist.* XVI. 52; THEOPHRASTUS, *Hist. Plant.* IX. 2.2; IX. 3.4; DIONYS. HALIC. *epit.* XX. 15; POLLUX VII. 101; See also my *Studies in Ancient Technology III* and SEIDENSTICKER, A., *Waldgeschichte des Altertums* (Frankfurt, 1886, 2 Bde)

137. STRABO V, cap. 218; CICERO, *Brut.* 22, 85

138. THEOPHRASTUS, *Hist. Plant.* IX. 3.1—4

139. PLINY, *Nat. Hist.* XVI. 52—56

140. PLINY, *Nat. Hist.* XIV, 134; XV, 61—62; XXXI. 68, 113; XIV. 127, 135; CATO, *r.r.* 25; COLUMELLA XII. 4.4; HORACE, *carm.* III. 8.10; MARTIAL XIII. 107, Geoponica VI. 4

141. PLINY, *Nat. Hist.* XVI. 56, 158

142. PLINY, *Nat. Hist.* XXXVI. 166

143. VITRUV. VII. 4.2; X. 9.2

144. PLINY, *Nat. Hist.* XXXV. 41
145. PLINY, *Nat. Hist.* XVI. 1
146. THEOPHRASTUS, *De Lapid.* 13 (edit. CALEY and RICHARDS)
147. CALEY, E. R. and RICHARDS, J. F. C., *Theophrastus on Stones* (Columbus, 1956)
148. THEOPHRASTUS, *De Lapid.* 16—17 (edit. CALEY and RICHARDS)
149. THEOPHRASTUS, *De igne* 37
150. READ, T. T., *The earliest industrial use of coal* (*Trans. Newcomen Soc.* vol. XX, 1939/40, pp. 119—135)
     DAVIES, O., *Roman Mines in Europe* (Oxford, 1935, pp. 153, 253)
151. PLINY, *Nat. Hist.* XXXIV. 96
152. CUNNINGTON, M. E., *Mineral Coal in Roman Britain* (*Antiquity* vol. VII, 1933, p. 89)
     COLLINGWOOD, R. G.: in FRANK, T., *An Economic Survey of Ancient Rome* (Baltimore, 1937, vol. III, pp. 34—37)
153. *Antiquity vol. XXXVIII*, 1954, p. 106 on article by KLIMA in *Archeologické Rozhledy*, vol. V, 1953
154. *Archaeologia vol. LXXXVII*, p. 137
155. SOLINUS, *Collect. rerum memor.*
156. WEBSTER, G., *A Note on the use of coal in Roman Britain* (*Antiq. J.* vol. XXXV, 1955, pp. 199—216)
157. HOUGH, W., *Fire as an agent in human culture* (*U.S. National Museum Bull.* No. 139, Washington, 1926)
     NEUBURGER, A., *Das Feuer als Hilfsmittel in Haus und Gewerbe* (*Der Mensch und die Erde*, Berlin, 1911, vol. VII, pp. 32 ff)
     BLAIR, C. J., *Heat in the Rig Veda and Atharva Veda*, Amer. Orient. Ser. vol. 45, New Haven, 1961
157a. RICHARDS, D. H., *The Chimney* (*J. Brit. Archaeol. Assoc.* vol. XXIV, 1961, pp. 67—79)
     SVORONOS-HADJIMICHALIS, V., *L'évacution de la fumée dans les maisons grecques du Ve et IVe siècles* (*Bull. Corr. Hell.* vol. LXXX, 1956, pp. 483—506)
158. rkḥ (II. 458.15), a fire, hence rkḥ (II. 458.9) Coptic ⲡⲱⲕ̅ⲅ̲ to fan a fire
159. ktjw. t, ktw. t (V. 145.1), hearth
160. k3p.t (V.103.16) from k3p (V. 103.9) to burn incense
161. SIR WILKINSON, G., *Manners and Customs of the Ancient Egyptian* (London, 1842, vol. II, pp. 120—121)
162. FISKE, D. L., *The Origins of Air Conditioning* (*Refrigerating Engineer* vol. 27, 1943, No. 3, pp. 123—126, 150)
163. *Jerem.* 36.22
164. *Isa.* 30.33; *Ezech.* 24.9
165. *Siphra* 55c; *Schabb.* III. 2 cod. K; *Bez.* IV. 5
166. *Kel.* V. 11
167. *Kel.* VII. 2 Cod. K
168. IZI-ḪA-MUN, abru, fire, stake. Baking is often carried out on or in ashes (NIMUR, timru, glowing cinders; hahu, ashes); but see *Ur Exc.* vol. IV, pp. 58, 69, 83; SALONEN, A., *Die Oefen der alten Mesopotamier* (*Baghdader Mitteilungen*, Berlin, vol. III, 1964, pp. 100—124)

169. Greek kakkabos, Latin cac(c)abus, acculus, pan, hence the OHG chachala and German Kachel, stove

170. SENECA, *de ira* I. 11.3

171. TACITUS, *Germania* 16

172. VITRUV. VII. 3.4; VII. 4.4

173. WINCKELMAN, *Sämtliche Werke* 1825, Vol. II, p. 38

174. KRELL, O., *Altrömische Heizungen* (Nürnberg, 1901)

175. LIPPMANN, E. O. VON, *Zur Geschichte der Vergiftung durch Kohlenoxydgas* (*Chem. Ztg.* vol. XXXIII, 1909, pp. 633—634)
    LUCRETIUS, *de rerum nat.* VI. 802

176. DACHLER, A., *Die Ausbildung der Beheizung bis ins Mittelalter* (Wien, n.o., pp. 141—142)

177. The 'ḥ (I. 223.13) Coptic ⲁⲓⲩ or the 'ḥw. t (I. 224.1)

178. ḥr śḏt (III. 395.15)

179. *Prov.* 26.21

180. *Isa.* 54.16; 44.12

181. *Koh. R.* 9.8(114b); *b. Ber.* 28a

182. *Amos* 3.15

183. *Tos. Sabb.* XVI. 18; *Bez.* II. 10

184. *Isa.* 44.26; 47.14; *James* 2.16

185. SALONEN, A., *Die Oefen der alten Mesopotamier* (*Baghdader Mitteilungen*, Berlin, vol. III, 1964, pp. 100—124)

186. BIRKENBIHL, M., *Entwickungsstufen der deutschen Kachel* (*Sprechsaal*, vol. 71, 1938, pp. 89—91)
    DEICHMÜLLER, J., *Tonöfen und Oefenmodelle der Lausitzer Kultur* (Mannus-bücherei Bd. 69, 1941)
    FABER, A., *1000 Jahre Werdegang von Herd und Ofen* (*Abh. Ber. Dtsches Museum* vol. 18, 1950, Heft 3)

187. SCHRÖDER, R., *Die geschichtliche Entwicklung der Zentralheizung vom Altertume bis zur Gegenwart* (*Tech. Gemeindeblatt*, vol. 13, 1910/11, pp. 247—251; 266—270)
    KÖRTING, J., *Aus der Geschichte der Zentralheizung bis zur Gegenwart* (*Technikgeschichte*, vol. 26, 1937, pp. 115—129)
    KRELL, J. R., *Heating, Past, Present and Future* (*J. Instit. Heating and Ventilating Engrs*, vol. 12, 1944/45, pp. 90—127)

188. Le général MORIN, *Note sur les appareils de chauffage et de ventilation employés pour les thermes à air chaud* (*Mém. Acad. Inscr. Belles Lettres*, 1e série, Tome VIII, 1874, pp. 345—370)
    BERGER, J., *Moderne und antike Heizungs-und Ventilationsmethoden* (Berlin, 1870)
    JACOBI, L., *Ueber Schornsteinanlagen und die Badeeinrichtung der Stabianer Thermen in Pompeii* (In: F. v. DUHN und L. JACOBI, *Der griechische Tempel in Pompeii*, Berlin, 1890, p. 30)
    KRELL, O., *Altrömische Heizungen* (München, 1901)
    DACHLER, A., *Die Ausbildung der Beheizung bis ins Mittelalter* (Wien, 1907)
    FUSCH, G., *Ueber Hypokausten-Heizungen und Mittelalterliche Heizungs-anlagen* (Hannover, 1910)

VETTER, H., *Zur Geschichte der Zentralheizungen bis zum Uebergang in die Neuzeit* (*Beitr. Gesch. Technik. Industrie*, vol. III, 1911, pp. 276—347)

PARIBENI, R., *Le Terme Diocleziane* (3. edit. Rome, 1918)

KRENCKER, D. & KRÜGER, E., *Trierer Kaiserthermen* (1929)

SCHWEEN, G., *Die Beheizungsanlagen der Stabianer Thermen in Pompeii* (Diss. T. H. Dresden, 1957)

PARET, O., *Die römische Hypokaustheizung* (Würtemberg, vol. VI, 1934, pp. 72—74)

MARTIN, A., *Erhitzung des Wasser- und Dampfbades* (*Proteus* vol. II, 1937, pp. 162—165)

BADERMANN, W., *Die Schornsteinheizungen der alten Römer* (*Prometheus* vol. 27, 1916, pp. 532—535)

THATCHER, E. D., *The open rooms of the Terme del Foro at Ostia* (*Mem. Amer. Acad. Rome* vol. XXIV, 1956, pp. 167—264)

STACCIOLI, R. A., *Le rotonde delle terme pompeiane* (*Arch. Class.* (Roma) vol. VII, 1955, pp. 75—84)

189. THÉDENAT, H., *Hypocausis, hypocaustum* (DAREMBERGSAGLIO, vol. II, cols. 345—350)

190. EPIPHANIUS, *advers. haer.* II. 52.2 (edit. *Patrol. gr.* MIGNE, vol. XLI, 955)

191. VITRUV. V. 10; PALLADIUS I. 40

192. SENECA, *Epist.* XC. 25; PALLADIUS I. 40

193. VITRUV. V. 10; MACROBIUS, *Saturn.* II. 11

194. VITRUV. VII. 4; PLINY, *Nat. Hist.* XXXV. 46

195. AUSONIUS, *Mosella* 339—340; SENECA, *de provid.* IV. 9

196. SENECA, *epist.* XC. 25

197. DIGEST. VIII. 2.13; XLIII. 21.3.6

198. CELSUS, *med.* I. 4; II. 17

199. GERALD JOYCE, J., *Silchester* (*Archaeologia* vol. XLVI, No. 2, p. 337)

200. PLINY, *epist.* II. 17.25; V. 6.25

201. SENECA, *de prov.* IV. 9

202. DIGEST. XXXII. 1.55

203. PLINY, *epist.* II. 17.23

204. STATIUS, *Silvae* I. 5.58—59

205. VALERIUS MAXIMUS IX. i.1; PLINY, *Nat. Hist.* IX. 168; MACROBIUS, *Saturn.* III. 15.3; CICERO, *phil. fr.* 5.76 (edit. MÜLLER); NONIUS MARC. 193—194

206. HILTON TURNER, J., *Sergius Orata, pioneer of radiant heating* (*Class. J.* vol. 43, 1947/48, pp. 486—487)

207. PLINY, *Nat. Hist.* IX. 168

208. VARRO, *de rer. r.* III. 3.10; COLUMELLA, *de r. r.* VIII. 16.5, MACROBIUS, *saturn.* III. 15.2

209. MARTIAL 13.90

210. VALERIUS MAXIMUS IX. i.1

211. CICERO, *de off.* 3.67; *de orat.* 1.178

212. ST. AUGUSTINE, *de Beata Vita* 26

213. PLINY, *Nat. Hist.* XXXI. 5; SENECA, *Quaest. Nat.* III. 24.3; ÅSTRÖM, P., *Fran Varberg till Vouni* (*Varberg Museum Årsbok*, 1963, pp. 147—159)

214. GINOUVÈS, R., *Sur un aspect de l'évolution des bains en Grèces vers le IVe siècle*

de notre ère (*Bull. Corr. Hell.* vol. LXXIX, 1955, pp. 135—152); KRETSCHMER, FR., *Die Entwicklungsgeschichte des antiken Bades und das Bad auf dem Magdalensberg* (Düsseldorf, 1961); MAUSSION DE FAVIE-RES, J. DE, *Note sur les bains de Damas* (*Bull. Et. orient. Syrie* vol. 17, 1961/2, 121—131)

215. LUCRETIUS, *de nat. rer.* VI. 800; LIVY 44.6.1; SENECA, *epist.* LXXXII. 5; PLINY, *Nat. Hist.* XXXIII. 152; VITRUV. IX. 21; SCRIBONIUS LARGO 130; CELSUS, *de med.* VII. 26.5; SUETONIUS, *Div. Aug.* 82.2; PETRONIUS, *Sat.* 73

216. CICERO, *Caelio* 67; VITRUV. V. 10.24; FESTUS p. 298b. 22M

217. PECLET, E., *Traité de la Chaleur* (Paris, 1850); *Nouveaux Documents relatifs au Chauffage et à la Ventilation des Etablissements Publics* (Paris, 1853)

218. VITRUV. V. 10.1—2

219. SENECA, *epist.* XC. 25

220. *Oeuvres d'Oribase* (trad. BUSSEMAKER et DAREMBERG, Paris, 1853, vol. II, p. 886)

221. WINCKELMANN, J. J., *Anmerkungen über die Baukunst der Alten* (1762, p. 49)

222. OVERBECK, J., *Pompeii in seinen Gebäuden, Altertümern und Kunstwerken* (Leipzig, 1884, p. 201)

223. JACOBI, L., *Das Römerkastell Saalburg* (Homberg, 1897, p. 250)

224. *The Mechanics Magazine* vols. 1—59, London 1814—153, No. 494, p. 286 CUNLIFFE, BARRY, *The Roman Palace at Fishbourne near Chichester* (*ILN*, *Archaeol. Sect.* no. 2189, June 27, 1964)

225. BOESWILLWALD, *Timgad, une cité africaine* (Paris, 1897) BROEDNER, E., *Untersuchungen an den Heizungsanlagen der römischen Thermen Nordafrikas* (*Germania* vol. XXXVI, 1958, pp. 103—113)

226. KRELL, O., *Altrömische Heizungen* (Nürnberg, 1901)

227. FUSCH, G., *Ueber Hypokausten-Heizungen und Mittelalterliche Heizungsanlagen* (Hannover, 1910)

228. VITRUV. V. 10.2; VII. 4.2

229. DE SICCI, *De balneis compendium* (Venice, 1553)

230. PLINY, *epist.* II. 17.23; V. 6.25

231. MAU, *Pompeiianische Studien*, p. 149

232. VETTER, H., *Zur Geschichte der Zentralheizung...* (*Beitr. Gesch. Technik Industrie* vol. III, 1911, pp. 276—347)

233. BADERMANN, W., *Die Schornsteinheizungen der alten Römer* (*Prometheus*, vol. 27, 1916, pp. 532—535)

234. BIÉVELET, H., *L'exploration archéologique de Bavai, Notes sur les hypocaustes de Bavai* (*Antiq. Class.* vol. XIX, 1950, pp. 81—92) BREUER, J., *Hydrothérapie et chauffage en Belgique à la période romaine* (*Rev. Centre neuro-psych. de Bruxelles*, 1952, pp. 25—28)

235. JECKLIN, F. & COAZ, C., *Fund einer römischen Heizanlage im Welsch Dörfli* (*Chur*) (*Anz. Schweiz. Alt. kunde* vol. XXV, 1923, pp. 78—82) STIGLITZ-TALLER, H., *Hypokaustanlage in Flavianus-Mautern* (J. Oesterr. *Arch. Instit.* vol. XLIII, 1956, Beiblatt 169—180)

236. HETTNER, F., *Zu den römischen Altertümern von Trier und Umgebung* (Trier, *Westd. Z.*, vol. 10, 1891, p. 57)

237. PARET, O., *Die Römer in Württemberg* (Stuttgart, 1932, vol. III, pp. 70—77)

MÜHLMANN, O., *Die Jenaër Hypokausten Anlage* (*Forsch. und Fortschr.* vol. XXXII, 1958, pp. 300—304)

238. KRETSCHMER, FR., *Der Betriebsversuch an einem Hypokaustum der Saalburg* (*Germania*, vol. 31, 1953, pp. 64—67) (*Saalburg Jahrbuch*, vol. 12, 1953, pp. 8—41)

239. SENECA, *epist.* 86.9

240. AUSONIUS, *Mosella* 337

241. MARTIAL, *Epigr.* X. 48

242. STATIUS, *Silvae* I. 5.58 ff

243. SENECA, *Epist.* 90.25

244. FORBES, R. J., *Studies in Ancient Technology* (Leiden, 1965, vol. V, pp. 168—188)

245. KRETSCHMER, FR., *Die Heizung der Aula Palatina in Trier, ein Versuch ihrer Deutung und der Aufkärung ihrere Betriebsweise* (*Germania*, vol. 33, 1955, pp. 200—210)

BROEDNER, E., *Einige Bemerkungen zur Heizung der Aula Palatina in Trier* (*Germania* vol. XXXIV, 1956, 277—278)

246. MARTIAL, *Epigr.* VI. 42.15; STATIUS, *Silvae*, I. 5.44—48

247. STEPHANY, FR., *Der älteste Deutsche Wohnbau und seine Einrichtung*, p. 82

248. WINCKELMANN, J. J., *Anmerkungen über die Baukunst der Alten*(1762, p. 49)

249. JACOBI, L. & COHAUSEN, VON (*Nassauische Ann.* vol. 17, 1882, p. 119

250. HORACE, *Odes* 19

251. FORBES, R. J., *Studies in Ancient Technology* (Leiden, 1965, vol. III, p. 51)

252. HOUGH, W., *Fire as an agent in human culture* (Washington, 1926)

253. DARYLL FORDE, C., *Habitat, Economy and Society* (London, 1934)

254. LIPS, J. E., *The Origin of Things* (London, 1949, chapter 1)

LIVERSIDGE, J., *Kitchens in Roman Britain* (*Archaeol. News Letter*, vol. VI, No. 4, 1957, pp. 83—85)

255. DANIEL, W. E., *Fuel and Heating through the Ages* (*Electrical Age*, vol. III, 1936/38, pp. 450—452)

256. BODEWIG, *Ein Ofen der La-Tène Zeit* (*Nassau. Altert.kunde* 1904/05, No. 4, cols. 114—118)

257. DALMAN, G., *Arbeit und Sitte in Palästina* (Gütersloh, 1935, vol. IV)

GALLING, K., *Biblisches Reallexiken* (Tübingen, 1937)

258. *Lev.* 2.5; 6.21; 7.9; 1 *Chron.* 23.29

259. MACALISTER, R. ST., *The Excavations of Gezer* (London, 1912, vol. II, p. 24)

SELLIN, E. & WATZINGER, C., *Jericho* (Leipzig, 1913, Fig. 36)

THOMSEN, P., *Reallexikon der Vorgeschichte*, vol. I, p. 318

260. *Hosea* 7.8

261. COF. KAUFM. *Men.* V. 9; *Kel.* V 2; VIII 7; *Schabb.* II 2

262. HIPPOCR. I. 676; GALEN, VI. 489; ISID. XX. 2.15; ARISTOPHANES, *Ach.* 86; PLINY, *Nat. Hist.* XIX. 18; DIOSC. I. 96; II. 81

263. *Matth.* 6.30; *Luke* 12.28

264. *Exod.* 8.3; *Lev.* 26.26

265. *Psalms* 21.10

266. *Gen.* 15.17

267. *Hosea*, 7.4.6; *Mal.* 3.19; *Sirach* 48.1

268. *Bab. b.* II. 2

269. *Bab. b.* II. 3

270. *Kel.* VIII. 3; *Ta'an.* III. 6; *Ohal.* XII. 1; *Tos. Kel. B.* k. VI. 9

271. *Kel.* VIII. 7; *Tos. Kel B.* k. VII. 9

272. *Schabb.* III. 2; *Pes.* III. 4; *Ab. z.* III. 9; *Kel.* VIII. 8; *Tos. Kel. B.* k. IV. 2

273. BLISS, *A Mound of Many Cities* (Lachish), p. 114
     MACALISTER, R., *The excavations of Gezer* (London, 1912, vol. I, p. 168)
     SELLIN & WATZINGER, *Jericho* (Leipzig, 1913, p. 88)

274. *Kel.* VIII. 9; *Tos. Kel. B.* k. VI. 17

275. *Tos. Bez.* III. 19—20; b. *Pes.* 31b; *Bez.* 34a; *Ab. z.* 35b

276. KLEBS, L., *Reliefs des Alten Reiches* (Heidelberg, 1915)

277. KLEBS, L., *Die Reliefs und Malereien des mittel. Reiches* (Heidelberg, 1922)

278. mk'r (II. 158.15, baker's furnace, hence mg (II. 164.4), glow of fire

279. KLEBS, L., *Die Reliefs und Malereien des neuen Reiches* (Heidelberg, 1934)

280. thr (V. 322.15) or trr (V. 318.18), Coptic ⲧⲣⲓⲣ , ⲑⲣⲓⲣ; Hebrew tannûr

281. 'bw (I. 223.20) fireman of the baker's furnace

282. MEISSNER, BR., *Babylonien und Assyrien* (Heidelberg, 1925, vol. I)

283. RAWLINSON, H. R., *Five Great Monarchies* (vol. II, p. 211)

284. IZI-NINDA-HAR-RA, akal tumri, baked in ashes

285. PLACE, V., *Niniveh and Babylon* (vol. I, p. 99), *Recueil des Travaux*
     (*Maspéro*), vol. XXX, p. 46; ULAL, tinûru, furnace

286. KI.NE, kinûnu, brazier

287. ašâku, ZIMMERN, B., *Beitrage zur Kenntnis der babylonischen Religion*
     (No. 26; No. IV, 38); *Mitt. Vorder-As. Ges.*, vol. XIV, p. 149

288. CT vol. VI. 27.16b

289. WILKENSON, CHARLES K., *Heating and Cooking in Nishapur* (*Bull. Metrop.
     Museum Art*, vol. II, 1943/44, pp. 282—291)

290. POLLUX X. 19.66

291. SENECA, *Quaest. nat. III.* 24

292. SAGLIO, E., *Caldarium and Calda* (DAREMBERG-SAGLIO, vol. I, cols.
     820—822)
     Anon., Antike Röhrenkessel (*Prometheus* vol. VIII, 1897, pp. 501—502)

293. GHIRSHMANN, R., *Fouilles de Sialk* (Paris, 1938, vol. I)
     WOOLLEY, L., *Carcemish* (*Irâq*, vol. I, 1934, pp. 146—162)
     WOOLEY, L., *Ur Excavations* vol. IV, pp. 29, 65 f.
     HILPRECHT, H. V., *The Excavations in Assyria and Babylonia*, pp.
     489—492
     BERTELONE, M., REGGIORI, A., MOLTONI, E. & STORTI, C., *Forno per
     ceramica di Roncolo* (Reggio Emilia) (*Sibrium*, vol. III, 1956/57, pp.
     185—204)
     SALONEN, A., *Die Oefen der alten Mesopotamier* (*Baghdader Mitteilungen*,
     Berlin, vol. III, 1964, pp. 100—124)
     WINTER, A., *Alte und antike Brennanlagen, die Regie ihrer Feuer* (*Keram.
     Z.*, vol. VIII, 1956, No. 10, pp. 513—517
     THOMPSON, F. H., *A romano-british pottery kiln*... (*Ant. J.* vol. 38, 1958,
     pp. 1/2, 15—51)

WINTER, A., *Der römische Töpferofen von Kastel* (*Keram. Z. Disch.* vol. 9, 1957, pp. 9, 482—484)

WINTER, A., *Technik des griechischen Töpfers in ihren Grundlagen* (*Techn. Beitr. z. Archäologie*, Mainz, 1959, pp. 1—45)

MATSON, F. R., *Techniques of the early bronze potters at Tarsus* (In: *Excavations at Gözlü Kule, Tarsus*, Princeton, 1956, pp. 352—361 of Vol. 2)

VERTET, H., *Les fours de potiers gallo-romans découverts en Bourbonnais* (*Bull. soc. antiq.* France 1961, pp. 121—122)

VAUTHEY, M. & P., *L'officine céramique de Terre-Franche* (*Allier*) (*Rev. arch. Centre* vol. II, 1963, pp. 319—334)

HARTLEY, B. R., *The firing of kilns of Romano-British type* (*Archaeometry* vol 4, 1961, pp. 1—28)

MAYES, P., *The firing of a second pottery-kiln of Romano-British type* (*Archaeometry* vol. 5, 1962, pp. 80—92)

CORDER, PH., *The structure of Romano-British pottery kilns* (*Archaeol. J.* vol. CXIV, 1957 (1959), pp. 10—27)

GILBERT, W., *The background of refractories technology* (*Refract. J. Gr. Britain*, vol. 39, 1963, pp. 2, 44—46, 48—50)

294. SCOTT, SIR LINDSAY, *Pottery* (In: SINGER, HOLMYARD and HALL, *History of Technology*, vol. I, 1954, pp. 376—412)

295. KLEBS, L., *Die Reliefs des Alten Reiches* (Heidelberg, 1915)

296. k̲rr (V. 61.9), heating (the pots)

297. KLEBBS, L., *Die Reliefs and Malereien des mittel. Reiches* (Heidelberg, 1922)

298. t3 (V. 228.16), potter's kiln

299. HEROD. I. 179; HOMER, *epigr.* 14; ATHENAEUS, *Deipn.* I. 28; PLUTARCH, *Polic.* 13

300. CICERO, *N. D.* I. 37,108; VITRUV. VII. 4.3; PLINY, *Nat. Hist.* 28.16; FESTUS, par. 344 B, 27; ARNOBIUS, *adv. gent.* VI. 14, p. 128

300a. WOOLLEY, *Ur Excav.* vol. IV, p. 7

   MACKAY, E. *Early Indus Civilisation* (London, 1935, p. 21)

   HOLWERDA, J. H., *Oudh. Med. Rijksm. Oudheden*, Leiden vol. XXVI, 1946, pp. 68 ff, 104 ff

301. JOPE, E. M., *Medieval Ceramics* (In: SINGER, HOLMYARD and HALL, *History of Technology*, vol. II, 1956, pp. 284—310)

302. SPEISER, E. A., *Excavations at Tepe Gawra* (*Ann. Amer. Schools Orient. Research* vol. IX, 1927/28, p. 50)

303. *Abh. Akad. Wiss. Berlin*, Uruk, *8th report*, Berlin, 1936 (p. 7, Table 27)

304. WAINWRIGHT, G. A., *Rekhmirê's Metal workers* (*Man*, 1944, No. 75, pp. 94—98)

305. h̲rj. t (III. 148.15, Coptic ϩ ρω, ϩ ρογ

306. The Coptic language has several words for furnace. The common word is ⲓⲏⲧⲱⲕ, ⲡⲓⲏⲧⲱⲓⲥ (Old Egyptian pr(n)tk3 (V. 332.6), literally "House of the fire" (holding the fire) derived from a verb ⲧⲱⲕ, ⲑⲱⲕ meaning to burn. Then there is the ⲧⲣⲓⲣ (Old Egyptian trr, Hebrew tannûr), a furnace, in which word we recognize the later "athanor" of the alchemists. The Coptic ⲕⲗⲟ for oven also means "a hole", and the Coptic ϭ ⲣⲱⲛ for furnace is not clearly defined

З о 9 о 7

307. *Daniel* 3.6
308. *Deut.* 4.20; *Isa.* 48.10; *Prov.* 27.21
309. *Gen.* 19.28
310. *Gen.* 15.17; *Isa.* 31.9
311. *Eccles.* 27.5; 28.30
312. *Deut.* 4.20; *Jerem.* 11.4
313. *Herodotus* III. 96
314. *Prov.* 17.3; 27.21
315. PLINY, *Nat. Hist.* XXXIII. 69
316. POLLUX VII. 99
317. DEICHMÜLLER, J., *Tonöfen und Ofenmodelle der Lausitzer Kultur* (Mannus-
     bücherei No. 69, Leipzig, 1941)
     DICKINSON, H. W., *Elinghearths* (*Trans. Newcomen Society* vol. XVIII,
     1937/38, pp. 274—277
     GOLDSMITH, J. M. and HULME, E. W., *Sketch of the history of natural
     draught furnaces* (*Trans. Newcomen Society* vol. XXIII, 1942/43, pp.
     1—13)
     HURST, J. E., *The history of the foundry cupola* (*Engineering*, vol. 124, 1927,
     pp. 830—831)
     KLOSEMANN, K., *Die Entwicklung der Eisengewinnung in Afrika und
     Europa* (*Mit. Anthr. Ges. Wien*, vol. 54, 1924, pp. 120—140)
     NICHOLLS, H. W., *Models of blast furnaces for smelting iron* (*Field Museum*,
     dept. of Geology leaflet No. 2, Chicago, 1922)
     VOGEL, O., *Zur Geschichte des Schmelztiegels* (*Glashütte*, vol. 65, 1935,
     pp. 722—723)
     WEIERSHAUSEN, P., *Vorgeschichtliche Eisenhütten Deutschlands* (Mannus-
     büchrei No. 65, Leipzig, 1939)
     WRIGHT, H. E.,*History of the development of blast furnaces in Great Britain*
     (*Iron Coal Trade Rev.* vol. 150, 1945, pp. 733—736, 777—780)
     JEFFREYS, M. D. W., *Some Notes on the Bikom blacksmiths* (*Man, April*
     1952, No. 75, pp. 49—51)
     COGHLAN, H. H., *Some experiments on the origin of copper* (*Man, July* 1939)
     COGHLAN, H. H., *Prehistoric Copper and some experiment in Smelting*
     (*Trans. Newcomen Soc.* vol. XX, 1939/40, pp. 49—65)
     COGHLAN, H. H., *Some Fresh Aspects of Prehistoric Metallurgy of Copper*
     (*Ant. J.* vol. XXII, 1942, pp. 22—38)
     SOUTHERN, H., *The historical development of furnaces* (*Edgar Allen News*,
     vol. 12, 1933/34, pp. 313—315; 330—333; 345—347; 357—359;
     374—376)
     COOK, R. M., *The double stoking tunnel of Greek kilns* (*Ann. Brit. School*
     Athens vol. LVI, 1961, pp. 64—67)
     PENNIMAN, T. R., ALLEN, I. M. and WOOTTON, A., *Ancient metallurgical
     furnaces in Great Britain to the end of the Roman occupation* (*Sibrium* vol
     IV, 1958/9, pp. 97—128)
     TYLECOTE, *Roman shaft furnaces in Norfolk* (*J. Iron Steel Inst.*, vol. 200,
     1962, pp. 19—22)
     FORBES, R. J., *Studies in Ancient Technology* vol. VIII (Leiden, 1964)
     NEEDHAM, J., *The Pre-Natal history of the Steam Engine* (*Trans New-
     comen Soc.* vol. XXXV, 1962/63, p. 30)

318. GILLES, J. W., *Der Stammbaum des Hochofens* (*Archiv. f. d. Eisrnhütten-wesens* vol. 23, 1952, No. 11/12, pp. 407—415)

MINGAZZINI, P., *Santuari o Alti-forni* (*Studi Sardi* vol. X/XI, 1950/51, pp. 3—17)

WURMBAND and SPIESS, *Stahl und Eisen*, 1907, pp. 1658 ff

FREISE, *Stahl und Eisen*, 1907, pp. 1618 ff

GILLES, *Stahl und Eisen*, 1936, pp. 252 ff

BECK, *Geschichte des Eisens*, vol. I, p. 514

319. HESIOD, *Theogony* 864
320, ELWIN, VERRIER, *The Agaria* (Calcutta, 1942, p. 181)
321. APOLLONIUS RHOD., *Argon. II.* 1002
322. BENOIT, F., *Soufflets de forges antiques* (*Revue Etudes Anc.*, 1948, pp. 305—308)

FOY, W., *Zur Geschichte der Eisentechnik insbesondere der Gebläse* (*Ethologica* vol. I, 1909, pp. 185 ff

FRÉMONT, CH., *Origine et développement de la soufflerie* (Paris, 1917)

FROBENIUS, L., *Kulturgeschichte Afrikas* (Berlin, 1933, pp. 197 ff)

HAMZA, MEHMUD, *The cylindrical tubes or nozzles of the ancient Egyptian bellows* (*Ann. Serv. Ant. Egypte* vol. XXX, 1930, pp. 62—63)

KLOSEMANN, K., *Die Entwicklung der Eisengewinnung in Afrika und Europa* (*Mitt. Anthr. Ges. Wien* vol. 54, 1924, pp. 120—140)

LOHSE, U., *Die Entwicklung der Gebläse bis zur Mitte des* 19. *Jahrhunderts* (*Stahl und Eisen* vol. XXXI, 1911, pp. 173 ff)

WYNNE, F. H., (*Trans. Instit. Mining Eng.* vol. XXXVI, 1903/04, pp. 231 ff)

PERCY, JOHN, *Metallurgy of Iron and Steel* (pp. 254—270)

WAINWRIGHT, G. A., *Rekmirê's Metal workers* (*Man*, vol. XLIV. 1944, No. 75, pp. 94—98)

CLINE, W., *Mining and Metallurgy in Negro Africa* (Paris, 1937)

THEOBALD, W., *Des Theopilus Presbyter Diversarium Artium Schedula* (Berlin, 1933)

NEEDHAM, J., *The Pre-Natal history of the Steam Engine* (*Trans. New-comen Soc.* vol. XXXV, 1962/63, pp. 3—58)

323. 'hn (I. 226. 15)
324. rkḥ śdt (II. 458.9) hence the Coptic ⲡⲱⲕⲣ, ⲡⲁⲕⲣⲉ and the Greek anthrakia, coal-fire
325. Egyptian nf, nfj (II. 250.10), Coptic ⲛⲓϥⲓ, ⲛⲓϥⲓ
326. FORBES, R. J., *Metallurgy in Antiquity* (Leiden, 1950)
327. LEPSIUS, C. R., *Denkmäler aus Aegypten und Aethiopien* (vol. II, Plate 13 & 49b)

STEINDORFF, *Das Grab des Ti* (Plate 134)

GARIS DAVIES, N. DE, *Deir el Gabrawi* (Vol. I, Plate xiv & Vol. II, Plate xix)

NEWBERRY, P. H., *Beni Hassan* (Vol. I, Plate xi; Vol. II, Plates vii & xiv; Vol. IV, Plate xx)

DUELL, P., *The Mastaba of Mereruka* (Chicago) (Vol. I, Plate 30)

328. LEGRAIN, *Délégation en Perse*, vol. XIV, p. 31
329. MEISSNER, BR., *Seltene assyrische Ideogramme* (Berlin, 1910, No. 1470)

330. C.T. vol. XI, iii, 26
331. *Job* 32.19
332. *Tos. Brz.* III. 15
333. *Iliad* XVIII. 468; VIRGIL, *Georg.* IV. 171; LIVY, 38.7; HORACE *Sat.* I.
      4.19; THEOPHILUS, III. 82—84)
334. *Iliad* XVIII. 468
335. HERODOTUS I. 67
335a. NEEDHAM, J., *Science and Civilisation in China* vol. IV. 2 (*Cambr. Univ.
      Press*, 1965 pags. 135—141)
336. SPIESS, O., *Archiv f. Anthropologie* 1918, No. 98, p. 114
337. AUSONIUS, *Mosella* 265—270
338. THEOPHILUS, *Divers. Artium Schedula III.* 82—84
339. GARIS DAVIES, N. DE, *The Tomb of Puyemrê at Thebes* (Vol. I, Plates
      xxiii & xxv)
      GARIS DAVIES, N. DE, *The Tomb of Rekhmirê at Thebes*
      GARIS DAVIES, N. DE, *The Tomb of the Two Sculptors* (Plate xi)
340. ELWIN, V., *The Agaria* (Calcutta, 1942, p. 181)
341. Coptic ϥⲱⲧ, used for the Greek "askos" in *Matthew* 9.17 and *Job* 32.19
342. CROS, G., *Nouvelles fouilles de Telloh* (Paris, 1910, p. 151)
343. *Isa.* 54.16; *Ezech.* 22.21; *Job* 20.26; 41.21; *Sirach* 43.4
344. VITRUV. X. viii. 1
345. HOMER, *Odys.* X. 19—20
346. GRAEF, B. and LANGLOTZ, E., *Die antiken Vasen von der Akropolis zu
      Athen* (p. 215 & Plate xxii)
      FURTWÄNGLER, A. und REICHHOLD, K., *Griechische Vasenmalerei* (Plate
      135 and vol. III, p. 85)
      DAREMBERG et SAGLIO, *Follis* (col. 1227) and *Caelature* (col. 784)
      LÜCKEN, G. VON, *Greek Vase Paintings* (Plate 107)
347. HOMER, *Iliad* XVIII. 372
348. HERODOTUS I. 68
349. THUCYDIDES IV. 100.1
350. DAVIES, O., *Roman Mines in Europe* (Oxford, 1935)
351. STRABO, VII. 3.9, cap. 303
352. THEOBALD, W., *Technik des Kunsthandwerks im zehnten Jahrhundert* (*Des
      Theophilus Presbyter Diversarum Artium Schedula*) (Berlin, 1933, p. 267)

CHAPTER II

REFRIGERATION, THE ART OF COOLING
AND PRODUCING COLD

1. *Introduction*

No doubt refrigeration is one of the essentials of modern life. We could not do without ice to cool our food and drinks nor without refrigerators to transport and preserve foodstuffs and in many cases air-conditioning makes life bearable in parts of the world where exploration or work would be impossible for many of us because of the climatic conditions.

However, we should realize that such niceties were only available during the last few generations. Ice or snow had been used by the very rich only when in 1805 Frederick Tudor started to harvest ice in New England to ship it to the southern States and the Caribbean. Both in Europe and America natural ice was used on a large scale until about 1880 artificial ice was produced cheaply by the new refrigerators. Cold stores and the long distance transport of frozen meat and other foodstuffs became part of our modern world a decade later. Some forty years ago the refrigerator entered the American home, deep-frozen foods appeared in the shops ten years later. Hence the story of modern refrigeration is very recent history (1).

Earlier generations were therefore limited to the occasional use of snow or ice. They could produce a fall of temperature on a limited scale by two methods only (2):

a. the "chemical" method of mixing a solid and a liquid or two solids, the complete dissolution of which consumes much heat, which is withdrawn from the surroundings. This is the principle of the so-called "freezing mixtures";

b. the "physical" method of evaporation of a liquid or rapid expansion of compressed gases, when again heat is consumed which is taken from the surroundings. This is the principle applied in our refrigerators, which the ancients used in a much simpler form and which they could not yet "translate" into machinery.

Freezing mixtures were first known in the latter half of the sixteenth
century, when Monardes and Villafranca mention them. They usually
consisted of mixtures of snow and nitre, though sometimes common
salt was used instead. Our earliest illustration of a cooler dates from
the same period and about 1630 "limonadiers" served cooled beverages
in the French capital. Research on this subject was begun by Porta
and Boyle.

Hence the ancients could produce cold only be certain primitive
forms of evaporation, apart from collecting snow or ice and storing

Fig. 17.
Snow and salt cooler, about 1500.
(From an engraving in the N.Y. Public Library Print Room).

it for use (3). We are reminded of the fact that Hippocrates considered
it dangerous to "heat, cool or make commotion all of a sudden in the
body. Why should one run the hazard in the summer of drinking
iced waters, which are excessively cold, and suddenly throwing the
body into a different state than it was before". The hot air in houses
could be made bearable by fountains or by sprinkling the marble
tiles with water, as is still done in southern climates, but this hardly
lowers the air temperature.

Apart from these effective means the ancients occasionally used
objects which they believed to have a "cold nature". Thus Neuburger
(4) reports an unspecified account of the Egyptian ladies of the fifth

century B.C. who "had the couch in their litters covered with a thick layer of green leaves and flowers, on which they stretch themselves out, covered only with a thin linen tunic. The curtains were drawn and then wet with cold water. In addition they rolled about their necks and arms two live snakes, and in each hand they took a quartz sphere, a mineral whose temperature remains constantly below that of the surrounding air". Whatever the truth may be of these earliest reports of air conditioning, we are certain that the idea that the dead need cooling was found amongst all peoples around the Mediterranean, even in Mesopotamia and Nubia (5). In a world of heat, sun and sand the idea of a "refrigerium" was born in analogy to the cool drink, which stilled thirst and assured life. In the cold countries of the north the heroes in Walhalla heated themselves by the drinks served by the Valkyries. The Celts left the door open for the spirits of the departed to enter and warm themselves near the glowing embers of the hearth. In the southern regions, however, there was a "locum refrigerii", a cool abode as the posthumous reward of the valliant warriors, which is already mentioned in the Gilgamesh epic.

Notwithstanding this appreciation of the cool shade we find no traces of the most important modern application of refrigeration, the preservation of foodstuffs by cooling. We find that it was "good in the eyes of Pharaoh and in the eyes of all his servants that food shall be for store to the land against the seven years of famine, which shall be in the land of Egypt; that the land perish not through the famine" (Gen. 41.36—37) and the preservation of surplus food was always a major problem in Antiquity. It was common knowledge that heat, if properly applied, was the great enemy of decomposition, or in modern terms "of bacterial life". Perishable goods like foodstuffs will be damaged if submitted continuously even to modest heat but their life is prolonged perceptably at low temperatures.

Still the ancients knew many natural caves, which could have been used for cold storage. Such natural caves, mostly in limestone formations and particularly those of volcanic origin, were known for their great preservative character. They were reported to be remarkably cool and dry, and the enclosed air was usually of exceptional purity. Some are actually cold when the rocks forming the walls are porous and infiltrating moisture evaporates rapidly. Yet they were not used for cold storage but foodstuffs were placed in cellars of houses. Such cellars are not always suitable for this purpose as their temperature may be well over 50° F and bacterial action is therefore not eliminated as it would at temperatures about ten degrees lower. The preservation of foodstuffs in cellars was therefore hardly effective, especially as the use of snow and ice was restricted to the cooling of wines and dainties on the tables of the very rich. As explained in the third volume of this series preserving foodstuffs was achieved by pickling, smoking or drying (dehydration) and the elimination of chemical preservatives, which in certain cases endangered human health, came only with the introduction of the refrigerator two generations ago.

2. *Snow and Ice in the Ancient Near East*

As we might expect the ancient Egyptian language has no term for "ice". Only in documents of the late XIXth dynasty do we find a word for "snow" (6) which is evidently derived from the Hebrew and which is written with an ideogram indicating that it fell from heaven". In Egypt it was a rare phenomenon, but it was frequent in Palestine. Both the Old Testament and Jewish Law (7) frequently mention hoar frost (kephôr), snow (šéleg), ice (ǵelîd, ḳéraḥ) and hail-stones (kêphat hab-bârâd). The Lord "scattereth the hoar-frost like ashes" (8) and it is compared with the barely visible manna in the early morning.

Snow was so common in ancient Palestine, that it was used as a symbol for purity and cleanliness (9) but also as a description of the signs of leprosy, when one's hand is "leprous like snow" (10), or of the battlefield covered with booty (11). "As snow in summer, and as rain in harvest, so honour is not seemly for a fool" (12), but "the cold of snow in the time of harvest" is like the "faithful messenger to them that send him, for he refresheth the soul of his masters" (13). Of course one needs warm clothes to protect oneself against the cold snow (14) and the wild animals take shelter like the "lion in the midst of a pit in time of snow" (15). In winter time "the streams of brooks are blackish by reason of the ice and the snow is hid in them" (16). Indeed, the Lord "maketh the snow to fall apace", "the hailstones are broken small", "he scattereth the snow", "hoar frost as salt he poureth on the earth, and being congealed it lieth on the top of sharp stakes" and "the water is congealed into ice, it abideth upon every gathering together of water, and clotheth the water as with a breast-plate" (17). "The waters are hid as with a stone, and the face of the deep is frozen" (18).

Jewish law advises taking "neither the road through fire nor that through snow, but the middle path" (19). Snow is used as the symbol of hell (20) in Jewish law, which frequently mentions hailstones, snow, hoar frost and ice as media which may transplant uncleanliness (21). It is a point of discussion whether frozen holy water retains its virtues (22).

The inhabitants of the Land of the Twin Rivers were quite familiar with the phenomena of cold, frost, ice and snow. This quartet occurs in the great Hymn to Shamash (23) and one ideogram is at the bottom of the Assyrian terminology for these phenomena, which was studied by Landsberger (24). The term "halpû" (25) describes the phenomena of frost and freezing in particular in such passages as "their arms were lamed like those of frozen people" or "frost bring thee rest" (26).

The properties of ice were well-known (27). A curse runs "the ground be ice and may you slip". A detachment of the army is told "if after the rain no ice is formed you may march" and Sargon describes a campaign in these words: "In the wildness of my heart I flung the entire province to the ground and made it congeal in its length and its breadth to ice". Ice was collected and stored of old. "Fields of ice", "ice-pits" and "ice-houses" have left their traces all over the Mediterranean and Black Sea regions. In Syria the snow of the Lebanon is still collected and stored in pits and cellars. We do not know exactly how long this custom goes back. In Europe they were fairly common in the days of Boyle and even down to the early nineteenth century (28).

We have definite information about a "cold-house" (bît halpî) in the city of Ur during the reign of Shulgi (ca. 2000 B.C.) (29). May be this was an "ice-pit" lined with timber. Three hundred years later we again hear of "ice-houses" (bît šurîpi), but in these cases it is not always clear whether ice was really stored in them. We know that the Greek "crystallos" means both ice and glass. In the same way "šurîpu" means both ice and translucent substances like certain ores, it is sometimes used as a synonym for verdigris or copper ore (mammûm, šuhtum) (30). Indeed other passages compare and identify the melting of ice and the smelting of ores (31). The "ice-house" in case occurs in a tablet the text of which runs thus: "Zimrilim, son of Iahdunlim, king of Mari and Tuttul and the land of Hana, builder of a bît šurîpi which before none had built on the banks of the Euphrates. The šurîpu he transported from..., on the banks of the Euphrates he built a bît šurîpi in Terqa, town beloved by Dagan". From this letter which dates back to about

1700 B.C. (32) and from others in the royal archives of the town of Mari we may conclude that there was a real "ice-house" in the town of Assur, but that the bît šurîpi of Terqa was rather a storehouse of copper ores (33) which were brought down by messengers from a distance of some 100—200 km. and which were carefully washed, picked and broken down at Terqa before storage and transport to Mari and other centres of metallurgy. It was built by an architect named Ahum who was sent from Mari to Terqa for this purpose.

Fig. 18.
Typical Egyptian scene of cooling wineflasks by fanning.

3. *Refrigeration by evaporation*

All over the East porous pottery is known to keep the water cool. Small quantities of water filtering through the pottery wall evaporate and withdrawn heat from the contents of the vessel. Von Luschan (34) claims that this principle was invented in Egypt whence the Arab world took the "qôl" (modern Arabic "kulle"). With this very thin porous pottery vessels von Luschan claims to have cooled water some 25° C below room temperature. The late-Latin "gillo" for wine-cooler goes back to this Arabic original.

In the long run such pottery absorbs some dirt and has to be cleaned which is achieved by drying and re-baking it. Dollinger, who repeated von Luschan's experiments did not achieve a temperature more than 5° C below room temperature, but even this is sufficient to produce a pleasant sensation for the hot and thirsty.

In Antiquity such porous pottery was certainly made and used and evaporation was even accelerated by fanning or by covering the wine jars with garlands of leaves and flowers which were kept wet (35).

Both in the Ancient Near East and India cold water and even ice were produced by filling shallow pottery vessels with water, covering them with stalks of corn or sugar cane and exposing them to draughts. Early travellers in India (36) report that small quantities of ice were thus made and the Esthonians used similar methods about 800 A.D. The Indians also believed that water containing salt kept cooler (37).

It seems that this method was also familiar to the ancient Egyptians though climatic conditions in their country did not allow the production of ice. This is what Athenaeus has to report (38):

Fig. 19.
Italian snow pit.
(After R. Boyle's Experiments and Observations concerning Cold, London, 1688).

"Protagorides, in the second book of his Comic Histories, when recounting the voyage of King Antiochus down the Nile, has something to say about ingenious contrivances to get cold water. His words are these: "During the day they place the water in the sun, and when night comes they strain the thick sediment and expose the water to the air in earthen jars set on the highest part of the house, while throughout the entire night two slaves wet down jars with water. At dawn they take the jars downstairs, and again drawing off the sediment, they thus make the water clear and in every way healthful. They then place the jars in heaps of chaff, and thereafter use it without the need of snow or anything else whatever"."

Galen tells a similar story in which leaves are used to cover the vessel. In ancient Egyptian literature all the concepts for cold and coolness are derived from the term for the north wind (39). The very late word for frost (40) is written with a sign denoting wind. Fans (41) were of course known of old and used to cool persons and drinks.

4. *Ice and Snow in the Classical World*

Being familiar with snow and ice, the ancients had of course, speculated on their origin. In the eleventh book of his Meteorologica Aristotle (42) tells us that rain, snow and hail fall from the clouds as a result of refrigeration. Rain and snow correspond with dew and frost respectively, they are due to similar causes and differ only in degree:

Fig. 20.
Producing ice in shallow vessels (India).

rain is due to the condensation of a large quantity of vapour, dew of a small quantity, snow is frozen cloud, as frost is frozen vapour. But there is no analogy to hail on the earth. He then goes on to say:

> "Now we know that hot and cold have a mutual reaction on one another (which is the reason why subterranean places are cold in hot weather and warm in frosty weather). This reaction we must suppose takes place in the upper region, so that in warmer seasons the cold is concentrated within by the surrounding heat. This sometimes causes a rapid formation of water from cloud. And for this reason you get larger raindrops on warm days than in winter and more violent rainfall... Sometimes the cold is even more concentrated within by the heat outside it, and freezes the water

which it has produced, so forming hail. This happens when the water freezes before it has time to fall. For if it takes a given time (t_1) to fall, but the cold being intense freezes it in a lesser time (t_2), there is nothing to prevent it freezing in the air, if the time (t_2) taken to freeze it is shorter than the time (t_1) of its fall. The nearer the earth and the more intense the freezing, the more violent the rainfall and the larger the drops or the hailstones because of the shortness of their fall. For the same reason large raindrops do not fall thickly. Hail is rarer in the summer than in the spring or autumn, though commoner than in winter, because in summer the air is drier; but in spring it is still moist, in autumn it is be-ginning to become so. For the same reason hailstones do some-times occur in late summer, as we have said. If the water has been previously heated, this contributes to the rapidity with which it freezes: for it cools more quickly. (Thus many people when they want to cool water quickly first stand it in the sun: and the inha-bitants of Pontus when they encamp on the ice to fish—they catch fish through a hole which they make in the ice—pour hot water on their rods because it freezes quicker, using the ice like solder to fix their rods). And water that condenses in the air in warm districts and seasons gets hot quickly..."

Wells with remarkable cool water were known in many regions (43) but snow and ice seem to have been collected to a certain extent (44). Thus Athenaeus tells us that (45):

"The ancients are also acquainted with the use of very cold water in drinking healths, but I will not quote them... Semos of Delos, in the second book of the Island History, says that in the island of Cimolos underground refrigerators are constructed in summer, where people store jars full of warm water and draw them out again cold as snow... (other examples cited tell of very cold water from wells and of instances when snow is used for drinking)...
Chares of Mitylene in his Records of Alexander tells how to keep snow, when the recounts the siege of the Indian capital Petra. He says that Alexander dug thirty refrigerating pits which he filled with snow and covered with oak boughs. In this way, he says, snow will last a long time."

and Seneca knew that the snow had to be packed hard together to keep well (46). However, we have little information on the gathering,

preservation and marketing methods of snow. There is no doubt
that snow-pits were used for many centuries. The Chinese classic
Shi-King has elaborate details on the religious ceremonies used for
filling and emptying the ice pits in which ice was preserved during
the summer months. Their use continued in the Mediterranean region
up to the beginning of this century. In Smyrna people rolled snow
into hollows in the mountains out of the sun and there it lasted till
summer. Ice was also brought down from Saint-Maximin and sold in
full summer in Marseilles. In Roman times chaff or straw seems to
have been used to cover the snow (47). The use of rough cloth was
limited to transportation (48).

Martial (49) quite rightly remarks that the cost of cold water obtained with such ice or snow may be greater than that of the wine
to be cooled. Some of this ice or snow was used in cooling pools
(frigidaria) in the baths (50) or in making cool water for handwashing,
for Petronius (51) tells us: "At last we sat down, and boys from
Alexandria poured water cooled with snow over our hands.".

We get the impression that the collection and use of ice was limited
(52) and that most of it was obtained from snow rather than from
ice cut from ponds. Seneca stipulates that in order to preserve it snow
should be packed (stipare) hard into pits or trenches and covered
with straw. In such circumstances the snow near the top will melt and
freeze again below and by the weight of the snow on top will be
converted into ice. Seneca also speaks of men not contended to use
snow but demanding ice from the bottom of the pits. "Water has a
varying price", he grumbles and wonders what the Spartans would
have thought of this business of putting up snow (54). On the other
hand both snow and ice seem to have been called "snow" unless there
was a good reason to distinguish them.

5. *Snow-cooled Drinks*

The greater part of this snow, however, was used in cooling drinks
for the tables of the very rich. This is what Pliny (55) says:

"Even the water supply is divided into classes, and the power
of money has made distinctions in the very elements. Some
people drink snow, others ice, and turn what is the curse of
mountain regions into pleasure for their appetite.

Coolness is stored up against the hot weather, and plans are
devised to keep snow cold for the months that are strangers

to it. Other people first boil their water and then bring even that to a winter temperature. Assuredly mankind wants nothing to be as nature likes to have it."

Apicius and others (56) mention frozen and snow-cooled dishes, but snow occurs more often as a refrigerant of drinks, especially wines (57). When Pliny the Younger writes, to his friend Septimius Clarus, reproaching him for not turning up at his dinner-table (58) he mentions "sweet wine and snow (the snow most certainly I shall charge to your account, and at a high rate, as it was spoiled in serving)". Xenophon relating the story of Hercules and the contest of Vice and Virtue (59) tells us that a charge which Virtue brings against Vice is that she buys costly wines and "runs around in summer to find snow" to make her drinks more tasty.

Seneca (60) tells us that "nothing is cold enough for some people— hot dishes and snow drinks—and now and then you will see them throw lumps of snow in their cups". Athenaeus (61) gives many quotations illustrating the use of snow in cooling wine:

> "That they also chilled wine in order to drink it rather cold is shown by Strattis in Keeping Cool: "No man would prefer to drink his wine hot; rather one likes it chilled in the well or mixed with snow". So also Lysippus in The Bacchants: "What's the matter, Hermon? How are we getting on? How else than this? The pater has sunk me down the well, me thinks, as one sinks wine in summer time"."

Also "if get drunk and drink snow", "what you want is wine cooled in the well and mixed with snow" or "so and so is the first man to know when snow is to be bought on the market". In this chapter he also mentions the story of the girl who tells Diphilus the poet: "No, it's not snow the wine is cooled with, we put one of your prologues in it!".

From the passages on the use of snow in Greek texts we can deduce the fact that they usually mixed snow with their wine directly. The Romans, however, put their ice on a strainer or metal or cloth and poured the wine through it avoiding contamination with foreign matter in the snow (62). In a few cases only they put their snow in the wine (63), in a few others they applied both methods in succession to achieve lower temperatures (64). However, in many passages in Seneca, Petronius, Pliny, Plutarch, Martial or Juvenal no indication is given what method was applied. It was costly and expressions such as "as rare as snow in Egypt" were common. One always ran the risk that the wine acquired an unpleasant taste from this contact with the snow (65). Hence some preferred indirect cooling by snow (66), or sieved, even melted snow before drinking it (66).

The medical profession generally condemned the use of snow and even cooled drinks. Hippocrates held that "waters of snow and ice are all bad, the clear, light, sweet part is separated out and disappears, the muddiest and heaviest part remains" (67). Here Pliny (68) agrees: "The thinnest part of it is gone when freezing". Hippocrates in his aphorisms warns against sudden temperature changes of the human body and hence condemns ice-cold drinks: "Cold things, such as snow and ice are harmful to the chest, and provoke coughing, discharges of blood and catarrhs" (69). Aulus Gellius informs us that he visited a rich man living at Tivoli together with some of his student friends and that they drank a good deal of water of melted snow (70), which, he says citing Aristotle: "is beneficial for crops and trees, but very unwholesome if drunk in quantities by men, producing wasting and diseases in the intestines". On the other hand Celsus reports (71):

> "Now Asclepiades, against the opinion of previous writers, affirmed that the drink should be kept constantly cold, indeed as cold as possible. I myself hold that each should trust in his own experiences whether hot rather than cold drink should be made use of".

Pliny (72) gives us further details on this physician Asclepiades, who was a fashionable doctor in the Rome of Pompey, and "would prescribe wine and cold water to his patients" and who "according to Marcus Varro preferred to win for himself the surname of "cold-water giver" (frigida danda). However, the majority of the famous doctors of Rome condemned the practice of using snow directly in wine or other drinks or to drink molten snow and several authors propagated these warnings (73).

Hence snow was used to cool water indirectly, which was then mixed with the wine. It was commonly believed that previously boiled water could be more readily cooled (74) and that it was more healthy (75). There is of course a difference as air and carbon dioxide have been driven out of such boiled water, which is the "aqua cocta" (76) which Nero claimed to have invented and which he called "Nero's decocta" (77).

There is a single passage of great interest in Lampridius (78) who tells us that Heliogabalus had mountains of snow erected near his villa, which is perhaps the first attempt at air-conditioning in world history.

7. Vessels for Cooling Drinks

We still have to discuss whether the ancients used special vessels for the indirect cooling of drinks with snow or cold water. The "psykter" was the typical wine-cooler of the ancients (79) though its form is hardly properly defined. In Plato's Symposium (80) Alcibiades asks for one of more than 8 cotyles for an ordinary vessel is not large enough. Athenaeus (81) tells us that in a parade of Antiochus Epiphanes were shown twenty-two golden wine-coolers (of these the largest held three hundred gallons, the smallest ten), one hundred-sixty silver "psykteres" of two to six metretes and three-hundred and twenty more of gold and silver but of unknown size. Other authors use the word "psykter" where most would say "krater". Moeris defines it as a large vessel in which cups were washed, but some authors say it was a large "krater" (wine-mixing bowl) which was placed on a support and containing pure wine.

Whatever the later indiscriminate use of this word may be it seems that it was used for a well-defined object in early days. Karo (82) described a series of pottery "psykteres" of the sixth and fifth century B.C. which may go back to metal originals. The oldest, sixth-century type is a double-walled amphora. The inner compartment into which the neck opens, was for the wine, while the outer compartment, which entirely surrounds the inner was for the snow-chilled (or hot) water. This water could be drained through a small opening at the bottom. This cooling liquid was poured into an opening below the neck.

This type of psykter had to make place in the fifth century for an entirely new type, which belongs to the so-called "red-figured pottery" which comes into use about 530—520 B.C. This new psykter was a top-shaped pottery vessel without a handle and destined to float in a large krater containing the cooling (or heating) liquid. Some of these psykteres had a lid.

The third and youngest type of vessel psykter was a large crater with an outflow opening near the bottom. It serves to cool the wine in the same way as our modern wine-cooler. Certain cylindrical pitcher-shaped vases found in Southern Italy and dating back to the fourth century B.C. are also believed to have been wine-coolers.

In later periods vases of widely different shape seem to have been used for cooling wine in the same way as many types of vessels were used to store cold water such as the "phiale, a flat vessel of bronze" which Athenaeus (83) mentions.

BIBLIOGRAPHY

1. ANON., *The Tenth Anniversary of "Ice and Refrigeration"* (*Ice and Refriger-*
   ation, vol. XXI, July-December 1901, pp. 1—17; 45—59; 89—103;
   125—135; 207—208; 223—230)
   The Ice Making and Refrigeration Industry (1890—1915) (*series of articles*
   in Ice and Refrigeration, vol. LI, 1916, No. 5, pp. 141—209)
   GOOSMAN, J. C., *History of Refrigeration* (*Ice and Refrigeration*, vol. 67,
   1924, pp. 297—299, 446—448, 541—542; vol. 68, 1924, pp. 33—34,
   110—112, 181—183, 226—228, 328—330, 428—430; vol. 69, 1925,
   pp. 70—71, 135—137, 335—336, 413—414, 478—480; vol. 70, 1925,
   pp. 99—101, 149—151, 203—205, 267—269, 372—373; vol. 71,
   1926, pp. 123—124, 197—198, 312—314, 503—504, 611—614)
   SCHMIDT, B., *Kühlung* (*Tageszeitung f. Brauerei*, vol. 29, 1931, pp. 622 ff)
   SCHMIDT, B., *Aus der Geschichte der Kälteindustrie* (*Wärme und Kälte-*
   technik, vol. 32, 1930, pp. 13—14)
   CROMMELIN, C. A., *Kunstmatige koude in vroeger tijden* (*Koeltechniek*, vol.
   IV, 1933, pp. 86—87)
   ANON., *Ancient Refrigeration* (*Refrig. Engineering*, vol. 33, 1937, pp. 94 &
   111)
   SMITH, EDGAR C., *Some Pioneers of Refrigeration* (*Trans. Newcomen Society*,
   vol. 23, 1942/43, pp. 90—107)
   PLANK, R., *Die Frischhaltung von Lebensmitteln durch Kälte* (*Deutsches*
   Museum, Abh. & Ber., vol. XII, 1940, No. 5, pp. 139—174)
   ANDERSON, O. E., *Refrigeration in America* (Princeton Univ. Press,
   1953)
   LINGE, K., *Werden und Wachsen der deutschen Kälteindustrie* (*Kältetechnik*
   Dtsch. vol. 8, 1956, pp. 1, 4—8)
   FORBES, J., *The Rise of Food Technology* (1500—1900) (Janus, vol.
   XLVII, 1958, 101—127, 189—175).
2. WIRKNER, C. G. VON, *Geschichte und Theorie der Kälteerzeugung* (Hamburg,
   1897)
3. FISKE, DAVID L., *Refrigeration is not new* (*Refrig. Engineering*, vol. 24,
   1932, pp. 201—205)
4. NEUBURGER, A., *The Technical Arts and Sciences of the Ancients*, (Me-
   thuen, London, 1930, pp. 122—124)
5. PARROT, A., *Le "Refrigerium" dans l'au-delà* (Leroux, Paris, 1937)
6. šrķ (ERMAN-GRAPOW, *Wörterbuch* IV. 204.14) *compare the Hebrew šéleg*
7. DALMAN, G., *Arbeit und Sitte in Palästina* (Gütersloh, vol. 1928, pp.
   236—237)
8. *Ps.* 147.16; *Job* 38.29
9. *Isa.* 1.18; *Ps.* 51.7; *Ps.* 147.16
10. *Exodus* 4.6; *Numbers* 12.10; 2 Ki. 5.27; *Neg.* I. 1—2; SIPHRA, *Tazria*
    2(61a)
11. *Ps.* 68.14
12. *Prov.* 26.1

13. *Prov.* 25.13
14. *Prov.* 31.12
15. *2 Sam.* 23.20
16. *Job* 6.15—16
17. *Ecclesiasticus* 43.13—20
18. *Job* 38.30
19. *j. Chag.* 77a; Ab. d. R. N. 28
20. *j. Sanh.* 29b; *Tanch. Reë* 10; *Pesikt.* 97b; *Jalkut Machiri on Ps.* 68.15b, b. Ber. 15b
21. *Ohal.* VIII. 5; *Mikw.* VII. 1; *Tos. Ahil.* II. 6
22. *Tos. Par.* IX. 8; *Teh.* II. 6
23. *K.B.* VI. 2.106.13; *AKA* 140:14
24. LANDSBERGER, B., *Lexikalisches Archiv* (Z. f. Assyr., vol. 42, 1934, pp. 156—160)

    MEISSNER, B., *Seltene Assyrische Ideogramme* (Berlin, 1910, Nos. 1506 & 1550)
25. We have SID ($\check{S}E_{12}$), kaṣû, to be cold (whence kuṣṣu, cold and EN-TEN-NA, kuṣṣu, winter) which is equivalent to $\check{S}E_4$ (halba/i), halpu, a frozen or congealed liquid or ice. Then there is the Sumerian AMAGI ($\check{S}EG_9$) (A, water plus MAGI. mabi, mami, frozen), šurîpu, ice. The word šurîpu is said to be a diminutive form of šarpu (Cun. Texts Brit. Museum 18.23; K. 4397,30) from a lost verb šârapu, to freeze.
26. IVR 40, No. 1, 2; J. Royal Asiat. Soc. 1927, p. 532,20
27. KB No. 1, Rs. 67; KLAUBER, Amer. J. Sem. Lang. 30, 278; HARPER 1305, Rs. 2f; SARGON, *Huit. Camp.*, line 215; RT 16,34, line 7
28. BOYLE, R., *Experiments and Observations concerning Cold* (1683)
29. *Altorient. Bibl.* I. 27, No. 10
30. JENSEN, *Keilschr. Bibl.* VI, i, 556
31. *Proc. Soc. Bibl. Arch.* 32, 1910, Tf. 4.25; V. R 47, 27, 28b
32. NOUGAYROL, J., *Une glacière centrale à Terqa sur l'Euphrate au début du second millénaire avant notre ère?* (C. R. Acad. Inscr. Belles Lettres 1947, pp. 265—272), see also HERZFELD, *Revue Assyr.*, vol. XI, p. 135
33. FORBES, R. J., *New evidence on Late Bronze Age Metallurgy* (*Sibrium*, vol. III, 1957, pp. 113—128)
34. DOLLINGER, H., *Poröse Tongefässe zur Abkühlung von Trinkwasser* (Naturw. Wochenschrift N.F., vol. XII, 1913, pp. 703 & 799)

    VON LUSCHAN, *Poröse Tongefässe zur Abkühlung von Trinkwasser* (Naturw. Wochenschrift N.F., vol. XII, 1913, p. 799)
35. PLANK, R., *Beiträge zur Geschichte der Kälteverwendung* (Z. ges. Kälte-Industrie, vol. 43, 6, 1936, pp. 125—131)
36. BLACK, J., *Lectures on the Elements of Chemistry* (Edinburgh, 1803)

    PARKES, FANNY, *Wanderings of a Pilgrim in Search of the Picturesque* (2 vols., London, 1850)
37. *Pantschatantra*, edit. Fritze, Leipzig, 1884, p. 160
38. ATHENAEUS, *Deipn.* III, 124
39. Cool (north) wind, ḳb(b) (Erman-GRAPOW, Wörterbuch V. 24.13), ḳb (V. 22.8), ḳbḥ (V. 26.5), to be cool and ḳbb.t (V. 25.10), cool

(or subsoil) water; also śnbb (IV. 161.15), śḳbb (IV. 304,6 & 7), ḳbḥ (V. 26.5), to cool, hence śḳbb (IV. 278.12 and IV.304.9) or ḳb (V. 26.5) to cool oneself and ḳb.t (V. 24.16) or ḳbḥ. w (V. 27.1), refrigeration. The cooling medium is described by śḳb. w (IV.305.10) or śḳbb (III. 439.4), hence śḳbb (IV. 305.13), the cooler for drinks and śḳbbwj (IV. 305.12) the cold storage for food or drinks.

40. ḥsj (III. 166.3)
41. nf. t (II. 250.10)
42. ARISTOTLE, *Meteorologica* I, XI. 348b
43. PLINY, *Nat. History* 31.21—23
44. LIPPMANN, E. O. VON, *Zur Geschichte des Kältemischungen* (*Z. f. Angew. Chemie* 1898, p. 739 ff.; *Abhandlungen und Vorträge*, Leipzig, 1906, pp. 110—124)
    GLOVER, R. T., *Iced water* (*The Challenge of the Greeks*, Cambridge, 1943, pp. 155—159)
45. ATHENAEUS, *Deipn.* III. 97, 124c
46. SENECA, *Quaest. Nat.* IV. 13.2; PLINY, *Nat. Hist.* 31.40; PLINY MINOR, *Epist.* I. 15
47. SENECA, *Quaest. Nat.* IV. 13.8; PLUTARCH, *Quaest. Conviv.* 6.6I AUGUSTINUS, *De Civit. Dei* 21.4
48. PLUTARCH, *Quaest. Conviv.* 6.6
49. MARTIAL 14. 116, 118
50. SUETONIUS, *Nero* 27.2; SENECA, *Quaest. Nat.* IV. 13.10; VOPISCUS, *Carinus, cap.* 15
51. PETRONIUS, *Satyricon* 31.3
52. SENECA, *Epist. Morales* 78.23; *Quaest. Nat.* IV. 13.7; PLINY, *Nat. Hist.* 19.55; Martial 9.90.5; Latinus Pacatus, *Panegyrici Veteres* 12(2).14.1; Paulinus Petricodiae, *Vita S. Martini Episcopi* 3.11
53. SENECA, *Quaest. Nat.* IV. 13.2
54. SENECA, *Quaest. Nat.* IV. 13.7—8
55. PLINY, *Nat. Hist.* XIX. 55
56. See also MACROBIUS, *Saturnalia* 7.12
57. GEER, R. M., *On the use of ice and snow for cooling drinks* (*J. Class. Weekly*, vol. 29, 1935/36, pp. 61—62)
58. PLINY, *Epist.* I. 15
59. XENOPHON, *Memorabilia* 2.1.20
60. SENECA, *Quaest. Nat.* IV. 13
61. ATHENAEUS, *Deipn.* III, (98)124
62. These strainers are called "colum nivarium" or "saccus nivarius", Martial 14.103; 14.104, see also Martial 9.23.8; 9.90.5
63. MARTIAL 5.64.2
64. SENECA, *Quaest. Nat.* IV. 13.9
65. SENECA, *Quaest. Nat.* IV. 13.8; Martial 14.117
66. PLINY, *Nat. Hist.* 31.21
67. HIPPOCRATES, *peri aeron* VIII. 50 (Loeb edition I. 92)
68. PLINY, *Nat. Hist.* 31.33
69. HIPPOCRATES, *Aphorisms* V. 24 (Loeb. edit.)
70. AULUS GELLIUS, *Attic Nights* XIX. 5

71. Celsus, *De Medicina* IV. 26.4
72. Pliny, *Nat. Hist.* 26.14; 29.15
73. Gellius 19.5; Macrobius 7.12.14—27
74. Pliny, *Nat. Hist.* 19.55; 31.40; Aristotle, *Meteorologica* 1.12.348b
75. Aristotle, *Meteorologica* I. 12; Galen, *de Morbis vulgar.* 4.10
76. Martial 2.85.11; 114, 116.2; Juvenal 5.50; Pliny, *Nat. Hist.* 31.23
77. Suetonius, *Nero* 48.3
78. Lampridius, *Heliogabalus cap.* 23
79. Suidas s.v. psykter
80. Plato, *Symposium* 312 E, Athenaeus *Deipn.* XI. 108, 502 d-e
81. Athenaeus, *Deipn.* V. 199 D—200 A
82. Karo, G., *Notes on Black-figured Pottery* (J. Hell. Studies, vol. 19, p. 141)
    Karo, G., *"Psykter"* (Daremberg-Saglio, vol. IV, pp. 750—751)
83. Athenaeus, *Deipn.* XI. 501

CHAPTER III

LIGHT

1. *Introduction*

Though John the Apostle reminds us that "men loved darkness rather than light (John 3.19)" still artificial light, like the dog, was one of his earliest companions. For when he acquired the art of making fire he also held the means of illuminating his cave or hut at will. We have discussed the origin of fire-making far back in the Old Stone Age and here we will simply quote two passages from Lucretius, where this Roman poet discusses the examples which Nature set to mankind and the natural means by which primitive man could provide himself with fire (1):

> "But often on mighty mountains it comes to pass", you say, "that the neighbouring tops of all trees rub together, when the strong winds constrain them to it, until at last a flowery flame gathers, and they blaze with fire!"
> Herein, lest by chance you should ask a silent question, it was the lightening that first of all brought fire to the earth for mortals, and from it all the heat of flames is spread abroad. For we see many things flare up, kindled with flames from heaven, when a stroke from the sky has brought the gift of heat. Yet again, when a branching tree is lashed by the winds and sways to and fro, reeling and pressing on the branches of another tree, fire is struck out by the strong forces of the rubbing anon the fiery heat of flame sparkles out, while branches and trunks rub each against the other."

However, when learning how to make fire mankind not only acquired a new source of heat and a means of cooking his food or keeping the prowling wild animals away at night but his fire was his first source of artificial light. Fires in braziers and fires baskets as. sources of light survived the invention of the torch and the candle The fire basket carried on a pole and called cresset had a wide-spread use in historic times and survived as the night watchman's "fire devil".

Cressets were used in the Near East, often bitumen provided the fuel. Primitive lighthouses carried open fires in beacon-tuns for many centuries.

Together with the domestication of plants and animals the development of new sources of light, the torch, the candle, and the oil lamp marks the progress of mankind through the New Stone and the Bronze Ages. Throughout these periods, and for many centuries to come, illumination depended on the supply of organic materials, e.g. on some form of carbon fixed by life forms. Not all carbonaceous substances will burn with a luminous flame. This will be clear when we think of such carbonaceous fuels as coke or charcoal from which the substances distilling at low temperatures have been driven out on purpose during their manufacture. The luminosity of a flame

Fig. 21.
Evolution of the Lamp.
(After O'Dea, Darkness into Daylight)

depends on two factors: the presence of volatile, low distilling constituents and their combustion in two stages. The wick of an oil or kerosine lamp sucks up liquid material which is then gasified in the flame and undergoes a kind of dry distillation forming gases and particles of carbon. These carbon particles then burn up in the outer mantle of the flame, after having radiated light waves because of the high temperature they acquire in the flame. As Faraday put it "every lamp, every candle therefore produces its own gases needed for the continuation of the flame". Indeed, any one who wishes to understand what goes on when a candle burns should read the very simple and lucid explanation given by this eminent scientist (2).

In an oil lamp not only a good wick is needed but also a good air (oxygen) supply to the flame. The fat or oil to be burned should have sufficient liquidity to allow a wick of good weave to conduct the required quantity to the burning part to support a luminescent flame.

By being able to regulate the oxygen supply one can adjust the combustion so as to avoid soot formation and to obtain the maximum luminosity. Only when Argand in 1794 invented wick-holders with a central air supply, and started to use properly woven wicks, and when he used a metal (later a glass) chimney to suck a good air-supply along the luminous surface of the flame to achieve complete combustion in the outer zone, it became possible to develop lamps which consumed more fuel per time unit than the old oil lamps with floating wicks and hence produced more light. This means that up to the days of Goethe mankind had lamps and candles of no more than one candle-power and that he could get more light only by increasing the number of lamps and candles though there were of course practical limits to such a procedure (3).

The torch or lighted splinter of resinous wood (German Fackel from Latin facula) was typical for wooded countries and, though it was the ancestor of the later tapers and candles, it was soon displaced in the Mediterranean and Arctic regions by lamps and other devices which used vegetable and animal oil supplies from land and sea as fuel.

The primitive open oil lamp in many cases originated with peoples at a very low stage of culture with a limited supply of oils none too suitable for burning in lamps. However, their mode of life did not require high candlepower lights. In tropical and subtropical regions lamps were long simple and undifferentiated because there was little need for artificial light, since the uniform day and the starlit night together with the simple habits of such peoples rendered more sophisticated illumination unnecessary.

Keeping such slight requirements in mind we must not forget that the eye is extremely adaptable. It has no difficulty in adapting itself to lighting in the whole range from the 20 foot-candle level of a fairly well-lit room at night (one foot-candle, the illumination produced when one square foot receives one lumen of light, is equivalent to 10.76 lux) to the 10,000 foot-candle level of a June sun in the open air. On the other hand our war experience has shown us that an illumination of 0.01 foot-candle of a road at night is sufficient for the wayfarer to pick his way with reasonable certainty, though the lowest limit of visual response is 0.0001 foot-candle. Hence, even with the primitive lighting devices which existed up to the end of the eighteenth century, lamps and candles were a boon to mankind, though they certainly limited life after dusk to a far greater extent than we can imagine. Even in the early nineteenth century the Eddystone lighthouse still burnt candles! Only when the scientists and engineers of the early nineteenth century turned their efforts to better lighting devices were striking improvements quickly achieved (4).

Until those days the supply of oils and fats which these lamps and candles consumed, their availability and price provide the keys to their importance as illuminants. This economic factor looms largely. Primitive islanders may have threaded wicks through the stormy petrels they caught and used them as lamps, mountaineers may have had ready supplies of resinous pine splinters, but the majority of mankind depended for its illuminant supplies on the fish oil produced by the fishing communites when their catches were abundant or on vegetable oils and tallow. In each case edible oils and fats were used for candles and lamps. In other words light consumed food and only more civilised and economically strong countries could spare a great measure of artificial illumination. Early last century the Elder Bretheren of Trinity House could still be greatly concerned at the habits of the lighthouse keepers, who supplemented their rations by eating the tallow candles provided, thereby greatly increasing the cost of keeping up the lights. Therefore in most houses curfew ("couvre le feu", cover the fire!) meant extinguishing the lights and going to bed.

Again the factor of fire was most important in these early days. Pine splinters were apt to scatter hot embers and were therefore dangerous with hangings, draperies and wooden floors. Spouted oil lamps tended to drip oil until the "crusie" or double-pan lamp came into use. Candle guards had to be used for many centuries to avoid the danger of fire. The light provided from such lighting devices was unstable and flickering, its position for reading and writing usually inconvenient. Certainly lamps and candles were more mobile, steadier and easier to manage than torches or pine splinters, but they had only one candle power. Candelabra (Latin candela, -b(a) rum: bearer) and multi-spouted lamps could supply more light but even then the illumination supplied was never anything like that of our modern electric bulbs supplying the same amount of light at only one-fiftieth of the cost five generations ago.

Earlier generations of archaeologists believed that after the open fire came the torch from which the lamp and then the candle descended. It is now clear that this evolution was not so simple and that oil lamps are far older than previously supposed. We will now discuss the different types of lighting devices separately.

2. *Lamps in Prehistoric Europe*

The discovery that a wick soaked in and fed by fat or oil will provide a lasting light, goes back at least to the Old Stone Age. These primitive lamps consisted of shallow saucers cut from stone, sometimes provided with a broad tongue projecting from the rim to form a handle. Thus in the cave of La Mouthe (5) in the Dordogne region a lamp of Magdalénien date was found cut in a piece of reddish sandstone. The hollow contained the remains of what once must have been an animal (bear?) fat. It has been suggested that these oldest lamps served the Upper Palaeolithic hunters of Western Europe when drawing their famous rock paintings in the depths of caves. However, at Tomonovka in Southern Russia dwellings were certainly lighted by lamps of a similar type cut from soft stone (6).

The wicks used were almost certainly of vegetable origin, moss or dry reed being used, though occasionally a lump of twisted hair may have served for this purpose. Sandstone or chalk served to carve the body of the lamp and some early specimens without a groove for the wick have long been held to be mortars for earth colours. In several cases we can trace the development of a spout and even decoration. The lamp found at La Mouthe was decorated with an engraving of an ibex on the base, later the lamp itself is sometimes roughly shaped into the form of an animal. A similar development has been found in the Far East (7) where even in Han times many lamps still retained the character of a "basin for holding wicks" sometimes shaped in the form of an animal or placed on a stand in the form of an animal.

Of somewhat later date are the pottery and stone lamps used in the neolithic mines and galleries cut for flint mining. Some of the English mines like Grimes Graves and Cissbury were provided with lamps hollowed out of chalk blocks of the type also found in neolithic camps of Sussex and Wessex (8). A large mass of Neolithic material shows (9) that the native population of Neolithic Europe used animal fats and possibly also raw linseed oil as a fuel for their lamps which were provided with flax and hemp wicks. In this thesis von Chorus gives the following stable showing this development:

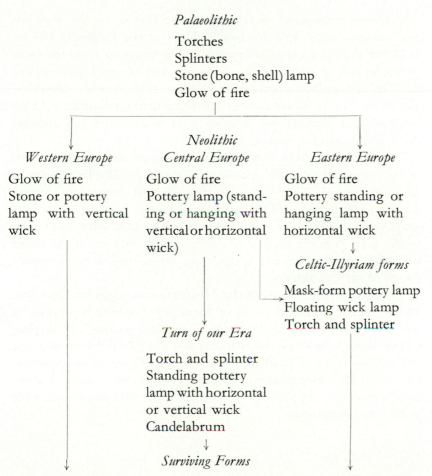

Palaeolithic

Torches
Splinters
Stone (bone, shell) lamp
Glow of fire

Neolithic

Western Europe	*Central Europe*	*Eastern Europe*
Glow of fire	Glow of fire	Glow of fire
Stone or pottery lamp with vertical wick	Pottery lamp (standing or hanging with vertical or horizontal wick)	Pottery standing or hanging lamp with horizontal wick

Celtic-Illyriam forms

Mask-form pottery lamp
Floating wick lamp
Torch and splinter

Turn of our Era

Torch and splinter
Standing pottery lamp with horizontal or vertical wick
Candelabrum

Surviving Forms

Stone and pottery lamps, candle, candelabrum, torch or splinter, float.

The prehistoric inhabitants of the Atlantic seacoasts had a fairly generous supply of fuel for their lamps as they caught whales and seals (10) which served them for many purposes. Though at present Eskimos also use caribou fat for lamp fuel, their ancestors probably obtained oil from the sea only. The use of seal blubber for heating and lighting has been specially prominent in the circumpolar zone with its long winter night and in the Baltic area oil from seal blubber was used for lighting up till modern times. Whale blubber was used for heating and lighting too. It was boiled down to yield the oil used in lamps and fires as late as the sixteenth century in Scandinavia and in the Faeroes even as the twentieth century (11).

Mathiassen compared the Eskimo stone blubber lamps with the oval pottery lamps from kitchen middens of the Ertebølle Culture of Denmark (12), analysis of samples of the scrapings from the inner surface of one of which revealed the presence of small quantities of fat. The archaeological evidence offers no clue to other subsidiary uses of this seal or whale blubber but it is worth noting that in Olaus Magnus' time blubber was employed in Scandinavia for greasing ships' planks and for treating leather.

These primitive stone lamps also afford us an interesting example of the conservatism of the ancient craftsmen (13). The Eskimos who migrated from Hudson's Bay to their present homes in western Alaska continue to obtain the soapstone for their blubber lamps from quarries by the Tree River in Coronation Bay, now some 1400 miles to the east. Possibly further research on the material from which European prehistoric stone lamps were carved might reveal similar proofs of early migrations.

The ancient stone lamps of the Mediterranean region are less well known probably because many of them have not been recognised as such but have been labelled "mortars" or "door-sockets" in the past. Calcite stone lamps have been found at Ur, gypsum lamps in Crete and various types of bowlshaped lamps, sometimes on pedestals are known to have been used in the Ancient Near East. In medieval Europe they reappear in the cressets of cloister walks and sometimes even in churches themselves.

3. *Torch and Taper*

When Hermes goes to warn Kalypso of the coming of Odysseus he sees her in her cave as "a fire on all the hearth blazed sprightly" (14). Firebrands and branches lit from the glowing embers soon supplemented the lighting of the cave or primitive but. Such torches were the first independent sources of artificial light and they may even antedate the primitive stone lamps which we discussed above. A few primitive tribes still have to resort to torches for lighting their homes. In some cases strange solutions have been found, in the Shetlands the fat bodies of the stormy petrels with wicks thrust down their throats are used as a kind of "natural lamp or torch".

Often primitive man has reached beyond the simple branch or faggot and selected substances which by their oil or resin content are more suitable for lighting than just dry wood. Thus *bark* has been used among the peasants and hunter-fishers of temperate and circumpolar Europe for tapers and torches down to the present day. The neolithic inhabitants of Switzerland and southern Germany also used spools of birch-bark as tapers or torches, the charred stumps of which have been recognised at Weiher bei Thayngen, Robenhausen and Federsee. A similar use of birch-bark persisted in certain Alpine valleys into the present century and still survives in the birch zones of northern Europe (15). The pitch contained in this birch-bark was used to repair a stone lamp found at Egolzwil.

Later torches were often carried in special socketed holders or in torch-cases filled with resinous material as shown in Greek vase-paintings. There we also notice early forms of *splinter lights*, often taking the form of two pieces of wood fastened to a staff, in the form of a St. Andrew's cross. Such splinters of resinous wood, especially pine wood, were carefully cut and dried and their illuminating power was often increased by treating them with combustible materials. Hence they are intermediate forms between the torch and splinter proper and the later tapers and candles. These splinter lights belong to the forest areas where such wood is plentiful. In Scotland for instance the use of pine splinters or "fir candles" as a source of lighting survived until recent times. In some regions different types of candelabra or similar devices were evolved to impale or hold these burning splinters.

Other primitive forms of tapers are the *rushlights*, a feature of the Welsh and English countryside. They consisted of peeled rushes (common soft rush, Juncus effusus), each of which had one (or two) strips left to support them. The peeled rush was dipped in fat or grease to give it a combustible coating like a thin candle or taper. The strip had the added effect of the later plaited candle wick in curving the burnt material to one side and in reducing the necessity of snuffing by bringing the carbonised point into contact with the air. Similar faggots or tapers were used during the Late Bronze Age in the copper mines of the eastern Alps.

Similar torches and tapers were used in the ancient Near East. In ancient Mesopotamia (16) the torch (German "Fackel" from Latin "facula", little torch (fax)) often consisted of a bundle of splinters dipped into bitumen or resin, sometimes bundles of rushes or springs of the vine were used. Assyrian reliefs show many instances of the use of such torches. We shall discuss their use in fire-telegraphy later on. In ancient Egypt several terms (17) denoted similar torches and tapers.

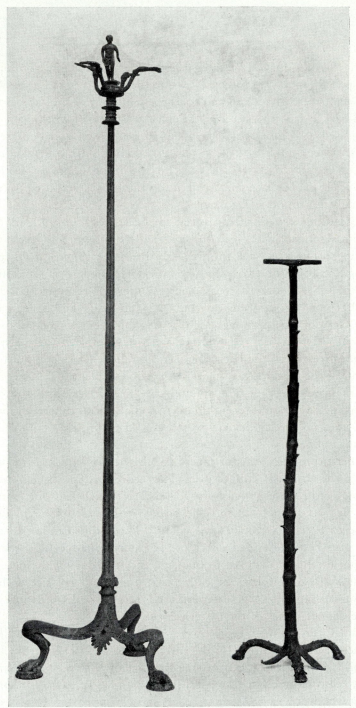

Fig. 22.
Etruscan candelabra.
(Photo British Museum, London)

The oldest of these "tk3.w" seems to denote a kind of taper made of fat built up around a wick, another denotes a taper with a flax or linen (maybe an oakum) wick, "gmḥ.t" but a term of New Kingdom date would seem to denote a real torch or bundle of splinters (w'3). Another late term "ḥ.t" for "wick, taper" is written with the ideogram of the carob-tree and products from this tree must have been used in compounding it (18).

In Ancient Greece (19) the glow of the hearth is the oldest source of light mentioned (20), no lamps are mentioned in the Homeric poems. However, torches and the like seem to have been used instead of lamps. We find the "pine-splinter" (das, dais) in common use (21), they were cut by the dadourgoi, the "torch-cutters" of Mount Ida (22) and other wooded regions. Apart from these the torch (lampas or lampter) is often mentioned (23). Instead of the pine splinters reeds smeared with pitch (24) or with the lees of grapes (25) could be bought from the "kapelos" (26), the "drug-store" of Antiquity. There was another kind of torch named "phanos" (27), but as this term is later applied to the lantern it is more probable that it indicated a fire-pot in which splinters or torches could be fixed in a mass of resinous or similar combustible nature. Other types of torches were manufactured from sticks of resinous wood bound with rushes, papyrus, or vine tendrils and treated with resin, pitch or wax, such as were used for the fire-pots mentioned above.

These different forms of torches and tapers had an important part to play in Greek religious life, they figure in the cult of the gods, in weddings and funeral rites (28). In classical Greece torches were still burnt for the gods in the market-place and in Roman times they played a large part in the mysteries of Mithras and the Magna Mater. These torches used in the later Roman ceremonies consisted of saplings beaten into a fibrous state with fat rubbed into them and formed into torches of the bundled type as depicted on Greek vases.

Lighting the home with such torches was dangerous and many famous buildings were thus consumed by the fire of torches dropped on purpose or by misadventure. As Thucydides tells us "in that same summer, too, the temple of Hera at Argos was burned down, Chrysis the priestess having placed a lighted torch near the garlands and then gone to sleep, so that the whole place took fire and was ablaze before she was awake". Pausanias writing many centuries later characteristically replaced the term torch by "lychnos" (lamp) (29). Therefore such torches or tapers were placed in special pans even in the palace

Fig. 23.
Syrian bronze candlestick.
(Photo British Museum, London)

of Odysseus (30) and Schliemann found such a torch holder of brownish clay during his excavations at Tiryns.

Such pans or fire pots on a support held torches and they are sometimes called lampter (31) but such pots are also often braziers used for heating, in which case they are called hysgara, hipnos, chytropous. They gradually developed into ornamental marble, stone and metal types. Apart from these fire-pots there were more developed types of candelabra, called lampter, lychnion or lychnia which were of the socket-type which holds the torch or taper or of the spike or pricket type onto which the torch was fastened or stuck. The ancient coins of Aptara (Crete) and other Greek towns show torch holders of various types. The pricket-type "candlestick" to hold the splinters or torches of resinous wood (Latin fax, taeda) or the tapers of vegetable fibres covered with combustible substances (phanos, funale) was considered to be the oldest form (32) by the ancients themselves. The Etruscans seem to have used them for their splinter lights and we have a few examples of Roman pricket candlesticks (e.g. in the Guidhall Museum, London) but in general the Romans seem to have preferred the socketed type, some of which like the example from Rheims now in the British Museum are made of pottery and even have an aperture to remove the candle-end.

The use of these chandeliers did not remain restricted to torches and tapers, they were later used as stands for a number of oil-lamps, sometimes made of wood and pottery for the poorer folk. But they are also used as candlesticks for the true candles. In the story of the candle the pricket figures again in the early Middle Ages and holds its own until well in the sixteenth century, when it is generally replaced by the socketed type, which begins to reappear during the fourteenth century. The chandeliers of the ancients also included hanging forms such as the "polycandelon" or disk supporting glass lamps, which began to be used more generally in the early Byzantine churches (33).

Pliny informs us of the fact (34) that:

"Aegina specialized in producing only the upper parts (sockets) of chandeliers and similarly Taranto made only the stems, and consequently credit for manufacture is, in the matter of these articles, shared between these two localities. Nor are people ashamed to buy these at a price equal to the pay of a military tribune, although they (candelabra) take even their name from the lighted candles they carry..."

But although it is admitted that there are no lampstands made of
Corinthian metal, yet this name specially is commonly attached to
them, because although Mummius's victory destroyed Corinth,
it caused the dispersal of bronzes from a number of the towns of
Achaia at the same time."

which goes to show that there was a certain amount of specialisation
amongst the Roman craftsmen.

4. *The Candle*

It will be clear from the above lines that the ancient authors were
none too correct in their terminology and used several word in-
discriminately for torches, tapers and even fire-pots or torch holders.
The same holds good for the word "candela" (35) which originally
meant a taper with a wick of oakum, the pith of reeds, papyrus or
any other vegetable fibre dipped in a bath of tallow, pitch or wax.
Sometimes special terms like cereus, funale or sebaceus give some
indication of the combustible substance used as a coating of the wick.
But apart from denoting a taper the word candela is also applied to
the true candle, the off-spring of the more primitive taper.

Tapers were burned in lamps or pots, wound in a coil or fastened
to a support. In certain European countries it still has a cult use.
Its principle is still applied in the float lights or night-lights, in wax
matches and in the long cords used in the now almost obsolete gas
lighter.

The candle was evolved when mankind disposed of a reasonable
supply of vegetable fats or of flocks and herds which yielded sufficient
animal fats for burning. Hence it cannot be older than the Early
Bronze Age and probably arose even much later.

Like the taper the candle is a self-contained form of illumination (36),
its fibrous core or wick being surrounded by a cylinder of fat or wax.
The wick of a candle is not in contact with the air and it does not
burn but chars. The charred end finally hinders proper burning and
all kinds of methods for "snuffing" the candle have been devised in
the course of the centuries. Not until Cambacéres introduced the
plaited wick (1825) and impregnation with appropriate salts allowed
Price to introduce his "snufless composite candles" in 1840 was this
daily trouble overcome.

As Hough (37) explained very clearly:

"The materials for candles are not many. In nature vegetable substances preponderate over those available from animal sources, yet only in a few places have vegetable fats and waxes been used for candles and most of these sporadic attempts belong to the modern period. In China and Japan illuminating substances are derived from the tallow tree (Stillingia sebifera) of eastern China, and the Rhus succedanea, of Japan. In both cases the wax of "tallow" occurs on the seeds, from which it is freed by means of heat and pressure. The Chinese tree tallow has a rather low melting point below summer temperature and it is found necessary to put on such candles a substantial coating of beeswax or insect wax.

The Chinese wax insect, or coccus pela, is found on the Ligustrum japonicum, L. obtusifolium, L. tibola and Rhus succedaneum. The eggs are gathered from nests on the above trees in the fall and kept wrapped in reed leaves. At the beginning of May the eggs are placed upon proper trees, usually Fraxinus chinensis, where they hatch about the 1st of June and begin wax making. In September the wax is scraped from the twigs where it has been deposited, melted with boiling water and cast into cakes. It is a white crystalline substance (Mtpt 152° F) resembling the best spermaceti. In the western Hemisphere wax was produced by the early settlers from the bayberry (Myrica cerifera), in Brazil from the Ceroxylon or wax palm."

Such fats being unobtainable the classical world made its candles from tallow or beeswax. The making of tallow candles by dipping usually coincided with the butchering of the winter stores of meat at which time much fat was accumulated.

Beeswax was available in fairly large quantities as the byproduct of the gathering and refining of honey (38), the main sweetening agent of the ancients (39). They were of course well aware that the bees collected wax to build their hives (40) from the different plants and flowers they visited. After the honey was extracted the wax was refined (41), by methods described by Palladius and Columella. The latter tells us, that "the remains of the honeycombs, when they have been well squeezed, after being carefully washed in fresh water, are thrown into a brazen vessel; water is then added to them and they are melted over a fire. When this has been done, the wax is poured out and strained through straw or rushes. It is then boiled over again a second time in the same manner and poured in such moulds as are thought suitable, water having been first added. When the wax has hardened, it is easy to take it out, since the liquid which remains in the bottom does not allow it to stick to the moulds."

Columella's recipe is of course incomplete and describes only the manufacture of crude wax. If we want to know how wax was properly refined we should turn to Pliny (42) who tells us much more:

"Wax is made after the honey has been extracted from the combs, but these must first be cleaned with water and dried for three days in the dark; then on the fourth day they are melted in a new earthen vessel on the fire, with just enough water to cover them, and then strained in a wicker basket. The wax is boiled again with the same water in the same pot, and poured into other water, this to be cold, contained in vessels smeared all round inside with honey. The best is called Punic wax; the next best is very yellow indeed, with the smell of honey, pure but produced in Pontus, the region of the poisonous honies, which makes me surprised at its established reputation; next is Cretan wax, consisting in very great part of bee glue, about which we have spoken in treating of the nature of bees. After these comes Corsican wax, which as it is made from honey got by bees from box, is supposed to have certain medical quality. Punic wax is prepared in the following way. Yellow wax is exposed to the wind several times in the open, then it is heated in water taken from the open sea, to which soda has been added. Then they collect with spoons the "flower", that is, all the whitest part, and pour into a vessel containing a little cold water. Then it is boiled again by itself in sea-water, after which they cool the vessel itself with water. When they have done this three times, they dry the wax in the open, by sunlight and by moonlight, on a mat of rushes. For the moon makes it white while the sun dries it; to prevent the sun from melting it, they cover it with a piece of thin linen cloth. The greatest whiteness, however, is obtained if after its exposure to the sun the wax is once more boiled. Punic wax is most useful for medicines. Wax becomes dark with the addition of paper ash, and red with an admixture of alkanet; by paints it is made to assume various colours for forming likenesses, for the innumerable uses of men, and even for the protection of walls and of weapons."

Fig. 24.

Making "dips". This hand-dipping process is used for making candles for certain industrial purposes. The dips are built up by adding successive layers of wax, the dipping and setting processes being continued until the required thickness and weight is reached.

(Shell photograph)

Dioscorides (43) has an equally detailed passage which runs:

"The best wax is that which is of a pale yellow, somewhat fat and of a sweet savour, and having the scent, as it were, of honey yet pure; which by kind is either Pontic or Cretan. The next in place to it, is that which is somewhat white by nature and fat. Now wax is made white after this manner. Having cut white and clean wax into small pieces, cast it into a new vessel and pouring thereupon as much sea-water, taken out of the deep, as shall be sufficient, boil it, sprinkling a little nitre upon it. And when it shall have boiled twice or thrice, taking off the vessel and letting it cool, take out the cake and scraping off the filth, if there be any about it, seeth it a second time, putting other sea-water to it; and when the wax shall have sod again, as has been formerly shown, take away the vessel from the fire and taking the bottom of a little new vessel first moistened with cold water, let it down gently into the wax, dipping it in a little with a soft touch, that a little of it may be taken and that it may be concreted together with istelf. Having taken it up, pull off the first cake and again let down the bottom, cooling it in water anew, and do this so long till you have taken up all the wax. Then piercing these little cakes with a linen thread, hang them up at some distance of each other and in the day-time setting them in the sun, sprinkle them every now and then with water and at night set them under the moon till they become perfectly white. But if any would make it extraordinarily white, let him work the other things in like manner, but let him seeth it often. But some instead of sea-water taken out of the deep boil it in the aforesaid manner once or twice in very sharp brine, then afterwards they take it out in a thin and round bottle having a handle, afterwards laying the little round cakes upon thick grass, they sun them until at last it becomes wonderfully white. But they do advise to set about this work in the spring when the sun both remits of its vehemency and yields dew so that it shall not melt."

This refined beeswax was used for encaustic painting (44) and for the manufacture of wax tablets (45). Pausanias tells us that the oldest Apollo temple was said to have been raised by bees from wax and feathers (46) and Virgil relates that Pan devised the art of joining reeds with wax (47). However, a large percentage of this wax was used for the manufacture of candles.

There are several methods for the manufacture of candles:

1.   Dipping and drawing the wick through molten fat or wax;
2.   Building it up by hand;
3.   Pouring molten fat or wax along the wick and thus gradually building up the body of the candle;
4.   Casting candles in moulds in which the wick has been fixed in advance.

The art of moulding candles was developed in the fourteenth century by the Sieur de Brez, but there was still the great difficulty that beeswax was apt to stick to the walls of the moulds and hence it was difficult to detach the finished candle from the moulds undamaged. Real improvement came only in the nineteenth century when Cambacéres introduced a good plaited wick (1825) and Chevreul and Gay-Lussac learnt to separate the high melting point of fatty acids or

"stearin" from fats (1823) and took out a patent (1825) for the manufacture of composite candles. The first efficient moulding machines
of the continuous wicking type designed to produce two to three
charges of 80—500 candles per hour were developed from the original
designed by Morgan (1834). During the latter part of that century
De Milly and Twitchell improved the manufacture and refining of

Fig. 25.

Jacob Ardaji, a shopkeeper in the Old City of Jerusalem, pouring molten wax onto
the wicks suspended on a revolving rack. The number of applications determines
the thickness of candles. Note the graceful lines produced by this manual process.
(Shell photograph)

stearin and about 1857 the first candles made from (petroleum) paraffin
wax were on the London market and soon displaced the tallow, wax
and composite candles.

The ancients used only tallow or beeswax candles produced by the
dipping process. The wick (hryallis, filum) of such dips was prepared
from certain types of papyrus (scirpus) or twisted fibres, sometimes
impregnated with sulphur and finally dipped (candelas sebare) into
the liquid tallow or wax. It is not easy to distinguish between tapers

(in which the mass of the wick preponderates) and candles (in which the wick forms but a small part of the total mass) in ancient texts, for the term "candela" denotes both. Usually the candela is a tallow candle (candela sebacea) and not a wax candle (candela cerea, cereus). Beeswax, though available and even imported from Olbia and the Black Sea region throughout the Roman Empire, remained expensive and the cereus seems to have been used by the rich only (48). The "candelae simplicae" were probably tapers. Ammian speaks of a "sebalis fax" when he wants to denote a candle made of tallow (sebum) (49).

This less precise terminology makes it difficult to decide whether the candle was known in Ancient Greece. Torches and tapers were certainly used before the oil lamp was introduced. Pine splinters and torches were used in the ancient religious ceremonies until the oil lamp is introduced in the fourth century, when it also appears among the votive gifts and in graves. Wax figures were used in magic and certain religious ceremonies but it is doubtful whether wax candles really figure in the Eleusinian mysteries as some modern authors claim.

The home of the candle seems to have been Italy, its use going back to the Etruscans. One of the earliest proofs of its use is a picture in an Etruscan tomb at Orvieto. When Apuleius speaks of the "brittle rushes which grow in marshy districts" used to manufacture "watch-candles" and funeral lights to burn by dead bodies while lying above the ground, he probably means tallow tapers. In heathen ceremonies the Romans always used wax candles where the Greeks used torches. Such candles were burnt in candlesticks or candelabra with spikes or sockets and fashioned of clay, wood or bronze. The socket often has an aperture to remove the candle ends. Candelabra found in the Saalburg were provided with sockets of different diameters for burning candles of different sizes. A fragment of a candle dating back to the first century A.D. was found in Vaison (near Orange) and is now in the British Museum. A chandler's apparatus is said to have been found in the ruins of Herculaneum.

From Rome the candle went east to Greece, at a fairly late date we find Greek words like "kandela" or "kerion" adopted from the Latin but often they are simply called "lampas". In the Near East too the candle is a late-comer. Beeswax (dônag) is mentioned in the Old Testament as something that melts easily. "The rocks shall melt as wax (keros) at Thy presence" and similar expressions (50) are fairly frequent but no mention is made of a candle. According to Jewish Law no wax (š'awâ) or fat should be used for the Sabbath light (51).

A comment on a passage in the Book of Proverbs (Prov. 6.23) stating that "the commandment is a lamp" runs "Like this lamp will burn also when one lights thousands of wax lights (ķerwínîn, from cerea or kerion) and tallow lights (sebâķin, from sebacus) and keep its light, thus he who spends for what has been ordered (charity) does not loose from his possessions" (52). Thus in Hellenism wax candles and tapers came into use in these parts. Wax was also used for waxed tablets for writing (53), in medical recipes (54) and to fill up small holes (55).

The candle came into its own in the Christian church. Already in early Christian tombs we find many candles depicted on the altars of saints and martyrs and they gradually become a very common item in old chuch accounts. Later Papal Bulls excluded the use of animal fats like tallow from altar candles, the beeswax content was to be at least 65—75% for the candles used on the High Altar, and a minimum of 25% for those used on lesser altars. Hence, though we have no clear data on the use of candles in such ancient authors as Livy or Pliny (56), we find the candle as a symbol of investiture in the hands of the acolyte from the fourth century A.D. onwards. The offering of candles from the emperor to the Pope is related to a similar offering made at the investitute of a priest and a bishop (57).

The first definite news on this use of wax candles was its connection with the Church festival of Candlemas, celebrated on February the second in commemoration of the presentation of Christ in the Temple. The late fourth-century pilgrim Etheria saw the celebration of "the meeting of the Lord (with Simon and Anna)" at Jerusalem on February 14th, 40 days after Epiphany. In 542, the date having been shifted to February 2nd, it was established through the Eastern Empire by Justinian. In the West it was introduced to replace the old heathen festival of "Hypopante" (celebrated on the first of February) but here it was called "The Purification of the Blessed Virgin". The rites of Candlemas are given in the eighth-century Gelasian Sacramentary and Pope Sergius I (678—701) instituted the procession with lighted candles. Pope Sergius II in 844 did much to further its celebration throughout the West. The well-known Golden Legend by Jacobus de Voragine (1228) has details on the blessing of the candles (58). The first specification of the candles for use in churches is given in Vincent of Beauvais' Speculum Majus (1250).

In medieval law culprits are sentenced to carry a lighted candle through the streets. Snuffing a candle forms part of the ceremony of excommunication (excommunicatio ardentibus candelis). The candle is also introduced as a measure of time and certain decisions have to be taken within the time a given candle burns. In the West tradition ascribes to Alfred the Great of England the invention of the candle timepiece (subdivided into equal segments). In the East such candles come into use during the T'ang dynasty (618—907) and they are the common means of time measurement during the Sung dynasty (960—1279). Incense sticks were used in the same way during the T'ang dynasty and later (58a). The thirteenth century documents mention an ordeal by two burning candles in the Fuero General de Navarra and there is the "oath over the candle" (iurare supercandelam). Hence the common use of the candle seems to have developed between 800 and 1200, though no Carolingian or early medieval pictures show this. The ordinance of William the Conqueror that "all fire and candles be extinguished at the ringing of a bell at eight o'clock" simply means lamps in general and does not refer to a common use of the candle. However, from 1200 onwards the manufacture of candles on a larger scale is well attested and taxation in different regions of Western Europe shows that its use has now spread beyond the walls of the churches to the houses and public buildings in general.

5. *Preclassical Lamps*

When we now turn to the typology of early lamps we should re-member that little attention has yet been given to this subject and that we have only vague indications about the development and life of the different types of lamps in use in the ancient Near East.

Shells, either used as found in nature or adapted for use, seem to have been the oldest types of lamps used in these regions. They have been found all over the Near East and even in Chanhu-Daro (India) and other sites of the Indus civilisation, which made great use of conch and Murex shells for inlay work, toyps, spoons, pastry moulds, etc. (59). As many shells have natural forms which more or less suggest their use as lamps we need not wonder that several such shell lamps were found at Ur. Here tricadna shells had been cut open to serve as lamps, their five projecting horns served as grooves to hold the wick. Imitations cut from stone are sufficiently true to nature to be identified. Some of the Ur stone lamps are alabaster imitation of shells.

Shells of the pecten (oyster and scallop) or the whelk type are mostly used. Their use as lamps spread east and west far beyond the

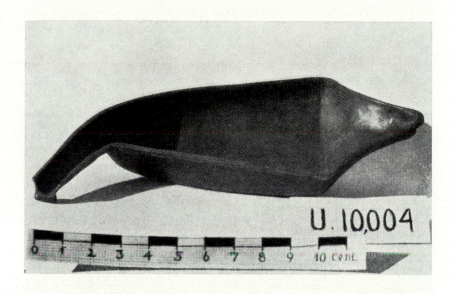

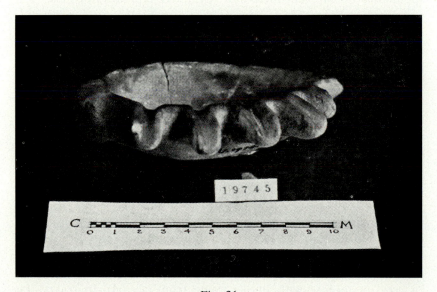

Fig. 26.

A multi-wick stone lamp (both forms derived from the shell), found at Ur.
(Photographs British Museum)

Near East and the Mediterranean. The "buckie lamps" of the Orkneys
and the Shetlands are suspended specimens of the Fusus antiguus or
red whelk. In such buckie lamps fish oil was burnt with a fibre wick as
in the lamp consisting of a single valve of the pecten used by the
Ainus of Japan and now in the Smithsonian Institution.

The early pottery lamps of the Near East often imitate such shells,
like those if the third millenium found at Tell Duweir (Palestine)
by the Wellcome Expedition. Later pottery types on this site deviate
from this original form, they are almost square, four-spouted and
flat-based. The pottery lamps imitating the scallop shell have often
been associated with Phoenician influence. Thus Walters refers to no
less than sixteen "cocked hat" type lamps, three of which were found
in Cyprus, two at Carthage, nine in Sardinia and two in Egypt (60).
Maybe we should associate this shell lamp with the worship of the
goddess to become Aphrodite in the Greek world, with whom the
scallop is closely associated (61). Unfortunately no true shell lamps
have been recovered from excavations in the Phoenician homeland
but only pottery imitations of the "cocked hat" type. Soon Greek
spouted lamps supplant these more primitive type in Phoenicia.

A similar change can be observed in ancient Palestine, where the
shell lamp develops by the acquisition of a flat base of a more and
more pronounced type, the pinched lip being transformed into a
definite wick-nozzle and the smaller body being deepened. Both at
Ras Shamra (Northern Syria) and later in Medieval Persia shell lamps
fashioned in bronze remained in vogue. Strangely enough we do
not find it in ancient Greece where the torch and the taper hold their
sway until the advent of the spouted lamp which has nothing in
common with the shell lamp.

The *open-bowl or saucer type lamp* seems to have originated in ancient
Egypt. Herodotus (62) tells us the story of King Mycerinus, who
being told that he had but a short time to live, turned the night into
day by lighting many lamps and thus cheating the gods out of the
time alloted to him. We have many illustrations of this simple type
of lamp (63) and probably many examples have not been recognised
as such by the excavators. Even Sir Alan Gardiner believed it to be
"a bowl of incense with smoke rising from it" (64). In reality this
sign looks more like a small bowl or flat saucer containing the oil
(mostly castor oil) and salt which Diodor, Strabo and Pliny mention.
Glass lamps were certainly not used in early times as Neuburger
claims, glass not being yet shaped into bowls or saucers. We also

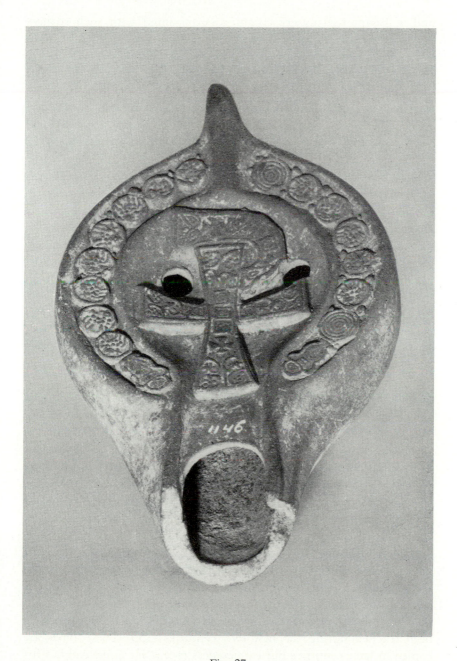

Fig. 27.

Roman oil lamp, decorated with the "chrysma" symbol, from Moura (Tunis).
(Rijksmuseum van Oudheden, Leiden; No. H.Q. 15)

find in Egypt red pottery columns surmounted with such shallow bowls as a kind of primitive lampstands. The simple open-bowl or saucer form developed into a spouted saucer lamp, the wick being allowed to hang over the side instead of floating in the middle. The plasticity of clay has been taken to invite such a development, which may also be due to the imitation of the shell lamp which we have already discussed. This spouted-saucer type lamp was used all over the Middle and Near East and it is still in common use.

The story and chronology of lamps in ancient Egypt is yet to be studied properly (65). Certain early Neolithic Egyptian stone bowls may well have been lamps, some have even spouts. However, in historic times the pottery floating wick type seems to have been a characteristic of the country. In Roman times it was translated into glass forms and it remained popular in the Middle Ages, being depicted in twelfth and thirteenth century manuscripts. Later authors like Clement of Alexandria always ascribe the invention of the lamp to the Egyptians, yet this may hold true only for the saucer lamp, for the shell lamp is missing and the popular cocked hat type is a cross of these two and originated somewhere else in the Near East, possibly in Syria. As the pottery lamp is so fragile and must have disappeared amongst the rubbish heaps of Egypt, we have little evidence of the development of these simple forms until we come to much later times.

The later terms for lamps (66) are all written with the "brazier" ideogram, that is with a sign interpreted by Sir Allan Gardiner as "a brazier with the flame rising from it". It looks more like a taper or rushlight in a holder, but this is difficult to decide. These terms are applied to pottery and metal forms current in later dynastic times, and we cannot always decide whether a particular type is meant. The pictures on tomb reliefs show bowls with upto three flames from floating wicks.

In Hellenistic and Roman Egypt Greek models of lamps completely displaced the older types (67) and closed-in lamps of various types are generally used. Though Roman models penetrated to all parts of the Empire during the first centuries of our era, Greek lamps held their own in Egypt and the apex of their development seems to have been reached during the first two centuries A.D. These types are copied in later centuries but carelessness creeps in. Solid handles for instance are signs of late work. After long copying of the decoration, of the original moulds such decoration becomes vaguer in later copies.

We find a gradual departure from the earlier rounded form and slightly projecting nozzle to ovoid and afterwards even pear or shoe shaped forms. The original white and grey colour became buff and pink. The nozzle becomes a mere hole at the end of the lamp and in the later lamp even a more or less well-marked groove from filling hole to wick hole can be found. To Byzantine times (fourth century A.D. and later) belongs a lamp, characteristic of the eastern Mediterranean, which has the shape of a hollow bowl with a cone or beehive-shaped receptacle inside it, to which the sides of the bowl form a rim. The inner receptacle has a small hole in the side serving as a nozzle and a filling hole at the top which is surmounted by a funnel in the more developed specimens. We also begin to find records such as "for the lighting of the lamps of the gods in the course of the year six metretes of oil a day" (68) in the papyri. Christian symbols begin to appear in the decoration (69) such as a Christian martyr repelling the great crocodile god Suchos with the symbol of the cross.

Another typical Christian feature is the use of hanging or standing lamps of glass for illuminating churches and other buildings. Such lamps, often called "candela", are mentioned by various authors from the fourth century A.D. onwards (70). Recent finds at Karanis have supplied additional data on these lamps which in the fourth and fifth centuries are either conical in shape or hemispherical bowls and which develop later into more complicated forms. Sometimes they were used as standing lamps and different types of standing brackets were employed such as the wooden tripods found at Karanis. More often they were hung singly or in groups in a candalabrum. All those that have ring-handles attached to their bodies or rims were presumably employed as single lights and hung by chains from a hook on the ceiling, or from a bracket jutting out of the wall. Multiple chandeliers of metal, sometimes of huge size and great magnificence have been found and are depicted in later manuscripts.

The use of a vertical glass tube in the centre of the vessel fixed to the base with molten glass was an obvious adaption of the Roman candlestick. The earliest known examples are the Gezer and Ophel lamps of the fifth and sixth centuries A.D. The glass tube to hold the wick becomes more and more common in Arab times, especially in beaker-lamps and today is the rule in the East.

Few details on the development of lamps in ancient Mesopotamia are given by the archaeologists (71). The primitive shallow saucer-type stone lamp with a pinched spout through which the wick passed

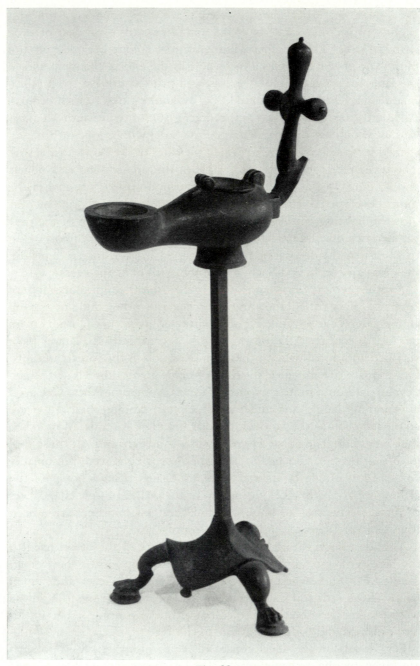

Fig. 28.
Bronze Christian lamp on standard (Egypt, second to fourth century A.D.).
(Rijksmuseum van Oudheden, Leiden)

gradually develop into the later pointed-shoe type lamp with a hole for the wick. This shoe-like lamp is often used as a symbol of the fire-god Nusku. From the third millennium B.C. onwards Tridacna (conch) shells were used as lamps and later imitations were fashioned from stone, bronze, silver and gold. The wick was usually made from wool or reed. The terms for lamps are usually connected with shells, vessels and with the word for "house" (bîtu) or "light" (nûru), we also find expressions such as "house of the wick". One wonders whether the term "bit nûri" (house of the lamp) indicates a real lantern in which a lamp was placed or whether it was just a lamp. The inhabitants of Mesopotamia were fully aware of the advantages of burning "earth oil" instead of the usual sesame oil (72) as this gave a better light even in the unrefined state. Torches made with the natural bitumen from the many seepages are shown in the bas-reliefs depicting military expeditions.

In the Old Testament only pure olive oil is mentioned for lamps, notably in connection with the tabernacle (73). The later Jewish law also mentions sesame, nut, fish, coloquinth and ricinus oil, but these should not be used for the Sabbath light and in the temple unless good olive oil be not available in foreign countries (74). "The light of the candela (lamp) and the sound of the millstone" belonged to town life (75) and "a good lamp goeth not out by night" (76). Such a lamp should have a good flax wick (77). It was kept burning for the master (78) and could be placed high on a standard or foot (lyknia) (79). As in the later crusie lamp a bowl might be fixed below the lamp to catch any dripping oil (80).

We often hear of the candelabrum in connection with the tabernacle or temple (81) to which belonged tongs (melḳâhájim) for inserting and pulling out the wicks, a knife for trimming the wick (mezammerôt) and pans (maḥtot) (82). The later glass lanterns (pânâs, Greek phanos) or candelabra might have a separate oil storage vessel (bêt ḳibbûl šémen) and a grip for the lamp proper (bêt ḳibbûl nêr) (83). The golden candelabrum of the temple with its seven arms plus lamps has a golden pair of scissors for the wick and a golden trimming knife. According to the Mishna the ordinary candelabrum had arms (kânîm) with cups (péraḥ) and rested on a foot (bâsîs, Greek basis) (84). In the Temple there were originally ten candelabra (85) but the Second Temple had only a single one. These candelabra with their lamps should be kept and trimmed regularly, at least once a day according to strict rules (86) laid down in Jewish law.

The present Chanukkah lamp is a direct descendant of the "seven-branched candlestick" of the Temple. It is made of a row of eight spoon-shaped lamps backed by a sconce-like panel decorated according to the country and the period, and sometimes provided with a narrow trough as a drip-catcher below. A pilot light may be added either as an extra lamp in the row or separately placed. The original eight-lamp arrangement is said to have arisen from the rededication of the Temple by Judas Maccabeus in 165 B.C. after its pollution by the pagan altar set up by Antiochus Epiphanes three years before. When relighted only one flask of holy oil sufficient for one day was available but this miraculously lasted for eight days. In commemoration of this miracle the Channukah lamp is lit one light or lamp at a time on successive days to cover the span of eight days of the festival period. Hence it is not, as popularly believed to be, a "candlestick" but a stand for a series of eight lamps.

In the ordinary home in ancient Palestine the lamp was usually near the stove. Salt was sometimes added to the oil as in ancient Egypt; it served not only to dry the oil thoroughly but also imparted a brighter yellow colour to the flame (87). It was allowed to use oil to light a fire except during the sabbathical year, when the wood should first be immersed in oil before putting it in the hearth. The earliest lamps were simple bowls, sometimes with a pinched rim to hold the wick. Gradually the bowl acquired a flat foot and the fold was enlarged until the bowl was completely covered up except for the hole for the wick and that for pouring in the oil. In Roman days lamps with special wick spouts are common. In Arab times special tubes for holding the wick became more general as did hanging lamps, which had been rarely used in earlier periods.

As the ancient house in Palestine had hardly any windows one had to use a lamp looking for small things like a coin (88) and outside the house they were certainly needed when there was no moonlight (89). In the story of the foolish virgins oil lamps are used in the narrow streets of the town where wood or splinters were not available. As the volume of the lamps was small it was necessary to refill them fairly often, hence the maidens carried jugs (aggeia) of oil. From other sources we know that a small bottle-like jug (ṣelôhît) was commonly used.

On the roads lamps were sometimes needed (90) but usually torches (lampades) or lanterns (phanoi) were carried as by the crowd which took our Lord prisoner (91). Throughout the desert journey the "column of fire" replaced the torches (lappîd) (92) which will no longer be needed in the New Jerusalem (93). In most cases the "lamp taken onto the path" (94) may be either a torch, a lantern or a real oil lamp.

6. *Classical Lamps*

In ancient Greece there was a long period during which the torch or the pine splinter, the "lampas", reigned and the oil lamp was not used. The Greek "lychnos" or "lychnon", Latin "lucerna" or "lych-

Fig. 29.
Mycenean bronze lamp.
(Photo British Museum, London)

nus" (95) always refers to a lighting device in which oil is sucked up by a wick to feed a flame. We are told that these terms are derived from "lux" (light) (96), Varro states that the term "lucerna" arose when the want for a Latin term was felt, and that previously candelae or torches had been in use, no oil being available in Italy for burning in lamps. Some have argued that the lamp was developed in ancient Greece from the torch by filling the torch-pans with oil and reducing the ratio of fibrous and combustible matter by the use of a single wick.

In reality lamps were known in Minoan Crete and Mycenaean Greece. We have Minoan clay lamps of a simple open-bowl type and also similar stone lamps both from Crete and Mycenae. Limestone stands were found on which such lamps must have been placed for illumination at festivities. Homer has one single reference to a golden lamp of Pallas (97). In Bronze Age Cyprus bronze lamps were occasionally found placed in niches or fastened to walls by means of a spiked attachment.

It should be observed that these few lamps found in Crete and on the Greek mainland are not of the spouted type and show no link with the shell type lamp common in the West-Semitic world and later also further south. This seems to support the claim put forward by Clement of Alexandria (98) that the Greeks took the lamp from the Egyptians. On the other hand we have no proof that the Greeks ever used a lamp of the floating wick type such as was common in Egypt. We have the report of Herodotus (99) that "at Saïs, when the assembly takes place for the sacrifies, there is one night on which the inhabitants all burn a multitude of lights in the open air round their houses. They use lamps in the shape of flat saucers filled with a mixture of oil and salt on the top of which the wick floats". This clearly refers to the kind of night-light still made to this day in Egypt by filling a pot with salt saturated with oil, into which a very long thin wick is set, and which we have already discussed. It seems necessary that the Minoan and Mycenaean lamps in our musea should be carefully examined to find out whether floating wicks were used or whether the wick overhung the side of these open-bowl lamps.

In the absence of shell-type lamps in Ancient Greece there can be no truth in the story by Josephus (100) that the Jews taught other peoples to light lamps on certain holy days. There is no doubt that once lamps came into common use in Greece they were not only used to illuminate interiors and, more rarely, exteriors, but also as votive offerings to deities and as tomb furniture and in religious ceremonies. Unfortunately early archaeologists neglected this subject and pending further research we must assume that the use of lamps died out after the Mycenaen Age to be resumed about 600 B.C., when lamps of the simple "cocked hat" type were re-introduced probably from the East, where they were in use in the Early Iron Age.

Lamps were found much less frequently in Greek sites than in the later Roman period. This may seem strange but we should remember that there was much less need for light in the ancient world, for there are more sunny days in the Mediterranean, the houses with their central light court and the ancient custom of not studying or working at night all cooperating. On the other hand votive lamps in temples or on the house altar or "lararium" were frequent.

We have ample information on the later Greek lamps (101). The earliest Corinthian "kothon" of the seventh and sixth century B.C. was a bowl of moderate depth on a low foot, with a horizontal curved handle and a curved-in rim which overhung the interior. Maybe the very oldest lamp was of the floating wick type but of this contention we have no definite proof. The development of this early Greek lamp shows two definite trends:

1. the form of the body gradually tends to assume the character of the later Roman enclosed lamp, the rim encroaching more and more on the centre, until it becomes a mere orifice and finally the top is closed in altogether;
2. the nozzle becomes more and more developed until it forms a tube of considerable length.

The earlier lamps were modelled by hand but from the sixth to the third century B.C. lamps were made on the wheel and finished with the typical Greek black glaze. The deeper body and the pronounced nozzle created a type of lamp called the "Attic" by Walters. Apart from this type we still find an open saucer lamp in use with a central socket which was either suspended or placed on a spiked support. In the Hellenistic Age, notably from the second century B.C. onwards, lamps were made in moulds, a process which may have been adopted from the East, but also we find lamps modelled by hand. The lamp base became flatter and we even find a low foot type. Maker's names begin to appear on lamps of the first century B.C. The black varnish is replaced by a kind of dark-grey metallic slip or a glaze corresponding with the contemporary pottery. The decoration is still fairly simple. Parthian lamps have a similar development between 200 B.C. and 200 A.D., some types with a downward projecting nozzle must have stood on a ledge.

Lamps are more frequently mentioned in the Classical Age of Greek literature. The fall of night is mentioned as "the hour when the lamp is lighted" (102). Pottery and bronze lamps are mentioned fairly often by the comedy writers of the fifth century (103) and in the fourth century a golden lamp burnt day and night in the shrine of Athena Polias in the Acropolis (104), "the wick in it is of Carpasian flax (asbestos?), the only kind which is fire-proof, and a bronze palm above the lamp reaches to the roof, and draws off the smoke".

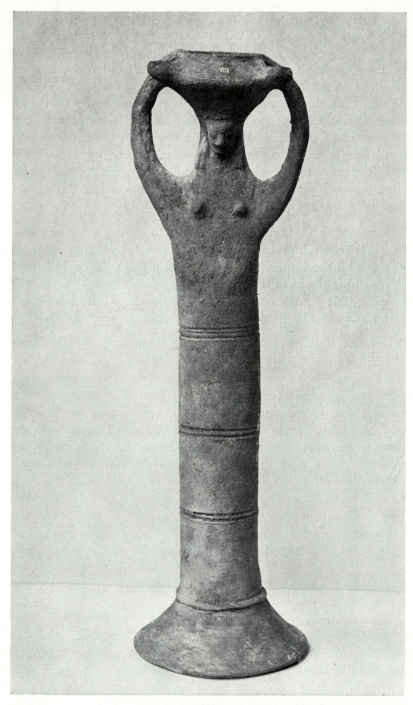

Fig. 30.
Archaic lampstand (Greece, sixth century B.C.)
(Photo British Museum, Londen)

Metal lamps were still fairly rare, the ratio of metal to pottery lamps in Greece was about 1:200, only in Roman times did metal lamps become really common. Moulds for lamps were made in the following way. The lamp form was modelled by hand, it was covered all round with clay which was then cut through horizontally in such a way as to obtain two moulds, one for the lid and the other for the lamp proper. Sometimes these two moulds were shaped separately, marks or bosses being used to obtain a proper fit. These moulds were separately lined with lamp clay firmly pressed in and before it had dried thoroughly the moulds were placed on one other and probably tied together. Later the mould was opened and the lamp was taken out. It was further dried in the air and burned at a low temperature, handles and other decorations being first added.

The pottery lamps had a filling hole and a spout for the wick but sometimes upto 12 funnels for wicks were employed. Callimachus mentions the following inscription on a lamp (105): "To the god of Canopus, Callistion, wife of Critias has devoted me, sumptuous lamp with twenty spouts, after having prayed for his son Apellis. Seeing my shine, one would say: Evening star, how didst thou fall from the sky?". Annular lamps of this multiple-wick type were sometimes used and suspended like chandeliers such as were common in Rome much later (106).

The manufacturers of these pottery lamps were not highly esteemed for Athenaeus informs us: "The drinking cups are kantharoi of pottery, as is likewise the lamp which is suspended from the ceiling, with wide-spreading jets of flame. That this cup got its designation from a potter called Kantharis is stated by Philetaerus in Achilles: "Ay, Peleus; for Peleus is a potter's surname—a lean lampmaker is he, Kantharus by name, miserably poor, no lordly person, I swear by Zeus" (107). The lamps were called lychnoi, dimyzoi, trimyzoi after the number of wick openings (108), the lip being called myxos or myxa. Standards for lamps were called lychnia, lychneia or lychnouchoi, many examples of artistic quality have been found. Some lamps were suspended from the ceiling, but later lamps are sometimes provided with a hollow cylinder leading through them vertically from top to bottom and thus the lamps could be moved up and down a vertical rod on a standard. The wicks could be adjusted by means of small tongs suspended from tiny chains or sharp thorns and thus the luminosity could be regulated, within narrow limits hoem er. Replenishing lamps was a troublesome business and hence attempts

were made to construct lamps fed from larger receptacles. Philon of
Byzantium and Heron of Alexandria (I. 34) tried to construct wicks
which were pushed forward automatically as they charred.

The lamp wick is usually called ellychnion or ellychnium (109)
such words as phlomos or phryallis (110) denoting a specific material
of which the wick is made. Such wicks were made from the mullein,
from asbestos (111), linen, oakum or papyrus (112). Pliny (113) also
reports that "the wicks made from fibres of the castor plant give a bril-
liantly clear flame but the oil burns with a dull light because it is much
too thick". Rushes (scirpus) served only to make the wicks of torches
or candles. The fuel used in these lamps was usually olive oil, to
which salt was often added. Apart from drying the oil, avoiding
spluttering and imparting to the flame a yellow colour, this salt may
have prevented the oil from getting overheated. For this latter reason
salt or sand were specifically used in tallow lights during the Middle
Ages. Naphtha was sometimes used in lamps (115) but this was a
fairly dangerous and rare substance in Greece. Another substitute
for olive oil was kiki (castor)-oil (116) which was, however, reputed to
give off a strong smell and hence its use was limited to the poor,
mainly in Egypt and other countries of the Near East where the castor
berry was grown.

The ancient lamps gave a weak light of warm colouring but with
an excessive oil consumption as related to its candle-power. The
ancients were loth to extinguish lamps (117). Often the flame was
smoky and Juvenal tells us that the fumes of the lamp brought in by
the boys blackened the busts of Horace and Virgil in the classroom
(118). The ancient lamps needed constant attention and snuffing. In
certain cases time was measured by the oil consumed in the reservoir.

In Carthage and other Phoenician sites one finds an early two-
spouted lamp (dimyxos, bilychnis) in general use, which may have
served as a prototype to the later classical annular or other lamps
with 8, 12 and 16 wicks. The body of the lamp in the Hellenistic Age
became the medium of potter and sculptor, shapes ranging from feet,
animals, shells to boats and the like. Here as in the Roman Empire
the trademarks or abbreviations of the potter's names inform us about
the trade movements of these mass-produced lamps.

In Italy, outside the Greek cities of the South, the use of lamps,
apart from a few isolated Etruscan examples, does not begin before
the third century. Rome obviously borrowed it from the Greeks of
Southern Italy, calling it "candela" first and then "lychnos" or "lucer-

na" (119). The earliest types were wheel-made open saucers, later the body was deepened and the top covered. The closing-in process was not yet complete by the second century B.C. After 200 B.C. most lamps are moulded and have decoration in relief, they are round or oval and the decoration is mostly limited to the rim. The typical lamp of the turn of our era is circular with decoration on the top, during the later Empire the oval form reappears and more elaborate specimen with many nozzles are made. This variety of forms is more notable in metal lamps.

The principal parts were the body (infundibulum), the top (discus), the ornamented rim (margo), the nozzle (rostrum, nasus, myxus) (120) with a hole for the insertion of the wick (ellychnium), the handle (ansa, manubrium) and the filling hole, which was often closed with a wooden plug. Sometimes we find a second hole for the insertion of a needle with which the wick could be adjusted. Whereas Greek lamps usually have a concave top, that of Roman lamps was flat or convex. The early lamps, dating before the third century B.C. are derived from the Corinthian kothon and the "cocked hat" type of the Near East through the Greek cities of the South. The later ones often clearly go back to metal types, notably the "delphiniform" black-glazed types of the first century B.C. Metal lamps were more popular in Italy than in Greece, most metal lamps were made of bronze though in the Rhine region a few lead lamps were found. The lamps stood in niches or on brackets or stands often wrongly called candelabra, though some of them are really also fit to bear candles. Other lamps were hung from chains.

The Roman oil lamp had won out on the earlier candle and 8-shaped tallow lamp. When about 75 A.D. the stamped mass-produced lamps begin to appear on the market the old 8-shaped tallow lamp also returns. In the second and third centuries A.D. Christian symbols begin to appear on Roman lamps and by this time lamp factories had arisen first at Rome then in the Po valley and Africa, later in Switzerland, Mainz, Trier, Cologne and several cities in Gaul. Bronze lamps were often modelled to animal and human shapes, iron lamps occur occasionally. All kinds of special lamps were designed and produced such as the trick lamp with double reservoir, which allowed the "magician" to empty it and still set it alight (121) or the "lucerna publicaris" (publicaria) used to search the body for fleas (122).

The lamp played an important part in ancient religious life and "photizein" means not only "filling with light" but also "becoming immortal". Lamps and lampstands appear in cult pictures of Minoan date, though they disappear. We have referred to the use of the lamp in Egyptian religious ceremonies and Herodotus tells us (124) that "all night long a lamp is kept burning in the appartment of the temple of Saïs". From the eighth century B.C. onwards lamps begin to reappear in the ruins of Greek temples. We have discussed the golden lamp in the cella of the temple of Athena Polias, the work of Callimachos. Multiwick lamps are very common in the sanctuary of Artemis Orthia at Sparta. On the north-east slope of the Acropolis sherds

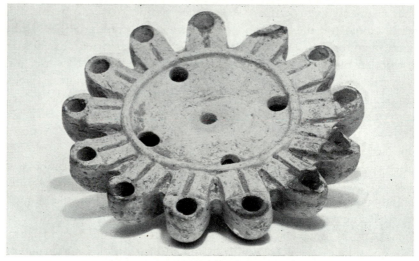

Fig. 31.
Multi-wick lamp of Roman date (First century A.D.), found at Holdeurn near Nijmegen (The Netherlands).
(Photo Rijksmuseum van Oudheden, Leiden)

of lamps were found which each had several hundreds of wicks (125). Lamps were very frequent in temples dedicated to Demeter. In the temple of Demeter Thesmophorus at Troizen remains of over 2000 lamps were found. Though the torch is characteristic of the ceremonies of the Demeter cult, lamps seem to have been found more suitable as votive gifts.

By the end of the Hellenistic period the penetration of oriental cults promoted the use of the lamp in many rites. The part of the lamp in the "festival of Herodes" (the Sabbath!) (126) was well known in the Greek world by that time and Herodotus had of course reported on many such uses from ancient Egypt. Indeed lamps are very frequent in the ruins of Egyptian temples at Delos, Philippi, Eretria and Pompeii. Lamps were now also used in private cult life and in certain oracles. Candles do not appear to have been used at this early date, though they are employed by the Arval Brethern about 240 A.D. and in the contemporary sun cult. Lamps were frequent in tree cults as we know from the writings of Prudentius, Chrysostomus, Cyrillus and others. During the Roman Empire they are very common on the house altar. Much earlier they had already appeared as ex-voto's in Roman temples and in graves and tombs. They appear amongst the welcome gifts or "strenae" at New Year's day from the first century A.D. onwards (127) and they can be used to chase away bad signs (128). Chrysostomus (129) mentions a strange custom of using lamps to choose the proper name for a new child. Lamps of different names are burned and the child is given the name of the lamp which burns longest to ensure it a long life. Not only were lamps dedicated in temples but the Greeks had adopted the practice of putting lamps in tombs from the Asiatics and the Romans took over this custom (130). The Christians dedicated such lamps in their catacombs only but the heathens buried them with the dead (131) for their future use.

7. *Roman lamp factories*

In the Hellenistic period the Greek lamp makers had given up making their products on the wheel and either modelled them by hand or fashioned them from moulds. The latter were modelled from a pattern lamp in a harder and finer clay than the pattern. The lower part contained the body of the lamp, the upper part the discus, both parts being joined by mortices and tenons. Plaster or baked clay were used for moulds.

The clay was impressed in the moulds with the fingers, the figured decoration applied by means of models or stamps, as in the case of Arretine and Gaulish ware, ornamental patterns were probably produced by a kind of wheel or running instrument as in pottery. Signatures in relief were taken from the mould. Each lamp factory had a large numer of moulds. The lamps of L. Caecilius Saevus show no less than 91 subjects; those of C. Oppius Restitutus 84, those of Florentius 51; but the subjects were not exclusive to one of them only.

The two halves of the lamp were joined while the clay was still moist and pared with a tool and the orifice for filling was then pierced.

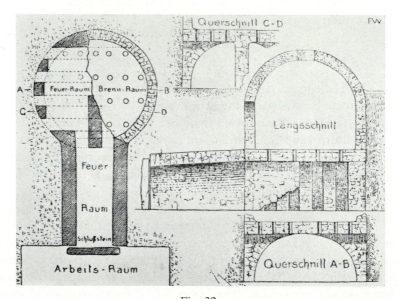

Fig. 32.
View of the Roman lamp factory at Wiesenau (Germany).
(After Fremersdorff)

Glaze, when used, was applied before baking, for which a moderate temperature seems to have been required. As soon as the moulded lamps had dried sufficiently they were stacked or put in batches close together in the furnace and baked.

The Romans started lamp factories producing on a fairly large scale and they also exported these mass-produced lamps (Firmenlampen) all over the Empire. One of these factories was excavated at Wiesenau near Mainz (132). The clay found on the spot had to be properly washed. These preparations were well executed for the clay found in the factory showed but slight variations in colour and it was well refined and capable of producing good thin pottery. It was usually leather coloured. The local loam had 23.53% of clay, 25.51% sand, 28.08% fine sand and 19.34% of calcium carbonate. There was little iron present and hence the final colour was not dark red. The baking temperature must have been around 1000° C. A glaze gave the lamps a colour which may have been intended to imitate metal. The clay (and the sand) were taken from a quarry no more than 50 yards from the furnace. Probably the loam was quarried in the summer and burned in winter after it had properly weathered. The furnace itself, near the banks of the river Rhine, had two holes one for entering and stacking the pottery in the furnace, a second hole served as a chimney for the combustion gases. The lower floor of the furnace was the proper combustion space with the typical praefurnium also found in hypocausts. Timber to be used as fuel was stacked near the opening of the furnace.

The glaze was probably applied after the first mild heating to dry the clay lamp and to give it some stability. Later mass-produced lamps no longer show a trace of glaze, which was to prevent the oil from leaking through the porous pottery. From fingermarks it was possible to establish how the dried lamp was hand-painted with glaze. From misfires and rejects it was also possible to establish that two systems were used to stack the moulded lamps in the upper furnace room.

Taking into account wells sunk in a limestone hill some 50—60 m. high and further indications it was possible to establish that this lamp factory and pottery was run by the military authorities of this part of the Rhine frontier. Winter quarters in this region were often dugouts in which proper light and lamps were imperative.

The excavations of Vindonissa (133) allow us certain conclusions on the extent of the Roman lamp trade. This military camp near

Basle (Switzerland) was built under the emperor Tiberius and left in the first years of Trajan, probably in 100/101 A.D. Under Claudius a large fire destroyed the greater part of the camp and hence two periods of its life can be clearly distinguished. Lamps were found in graves and dwellings, upto 1912 1100 lamps had been found and in 1916 another 500. Over 750 of these are decorated with some 325 different designs.

Generally speaking their form is very simple. The greater part

Fig. 33.

Mould for clay lamp (Eastern Mediterranean, first century B.C.).

(Photo British Museum, London)

of the decorated lamps seem to have been made north of the Alps, probably at Lugdunum (Gaul). Even though many forms are imitations of Roman and Italian lamps few bear stamps of Roman manufacturers. This goes to show that there was a large export of lamps from Gaul to Helvetia and Germania during the first century A.D. Few direct Italian imports have been found, most of them hailing from the shops of CELER and HILARIO in Upper Italy.

Some 250 lamps bear the trademark of a firm. Here again we find a large variety of qualities and makes. The best dark-red quality is of Italian make. The second-best yellowish-red lamps are probably of local manufacture but most of the mass products hail from Gaul and Germany and only a small percentage of the total is of Italian make. According to the trademark MVTF (Mutinae fecit) the centre. of Italian lamp manufacture was in Modena and started about 75 A.D., but a few must hail from Pompeii. All lamps with broad grooves leading to the nozzle were made after 100 A.D. About one third of the stamped lamps bear the name of FORTIS, a few that of COMMUNIS, others that of ATIMETUS or FIRMUS. Fortis may

Fig. 34.
Spoiled set of lamps from lamp factory (50 A.D.).
(Photo British Museum, London)

have been the inventor of the deep-groove lamp at Modena, his full name being L. Aemilius Fortis. STROBILIS had his shop near Modena at Magreta, VERECUNDUS also hails from this region. Only few of these manufacturers survived towards the end of the second century A.D.

Open lamps used for tallow were found too, often the top is removable to allow proper filling. These lamps occur more frequently in the second century A.D. and later there seems to have been a general regression towards more primitive native types such as the 8-shaped

lamps, cocked hat types and simple open bowls, some of which have
a central wick. It would therefore seem that by the second half of the
first century A.D. the lamp manufacturers of Gaul and Germany
started off on their own original types of lamps based on primitive
types of the region. Only 13 bronze and 8 iron lamps were found at
Vindonissa, some of which are of the chandelier type.

Further proofs of the conclusions reached at Vindonissa were
found from the surveys of the Austrian lamp collections (134). Here
again we find imports from many lamp factories in Upper Italy such
as that of CELER at Tortona, HILARIO at Parma and MENAN-
DER, CERINTHUS, FORTIS and STROBILIS in or around Modena. Another collection of 33 lamps came from the neighbourhood
of Este, seven models of which date back to the first century A.D.
These ateliers seem to have had more or less a monopoly of world-
wide trade which they lost by the second century A.D. when their
lamps were imitated locally in the different provinces.

The world-wide trade in lamps is echoed by a find in Pompeii (135)
where in the year 1881 a wooden box was found in the tablinum of
house 9, isula 5, regio VIII. This crate, which was still packed when
the disaster of 79 A.D. overtook the city, contained 37 lamps from
another part of the Empire and it was most probably repacked in
Italy and not shipped directly from their place of manufacture in
southern Gaul, for 24 of the lamps bear the stamp STROBILIS,
6 COMUNIS, 4 ECHIO, 2 FORTIS and one is uninscribed. This
strongly suggests that these lamps represent a consignment received
at Pompeii from a wholesale-dealer.

We have further proofs that exports from Italy to Africa and Egypt
were not confined to a few articles for the luxury trade but included
Italian clay lamps and bricks. Italian lamps are not only recorded by
the papyri (136) but also by excavations (137). In North Africa we
have abundant evidence to establish the development of this lamp
trade (138). At first one finds in Tunis lamps of the cocked hat type,
then imported Greek lamps, then round Romano-African lamps
without a handle and finally the typical Roman types with an elongated
spout, handle and fully decorated. The decorations often reproduce
masterpieces of sculpture and as the originals were not available to
any possible local lamp maker these lamps must have been imported,
though the subjects could have been copied from coins, gems and
vases. Inscriptions inform us of the imports of Roman lamps (139),
some coming from Alexandria (140).

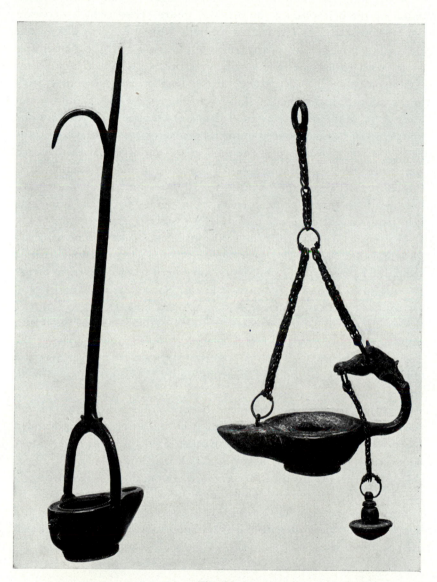

Fig. 35.
Roman Bronze Hanging Lamps.
(Photo British Museum, London)

Before long the African lamp makers began to offer competition, imitating the mythological, animal and genre scenes which decorate the Italian lamps. At Carthage a jobber's warehouse was discovered (141) containing not only many lamps but also moulds for ornamenting lamps with various designs which were probably sold to small local establishments. Probably some of the smaller lamp manufacturers in the country had sufficient skill to produce their own moulds from fine lamps. Many of the unsigned lamps of cheaper make are obvious imitations of those produced in the larger factories of Italy. The Arabs of the region of Kasserine, Sbeitla, Feriana and Thala are said at one time to have sold great quantities of red ware of ancient manufacture, the source of which they would not disclose but which must have been made in their vicinity. Lamps from the factory of L. Pompeius Pontianus in Carthage are found only in Africa and Sardinia (142). L. Hortensius, L. Caprarius and C. Iunius Alexis had the same markets. On the other hand lamps bearing the stamp of the Pullaeni family, which had a domain at Uchi Maius, have been found in Africa, Sicily, Ostia, Roma, Dalmatia, Transpadene and Narbonese Gaul and Spain. Hence these African lamps were not made in villages but in factories belonging to real lamp manufacturers who gradually ousted the Italian imports and even carved out a market for themselves outside the province of Africa. Christian lamps from Africa were used at Syracuse (143) and in the region of Camarina, Sicily (144) during the fourth century A.D.

In Britain too Italian pottery and bronze lamps were first imported during the first and second centuries A.D. but imports soon declined when local products increased. In Roman Spain we also find pottery lamps from Latium (145), Campania (146), Mutina (147) and Africa (148), together with other earthenware containers. In Sicily, during the early Empire, pottery lamps were imported from Campania to Catana (149), Selinus (150), Solus (151) and other localities (152) and lamps from Modena were found at Catana too (153), dating back from the second century and hailing from FORTIS' shop.

8. *Some Applications of Lights and Lamps*

However hard the Hellenistic inventors like Philon and Heron tried (154), they could only improve the oil-supply of lamps but they could not increase the poor light-intensity of the ancient lamps. Still every house had its lamps standing in niches, hanging on brackets or

suspended from chains attached to the ceiling. Sometimes the lamp
stood in front of the house altar and also served the inhabitant as a
source of light. Lamps were used in bedrooms (155), but this use does
not seem to have been frequent (156) for there was a danger of fire
and many fires caused by oil lamps are reported (157). In rare cases
we hear of lamps used for study during the night (158). They figure
largely at meals (159).

We are informed that the miners bound lamps to their foreheads
when working deep down in the mines (160). However, outdoor
lamps would tend to cause trouble because of gusts of wind and
draughts and hence they were protected by a transparent medium,
in other words they were carried about in *lanterns*.

We have a host of terms to denote lanterns, such as "lanterna,
laterna, lampter, lychnouchos, phanos and hypnos" (161) the Latin
lanterna being derived from the Greek lampter (162). "Phanos" is
a later term as is "hypnos". The "laternarius" was both the manu-
facturer of lanterns and the slave who accompanied his master at night
to light his way (163), for only the Spartans went home at night
without a light (164). Hence nearly all lanterns on ancient monuments
are in the hands of slaves. However, they are even found in tombs
and they were used for signalling and also on ships (165). Diodor
speaks of the lights of the ship of a general and when Scipio crosses
to Africa "the warships would show single lights, at night, the trans-
ports would have two, while the commander's ship would be distinguished by three lights" as Livy tells us. Representations of such ships'
lanterns can be found on two engraved bronzes of archaic style and
their use therefore goes back to at least the eighth century B.C.

It has been suggested that the origin of the lantern was a woven
basket into which the lamp was placed to protect it from rain and
wind, but unfortunately too few lanterns have survived from earlier
periods. The body of most of the ancient lanterns was made of bronze
or iron, but also of pottery and wood (166). The earliest forms are
cylindrical and fitted with a bow. Hellenism brought square or cylindrical lanterns with a conical top and from 150 B.C. onwards we find
pottery lanterns with holes in the body to be used as tablelamps or
lanterns. The lanterns with a bronze framework and transparent
windows seem to have been invented about the first century A.D.
Certain types of lanterns were used for ceremonial or votive purposes.

The most common transparent material used for the windows of
lanterns was horn, plaques of which were shaved to the correct

Fig. 36.
Terracotta Lantern found in Roman Gaul, height 23.5 cm.
(Rijksmuseum van Oudheden, Leiden, Inv. No. R. 1952)

thickness (167). They were quite resistent to heat and humidity and gradually superseded the parchment (derma) (168), stretched bladders (vesica) (169) and oiled linen (170) windows also used in earlier forms, since the fifth century B.C. Glass windows are not used generally before the seventh century A.D. (171). The covers of some lanterns were removable (172).

Hence in Antiquity torches, tapers, lamps and lanterns were available and public lighting was possible in principle. However, in general everybody saw to his own means of lighting his way (173). Proper lighting was only effected at triumphs or processions. Thus we are informed (174) that Caesar at his Gallic triumph "mounted the Capital by torchlight with forty elephants bearing lights on his left and his right". Theatres were properly lighted (175) for "Caligula exhibited stage-plays continually, of various kinds and in many different places, sometimes even by night, lighting up the whole city" and Domitian gave "gladitorial shows at night by the light of torches". The thermae had sufficient lamps (176), the smaller thermae of Pompeii had some 1000 lamps. Certain lamps bearing the inscription SAECUL may have been connected with the Ludi Saeculares at which illumination took place (177). Again, when Cicero wanted to catch the Catiline supporters Rome was lit up and Claudian describes how Milan was illuminated with torches and lamps for the marriage of the Emperor. Certain public buildings like the townhall of Tarentum had huge lamps with upto 350 wicks (178).

However, such occasional or local illumination was still far from real provision of public lighting. We are always told that Antioch was the first city in the world to light its street properly about 350 A.D. (179). These reports by Libanius (314—393) and St. Jerome (345—420) are confirmed by those of Basil the Great who tells us that Caesarea in Cappadocia had such a system of lighting about 371 A.D. On the other hand we have many terracotta figurines of a lamplighter (Luchnaptas, Lampadarius), who seems to have been a well-known figure in Alexandria and other Ptolemaic towns (180). We are fairly certain that the larger streets in Hellenistic towns, such as the two large avenues of Alexandria, with their porticos must have been properly illuminated by the countless lamps and lights in the shops and over the doors or house-entrances. Ammianus Marcellinus informs us that at night Rome was as bright as during the day.

In the Via dell'Abundanza (Pompeii) there were at least 285 lamps on counters and above doors on a stretch of some 500 m. "Second

Fig. 37.
Roman Bronze Lantern.
(Photo British Museum, London)

street" in the same town had 396 lamps in 132 shops over 576 m. and the 700 m. long "High Street to Stabiae" had some 500 lamps (181). Then there were the lamps on the corners of the streets under the statues of the gods or house and family spirits (lares compitales) (182) about which custom Tertullian complains (183) and which were finally forbidden by Theodosius the Great (184). Then again many temples (185) and often graves (186) were brightly illuminated at night and traffic at night may not have been as uncomfortable as generally supposed. By the sixth century A.D. street lighting was quite common in the Orient. In Western Europe we have to wait until many centuries later before any attempt was made to establish proper public lighting services (187).

Light played an important part in the development of *fire-signals* and optical telegraphy, that is not only in longdistance communication in wartime but more particularly in the development of means of communication which are essential for the growth of large empires, when news from all parts has to reach the capital as soon as possible. Riepl's work on this subject is still a classic (188), but its warnings are often little heeded by authors. Whatever interpretations have been given to ancient texts, it is still true that no important development in optical telegraphy took place before the days of Polybios (second century B.C.) when the first logical system of signalling was developed. However, development soon came to a standstill until this means of long-distance communication was studied and developed during the French Revolution.

Light signals of a very primitive and general nature have played their part in warfare from the earliest days. Ancient historians report how fires, clouds of dust or columns of smoke were observed by army commanders and sometimes used to mislead the enemy. Even the glittering of arms and shields sometimes constituted a welcome sign of the enemy and clever generals avoided such warnings and covered shields and arms in order to approach the enemy without being seen (189). In general camp fires were visible at large distances (190), they might form a welcome sign of reinforcements arriving in the nick of time (191). Hence they were sometimes left burning to confuse the enemy or to trick him into over or under estimating the size of the approaching army (192). In some cases, such ruses being well-known, generals even played a game of "double poker" (193). Other similar tricks were setting a camp afire (194) and attaching fire-brands to the horns of cattle (195). The campfire could be avoided on certain occasions (196) or putting it out and then relighting it might work (197). By day such signs as clouds of smoke and dust were both observed and used as a ruse (198), as were banners and flags. Such tactical uses of light were also practised by Greek and Hellenistic generals (199).

Optical signals were also given at sea by ships (200), some of which could be distinguished by certain pre-arranged signs (201). Here we approach the earliest forms of telegraphy which always involves pre-arranged signs to convey a certain message (202). Such fire-signals, the Greek "pyrsos" or "phryktos", occur in the earliest texts as well as in Latin literature (203) and they have been used upto the present day. In certain cases these fire-signals are given from watch or signal towers built on prominent hills and headlands and belonging to a system of defence (204).

The pre-classical civilisations had used torches made of rushes and bitumen to give signals (205). We hear of a witch, who "lighted a fire at every double-hour's distance and sent a messenger after every double-hour" (206) and Assurbanipal, the Assyrian king, tells us that he "saw the torches flare up; at every hour's distance on the way light appeared" (207). In the archives of the palace of Mari, which go back to the days of Hammurabi, king of Babylon, that is ten centuries before Assurbanipal, the expressions "to lift the fires" (išatam našûm) and "to lift the torches" (diparam našûm) are quite common (208). Thus we find a letter written by Banum to king Zimrilim of Mari running thus:

> "Yesterday I left Mari and spent the night at Zuruban. All the Benjaminites have lifted their torches. From Samanum to Hum-Muluk, from Hum-Muluk to Mišlam, all the cities of the Benjaminites of the Terqa district have lifted their torches in response. Still, until now I have not been able to determine the reasons behind these torches. Now I will investigate this and I will pass it on to my master. May the guards of the town of Mari be watchful and may my master not pass beyond the gateway".

A further letter states that "The Benjaminites have not ceased to revolt and I have had torches lifted to call up auxiliary forces. Possibly because of these torches the heart of my master may grow anxious. But the heart of my master should not be anxious, My lord should know this".

A letter by one Sammetar to the king runs: "Where the attack of the enemy is signalled I will come to the rescue and my lord shall ordain that the army be immediately assembled. Certainly the enemy is very numerous. At the lifting of my torches there, where an attack is signalled, may Iasim-Dagan and the army hasten thence promptly". A letter from Ishmeh-Dagan to his brother Iasmah-Hadad of Mari suggests that there existed series of watch-towers which permitted signalling from city to city: "Because you lifted two torches this night the entire country may come to your aid. Let tablets be written to the entire country, to the land of Anadariq upto the district of Ḥasidanum, upto the district of Nurrugin and let them be carried by your swiftest young men. Write in these terms: A great number of enemies have come in the middle of the country for a razzia, that is why the two torches have been lifted. Do not come to assist us!".

In a further letter the king reproaches Zidria for having gone beyond his orders of lifting the torches from Mari to Ḥana only. Zidria replies that he had an order to lift a torch when he saw one, but now when he sees one he will not lift a torch but when he sees two he will assemble the entire forces all over the country and lift two torches! Hence "lifting a torch" was a simple signal meaning either "revolt" or a call to the arms because of an invasion. Hence in these letters the expression is also used metaphorically to indicate "inciting to revolt" or "remain unpacified". In a few cases the signal was the confirmation of a message on a tablet sent by special messenger, as is still the case in these districts. In no case, however, is a full message signalled to be decoded on the spot. Hence we cannot yet call this fire-telegraphy.

Similar fire-signals are mentioned in the Old Testament. "Now there was an appointed sign between the men of Israel and the liers in wait, that they should make a great flame with smoke rise up out of the city" (209). The prophet Jeremiah (210) incites the inhabitants of Jerusalem "to flee out of the midst of Jerusalem, and blow the trumpet in Tekoa, and set up a sign of fire in Beth-haccerem; for evil appeareth out of the north, and great destruction". Indeed the ostraca found by J. L. Starkey at Lachish (211) inform us that a commander of a post north of Azekah writes the military governor of Lachish, Ya'ush, that "we are watching for the signals of Lachish, according to all the indications which my lord hath given, for we can not see Azekah", which refers to the approach of the Chaldeans who are soon to besiege Lachish (589 B.C.). Such pre-arranged fire-signals also occur in the later Mishnah (212) where we read that "formerly fires were lighted on the mountains" to warn the Jewish communities outside Jerusalem and even in Babylonia that the new moon had appeared when this phenomenon was not too clearly visible. Long staves of cedar wood were used to which reeds, branches of the olive tree and oakum were attached by means of a cord. These torches were lighted on the top of a mountain and "agitated in all directions until they saw the next fire on the second, the third mountain, etc. This began on the Mount of Olives and went to Sartaba, from Sartaba to Agrippina, thence to Chauran, to Beth-Baltin" and further down to Mesopotamia. Here again we have but the most primitive form of optical telegraphy, which remained in use upto the Arab period (213).

In the Greek world the use of optical signalling devices, such as torches or fires, goes back to the archaic period (214). This invention was ascribed to Sinon by Pliny, but more often to Palamedes, son of Nauplion. The most spectacular story of how such news was quickly transmitted from cape to cape and island to island is the story of how the fall of Troy was reported at Argos (215). Diels argued (216) that the distance between the steps was 150 km or 180 km. in two cases, which distance could not possibly be covered by fire-signals, but Darmstaedter mentions that fires on mountain-tops in the Tyrol have been seen at distances of 80 km. and could certainly be perceived much further off in the clear sky of Greece. Lighthouses are visible up to 90 km. away. Appian mentions (12.67) a fire seen at a distance of 187 km. and Darmstaedter calculates that a fire lit on the top of Mount Ida would be visible at 240 km. Whatever the truth may be, here again we have a single signal transmitting a pre-arranged message. This is also the case when Mardonius transmits the news of the capture of Athens (217) "by fire signals along the islands" to Sardes. In Persia such a signalling system was coupled with the messenger service (218), which allowed news to reach Susa from the frontiers of the empire within one day. Thus too the news of the battle of Plataea came to Mykale in a few hours (219) and the results of the battle on the river Sagra were known on the same day in Peleponesian Greece (220). Similar systems were in use in the different Hellenistic kingdoms (221) and it was used in Roman warfare and tactics (222).

In all these cases one simple signal was used to transmit the message. The seemingly complicated message transmitted by the post on Sciathus to the main fleet at Artemisium (Herodotus VII. 183) can be given in two pre-arranged signals and the message from Kerkyra, discussed by Thucydides (3.80) can be solved by one sign transmitted over a distance of 80 km. The difficulty lay in the invention of a variety of signals. One could simply hold up a torch, move it up and down vertically or give it a circular movement (223). There was also the possibility of inventing a code based on the simultaneous lifting of one or more torches or on the subsequent showing of one or more torches (224). The principle of intermittent visibility was used in the so-called "pyrseutic methods" later propagated by Sextus Julius Africanus. It was the first step on the way to a "Morse code" which allowed the transmission of unpremeditated messages, by spelling out words and sentences in alphabetic signs. The older systems used pre-arranged signs or sequences of signs which could then be decoded. Failing an electric relay system, the only progress Antiquity could make was the development of systems using many torches at relatively short distances of each other. However, such groups of torches at say three feet distance of each other are no longer distinct groups of torches at distances over 1000 m. Hence we will find that Polybius (225), who in 150 B.C. describes the development of this "fire-telegraphy", had to use upto 10 men at each station with ten torches to get a reasonable variety of signs to spell out a message. This important passage runs as follows:

"It is evident to all that in every matter, and especially in warfare, the power of acting at the right time contributes very much to the success of enterprises, and fire-signals are the most efficient of all the devices to aid us to do this. For they show what has recently occurred and what is still in the course of being done, and by means of them anyone who cares to do so, even if he is at the distance of three, four, or even more days' journey, can be informed. Thus it is always surprising how help can be brought by means of fire messages when the situation requires it. Now in former times, as fire-signals were simple beacons, they were for the most part of little service to those who used them, for the service had to be performed by signals previously determined upon, and as facts are indefinite, most of them defied communication by fire-signals. To take the case I just mentioned, it was possible for those who agreed on it to convey information that a fleet had arrived at Oreus, Peparethus, or Chalcis, but when it came to some of the citizens having changed sides or having been guilty of treachery, or a massacre having taken place in the town, or anything of the kind, things that often happen, but cannot be foreseen—and it is chiefly unexpected occurrences that require instant consideration and help—all such matters defied communication by fire-signal. For it was quite impossible to have a preconcerted code for things which there was no means of foretelling".

Aeneas, the author of the work on strategy (abt. 350 B.C.), wishing to find a remedy for the difficulty, advanced matters a little, but his device fell far short of our requirements, as can be seen from this description of it. He says that those who are about to communicate urgent news to each other by fire-signals should procure two earthenware vessels of exactly the same width and depth, the depth being some three cubits and the width one. Then they should have corks made a little narrower than the mouths of the vessels and through the middle of each cork should pass a rod, graduated in equal sections of three fingerbreadths, each clearly marked off from the next. In each section should be written the most evident and ordinary events which occur in war, e.g. on the first "Cavalry arrived in the country", on the second "Heavy infantry", on the third "Light-armed infantry", on the next "Infantry and cavalry", next "Ships", next "Corn" and so on until we have entered in all the sections the chief contingencies of which, at the present time, there is a reasonable possibility in war time. Next he tells us to bore holes in both vessels of exactly the same size, so that they allow exactly the same escape. Then we are to fill the vessels with water and put on the corks with the rods in them and allow water to flow through the two apertures. This being done it is evident that, the conditions being precisely similar, in proportion to the amount of water escaping the two corks will sink and the rods will disappear in the vessels. When by experiment it is seen that the rapidity of escape is in both cases exactly the same, the vessels are to be conveyed to the places in which both parties are to look after the signals and deposited there. Now whenever any of the contingencies written on the rod occurs, he tells us to raise a torch and to wait until the corresponding party raises another. When both the torches are clearly visible the signaller is to lower his torch and at once allow the water to escape through the aperture. Whenever, as the cork sinks, the contingency you wish to communicate reaches the mouth of the vessel he tells the signaller to raise his torch and the receivers of the signal are to stop the aperture at once and to note which of the messages written on the rods is at the mouth of the vessel. This will be the message delivered, if the apparatus works at the same pace in both cases.

This is a slight advance on beacons with a pre-concerted code, but it is still quite indefinite. For it is evident that it is neither possible to foresee all contingencies, or even if one did, to write them on the rod. So that when circumstances produce some unexpected event, it is evident that it cannot be conveyed by this plan. Again none of the things written on the rod are defined statements, for it is impossible to indicate how many infantry are coming and to what part of the country, or how many ships or how much corn. For it is impossible to agree before hand about things of which one cannot be aware before they happen. And this is the vital matter; for how can anyone consider how to render assistance if he does not know how many of the enemy have arrived, or where? And how can anyone be of good cheer at better tidings, or in fact think anything at all, if he does not understand how many slips or how much corn has arrived from the allies?

"The most recent method, devised by Cleoxenus and Democleitus and perfected by myself (Polybius), is quite definite and capable of dispatching with accuracy every kind of urgent message, but in practice it requires care and exact attention. It is as follows: We take the alphabet and divide it into five parts, each consisting of five letters. There is one letter less in the last division, but this makes no practical difference. Each of the two parties who are about to signal to each other must now prepare five tablets and write one division of the alphabet on each tablet, and then come to an agreement that the man who is going to signal is in the first place to raise two torches and wait until the other replies by doing so too. This is to ascertain that both are ready for the signalling. These torches having been lowered, the dispatcher of the message will now raise the first set of torches on the left side indicating which tablet is to be consulted, i.e. one torch if it is the first, two if it is the second, and so on. Next he will raise the second set on the right on the same principle to indicate what letter on the tablet the receiver should write down.

When they part after coming to this understanding each of them must first have on the spot a telescope (sighting tube!) with two tubes, so that with the one he can observe the space on the right of the man who is going to signal and with the other that on the left. The tablets must be set up straight in order next the telescope, and there must be screens in front of both spaces, ten feet in length and of the height of a man so that the torches may this be seen distinctly when raised and disappear when lowered. If when all has been thus got ready on both sides, the signaller wants to convey, for instance, that about a hundred of the soldiers have described, he must first of all choose words which will convey what he means in the smallest number of letters, e.g. instead of the above "Cretans a hundred deserted us", for here the letters are less than half in number, but the same sense is conveyed. Having jotted this down on a writing-tablet he will communicate it by the torches as follows: The first letter is *kappa*. This being in the second division is on tablet number two, and, therefore, he must raise two torches on the left, so that the recipient may know that he has to consult the second tablet. He will now raise five torches on the right, to indicate that it is *kappa*, this being the fifth letter of the second division, and the receiver of the signal will note this down on his writing tablet. The dispatcher will then raise four torches on the left as *rho* belongs to the fourth division, and then two to the right, *rho* being the second letter in this division. The receiver writes down *rho* and so forth. This device enables any news to be definitely conveyed.

Many torches are of course required as the signal for each letter is a double one. But if all is properly prepared for the purpose, what is required can be done with whatever system we follow. Those engaged in the work must have had proper practice, so that when in action they may communicate with each other without any possibility of a mistake. From many instances it is easy for all who wish to learn how great the difference is between the same thing when it is first heard of and when it has become a matter of habit. For many things which appear at the beginning to be not only difficult but impossible are performed quite easily after time and practice. There are many other examples which confirm this, but the clearest of all is the case of reading...".

The combination of signals and clepsydrae which Polybius discusses at the beginning of his story no doubt came down from the Carthaginians. Polyaenus, the author of a Strategemata (Second century A.D.) tells us (226) that this system of signalling was used by them during their invasion of Sicily to "wire" home for reinforcements or food. There must have been signalling station at Kossyra between Sicily and Africa. This system may have been used by Dionysios the Elder (410—367 B.C.), tyrant of Syracuse. Up to 24 messages or even letters of the Greek alphabet could thus be transmitted and if the speed were something like 20 letters per hour, one night might be sufficient for a long message. On the other hand short messages may have been conveyed which were then completed by instructions sent be messenger or "hemerodromus". However, even Polybius' improvements on this primitive signalling were still far from fool-proof and we saw that it required many men and stations to be trans-mitted over a reasonable distance. There was also the danger of the enemy reading the signals too. Even in Antiquity false signals and lights were used to mislead the enemy or ships (228) and it was tried to circumvent such false signals or mistakes by controls (229). Still the only proper solution was a simplification of Polybius' system. It took over 2000 years before a system working with one man and one signalling apparatus or semaphore could achieve this, though an improvement was suggested by Sextus Julius Africanus (first half of the third century A.D.) but this fragment may go back to an earlier invention which Africanus reports. It runs (230):

"The Romans use a system, according to my opinion a most remarkable one, to tell each other all kinds of things by means of fire-signals. They divide the places for signalling in such a way that they have fields in the middle, to the right and to the left, then they divide the letters in such a way that those from *alpha* to *theta* have their place to the left, those from *iota* to *pi* in the middle and those from *rho* to *omega* to the left. If they want to transmit the sign *alpha*, they raise the fire signal once to the right, for *beta* twice, for *gamma* thrice, etc. If they wish to transmit *iota*, they raise the fire-brand once in the middle, etc. this they do to avoid transmitting the letters by numbers of fire-signals. Those who receive the signals, write down the letters received in the form of fire-signals and transmit them to the next station which then transmits them to the following one and so on until the last of the fire-signalling stations".

This was a slight improvement, for by increasing the distance between the torches to say 10 m. the visibility could be increased to about 10 km. Six heavings of torches per minute became possible and it involved less mistakes. This improved Polybius system is a true precursor of that of Morse, however slight the improvement was.

We have no proof that the Romans ever added a system of fire-

signals to the very efficient cursus publicus. The only example we
have of such a message being transmitted by fire-signals was upon
the assassination of Sejanus, which news was transmitted from Rome
to the emperor Tiberius at Capri (231). Fire-signals in wartime do
occur in Roman war records and unfortunately they were misunder-
stood in a number of cases (232). A proper system of watchtowers
for the transmission of fire-signals was never centered upon Rome.
Such systems did exist along the lines in Europe and Great Britain
at a later date, but in early records the enemies of Rome use such
signals more frequently than the Romans themselves. One of the
earliest Roman signalling systems was organized during the siege
of Dyrrachium (233) during the civil war. Later on, the lines the
watchtowers at a distance of $1^1/_2$ to $2^1/_2$ km. proved very suitable
for such a system and such systems seem also to have existed on
certain inner defence-lines (234). Unfortunately there was no evolution
of the fairly primitive "pyrseutic method" we have described above
and later suggestions like that of Vegetius (235) are in fact a step
backwards from the ideas of Polybius and allow but the transmission
of certain premeditated signals. It remained on the level of the signalling systems used by African tribes until the inventors of the French
Revolution era turned it into an efficient and simple system for transmitting any message. Electricity using the Morse code turned it into
the rapid communication system we use now.

We have still to discuss an important application of lights, the use
of harbour-lights and *lighthouses* to further shipping. There is no
doubt that in ancient times the watchtowers built on the coast and
near harbours sometimes served as signal towers for shipping. Faggots
or torches were occasionally burnt on them to guide and warn ships.
Thus Homer tells us (236) that "when the sun has set blaze forth the
beacon fires. High rise the flames, and to the dwellers round their
signal flash, if hap'ly over sea may come the needful aid", or he speaks
of the "watchfire's light, which, high among the hills some shepherd
kindles in his lonely fold" or of Odysseus who "not far remote my
Ithacans I saw fires kindling on the coast".

Such warning or guiding signs were purely incidental forms of
fire-telegraphy such as we have discussed. In several cases watchtowers (skopai) were built to serve on occasion as beacons. Herodotus
(237) mentions a "watchtower of Perseus in Egypt". Polybius tells
us that at Hercte (now Monte Pellegrino near Palermo) (238) "there
is a knoll which serves for an acropolis as well as for an excellent post

of observation (skopè) over the country at the foot of the hill". In the story of Medea (239) she promised to give her friends "a signal from the palace during the day by means of smoke, during the night by means of fire, in the direction of the look-out (skopè) which stood high above the sea". But even in cases when such watchtowers as expressily said to have been built to guide the mariners, such as "the tower in Caepio (Spain) which stands upon a rock that is washed on all sides by the waves, and, like the Pharos tower, is a marvelous structure built for the sake of the safety of mariners" (240), nothing allows us to conclude that permanent fires were kept burning during the night. In fact such towers like other monuments or landmarks like the Colossus of Rhodes or even the Pharos of Alexandria guided the mariners by day only. The texts show us that not until Roman times were some of such towers provided with permanent fires during the night.

Sailing by night by the stars and the contours of the land only, except for occasional pre-arranged lights must have been difficult. However, Mrs. Semple (241) has drawn attention to the fact that there were temples to Poseidon or Venus on many capes and promontories along the ancient Mediterranean coast. In such temples and sanctuaries fires were kept burning and many of them may, in fact, have provided the mariner with ample bearing for sailing or rowing at night. Her careful investigation of these templed promontories yielded:

> "One hundred and seventy-fire of these promontory shrines, besides twenty consecrated headlands, known to the ancients as sacred, but lacking any surviving record of altar or temple. Numerous other cases not here included, rested upon suggestive but incomplete evidence. These sanctuaries were found distributed from the tip of the Sinai peninsula in the Red Sea, a notorious spot for conflicting winds and currents dreaded by Egyptian, Greek and Roman seamen, all the way west to the angle of Portugal at Cape St. Vincent, where a rude cairn of stones marked the consecrated worship of an ancient Melkart or Heracles. They reached also from the Crimean Bosporus, where they clustered thick along the sea ways leading to the Scythian grain fields, south to Egypt and west to the headland of the Pyrenees, where these mountains stretch out the rocky skeleton of an arm before they dive beneath the waves of the Mediterranean.
> The form of these headland sanctuaries was varied. One was

the imposing Doric temple to Poseidon at Sunium or the rich fane of Venus of Eryx. A simpler form was the sacred grove with its shrine or marble canopy over the statue of the god, like the sacred precinct of Artemis on the northeast promontory of Euboea. Most primitive was the wave-wrought cave which nature provided as a local shelter for altar or wooden image of the deity. Most of these headland sanctuaries date back to the grey dawn of history".

Fig. 38.

Templed promontory in Greece.

(After Semple)

The Pharos of Alexandria is usually held to be the oldest lighthouse in the world, but the earliest texts (242) do not specifically refer to any fire kept in this monument during the night. Caesar, for instance, says "the island of Pharos gives its name to a tower, a miracle in size and engineering. Lying opposite Alexandria it forms one side of the harbour, and earlier monarchs had connected it with the city by means of a narrow causeway like a bridge, about threequarters of a mile long and resting on piles driven into the sea-bed". Incidently this passage conterdicts the false contention of later authors like Isidore of Seville and Hrabanus Maurus (243) who wanted to derive the word pharos from "phos" (light) and "orasis" (to see)! Indeed the island bore the name Pharos some five centuries before the Pharos tower was erected.

This huge monument and landmark has been carefully studied (244). When Alexander the Great founded Alexandria he left the planning of this new port to Deinokrates of Rhodos and to Kleomenes of Naucratis. The Pharos was not begun until a generation later "when Phyrrus became king of Epiros" (245). The architect was Sostratos of Knidos, son of Dexiphanos. It took nearly twenty years to build and cost some 800 talents. It was dedicated by Ptolemaios Soter about 280 B.C. to the "gods saving the mariners". It remained practically untouched until the days of Ammianus Marcellinus and Epiphanios (fourth and fifth centuries A.D.).

Repairs started during the reign of Anastasios (491—518) A.D. and Procopius of Gaza (246) foretold the ruin of the tower. This "tower on an island" (247) is also shown on the coins of Alexandria from 95—190 A.D. but its structure remained a matter of conjecture for a long time as the Arab geographers and historians who reported its history and repairs until it was definitely destroyed by the earthquake of 1303 were rather vague about its form and construction. Recently, however, a document was found written by one Ibn al-Shaikh who resided at Alexandria in 1165 and the greater part of the next year to return to his native Malaga in 1166. There he wrote his Kitab Alif Ba giving a detailed description including dimensions of the Pharos which allow us to give a more trustworthy plan of this ancient monument (248).

We know now that it is wrong to believe that this Pharos was originally anything more than a day-time landmark, the bronze statue of Isis Pharia guiding the ships which wanted to enter the harbour of Alexandria. Caesar and Strabo know nothing of fires on the Pharos at night-time, Lucan and Pliny do mention them (249). Though the former contention is still upheld by some (250) we must agree with Hennig (251) that the Pharos of Alexandria became a lighthouse only between 41 and 65 A.D., when at night fires of wood mixed with tar, resin or asphalt were burnt in its lanterns so that it was visible to mariners "at a distance of 300 stadia (some 48 km.)" (252).

Indeed, the first buildings erected to serve as lighthouses were the towers of Boulogne and Ostia. The lighthouse of Boulogne owes its origin to the act of Caligula who wanted to commemorate his "victory" after his campaign to the Atlantic seaboard and "erected a lofty tower, from which lights were to shine at night to guide the course of ships, as from Pharos" (253). Its use as a lighthouse is believed to have started in 46 A.D. and it has for centuries served the mariners sailing the Channel. The lighthouse of Ostia dates back to

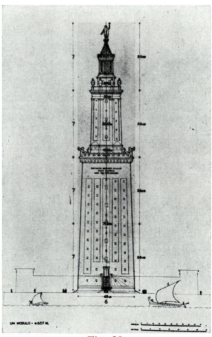

Fig. 39.

The Pharos of Alexandria, restoration as suggested by Palacios.

42 A.D. when the emperor Claudius "constructed the harbour of Ostia by buildings curving breakwaters on the right and left, while before the entrance he placed a mole in deep water. To give this mole a firmer foundation he first sank the ship in which the great obelisk (now in front of St. Peter's) had been brought from Egypt, and then securing it by piles, built upon it a very lofty tower after the model of the Pharos at Alexandria, to be lighted at night and guide the course of ships" (254). This report was confirmed by modern archaeology (255).

Many more lighthouses followed at Rhegium, Ravenna, Brundisium,

Dyrrachium, Puteoli, Dover, Misenium and at Coruna about 100 A.D., during the reign of the emperor Trajan, the lighthouse was built which still stands over the harbour on a cliff. A coin of 86/87 A.D. of the town of Laodicea shows a lighthouse, built in two steps, on top of which stood a statue of Athena or Dionysos. This lighthouse stood on the north jetty exactly on the spot of the present lighthouse of Latakia (256). There was a lighthouse at Salona (257) and at Heraclea (Bythinia) (258). By the end of the first century A.D. there must have been some thirty lighthouses which number was slowly increased during the following century, after which a standstill in building lighthouses becomes evident from the documents.

As many of these lighthouses, in which the fires received constant attendance during the night, were called pharos after the famous Pharos of Alexandria, we need not wonder that the later encyclopedists identify the word "pharos" with a lighthouse. Thus Solinus (259). says:

> "Hence one calls buildings erected in harbours to illuminate the approaches (ad praelucendi ministerium) pharus".

Isidore of Seville (260) declares: "A pharos is a very high tower which the Greeks and Romans, because by its flames it is visible at great distances to mariners, call after Pharos which Ptolemy erected at Alexandria at the cost of 800 talents. Its aim is to give fire-signals to the nightly course of ships, to mark shallows and harbour-entrances, so that the ships surprised by the dark do not run into cliffs".

In Byzantine and Arab times the number of lighthouses slowly increased and often fires burnt on the many watchtowers which the Arabs built all along the north coast of Africa. Hennig (261) is right in stating that, though during the Dark Ages many lighthouses ceased to function for some time, when decentralisation of authority was rampant, the idea of the lighthouse was never lost in the Mediterranean, Black and Baltic Seas and on the Atlantic coast several continued to function until by 1200 a new period began of construction and reconstruction of lighthouses along the coasts of Europe.

BIBLIOGRAPHY

1. LUCRETIUS, *De Rerum Natura* I. 896—900; V. 1091—1100
2. FARADAY, M., *Chemical History of a Candle* (*edit. W. Crookes*, London, 1861)
3. WALSH, JOHN W. T., *The Art of Illumination, history of the Art* (The Illuminating Engineer, col. XXIV, pp. 84—87)
   BÖSENBERG, A., *Lampen und Leuchtkörper aus früheren Zeiten* (Licht und Lampe, 1926, pp. 46—48, 81—83, 170—172)
4. O'DEA, W., *Darkness into Daylight* (London, 1948)
   ROBINS, F. W., *The Story of the Lamp* (Oxford Univ. Press, 1939)
   WEULE, K., *Chemische Technologie der Naturvölker* (Berlin, 1922, pp. 36—42)
   HOUGH, W., *Fire as an agent in human culture* (U.S. National Museum, Bull, No. 139, Washington, 1926, pp. 184 ff)
5. BERTHELOT, *Sur une lampe préhistorique dans la grotte de la Mouthe* C.R.A.I. vol. CXXXIII, 1901, p. 666)
6. GOLOMSHTOK, E., *The Old Stone Age in European Asia* (Trans. Amer. Phil. Soc. N. S. vol. XXIX, 1938, pp. 308—324)
7. ALLEN, M. R., *Early Chinese Lamps* (Oriental Art, vol. II, 1950, pp. 133—140)
8. CLARK, J. G. D. and PIGGOTT, S., *The age of the British flint mines* (Antiquity, vol. VII, 1933, pp. 166—183)
9. CHORUS, H. VON, *Das Beleuchtungswesen der vor- und frühgeschichtlicher Zeit* (Berlin, 1938)
10. CLARK, J. G. D., *Prehistoric Europe, the economic basis* (London, 1952)
    BIRKET-SMITH, K., *The Caribou Eskimos* (Copenhagen, 1929, vol. I, p. 47)
11. ANNANDALE, N., *The Faroes and Iceland* (Oxford, 1905, pp. 37 & 47)
12. MATHIASSEN, TH., *Archaeology in Greenland* (Antiquity, vol. IX, 1935, pp. 195 ff)
13. CHAPPLE, E. D., and COON, C. S., *Principles of Anthropology* (London, 147, p. 256)
14. HOMER, *Odyssey* V. 68
15. RÜTIMEYER, L., *Ur-ethnographie der Schweiz* (Basel, 1924, pp. 80—94)
16. MEISSNER, BR., *Babylonien und Assyrien* (Heidelberg, 1925, vol. I)
    NEUBURGER, A., *The technical arts and sciences of the ancients* (London, 1930, pp. 234—247)
    SALONEN, A., *Die Hausgeräte der alten Mesopotamier* (Helsinki, 1965, pp. 138—146)
17. The oldest term in Erman-Grapow Wörterbuch der aegyptische Sprache is tk3.w (V. 331.9), Coptic TIK, ⲐIK, which was derived from tk3.w (V. 331.6), flame, light and which was written with the brazier ideogram. From it is derived the word tk3.w (V. 332.2), to make or light a candle or torch and tk3.w (V. 332.), the day of the torch.

A somewhat later term is gmḥ.t (V. 171.14) written with the ideogram of textiles and denoting both wick and candle or taper.
The youngest term is w'3 (I. 280.1) written with the "branch" ideogram.

18. h'.t (III. 39.18) with the "carob" ideogram.

19. MILLER, J. M., *Die Beleuchtung im Altertum* (Berlin, 1885)
    GRAHAM, J. W., *Light-wells in classical Greek houses* (*Hesperia* vol. XXVII, 1958, pp. 318—323)

20. HOMER, *Odys.* VI. 305; XVII. 569; XIX. 388—389; V. 59; VI. 7, 13, 69; XIV. 518; *Iliad* IX. 470

21. HOMER, *Iliad* XI. 554; XVII. 663; ATHENAEUS, *Deipn.* XV. 700b; ARISTOPHANES PL. 1194; THUCYDIDES 7.53.24; XENOPHON, *Cyrop.* 7.5.23

22. THEOPHRASTUS, *Hist. Plant.* III. 9.3; *Caus. Plant.* V. 16.2

23. HOMER, *Odys.* XVIII. 306, 343; XIX. 63 (Hesych. s. v. lampter; POLLUX VI. 103; X. 116); VII. 100; AESCHYL, *Choeph.* 536; EURIP. *Troad.* 535; EURIPD. *Hel.* V. 818; SOPHOCLES, *Aiax* 285

24. SCHOL. *to* ARISTOPHANES, *Vesp.* 1373

25. ARISTOPHANES, *Lysist.* 308; ATHENAEUS, *Deipn.* XV. 701a

26. LYSIAS, *De caed. Erat. par.* 24

27. ATHEN., *Deipn.* XV. 59 & 700b; POLLUX VI. 103; X. 116—117

28. VASSITS, M., *Die Fackel in Kunst und Kultus der Griechen* (Diss. München, 1900)

29. THUCYDIDES III. CXXXIII. 2; PAUSANIAS, *Descr. of Greece* II. 17

30. HOMER, *Odys.* XVIII. 307; XIX. 63

31. SAGLIO, E., *Candelabrum* (Daremberg-Saglio vol. I, pp. 869—875)

32. VARRO, *Ling. Lat.* V. 119; PLINY, *Nat. Hist.* XXXIV. 11; MARTIAL XIV. 43; SERVIUS AD AEN. I. 727; ISIDORE, *Orig.* XX. 10.5

33. FORBES, R. J., *Studies in Ancient Technology* (Leiden, 1965, vol. V, p. 191)

34. PLINY, *Nat. Hist.* XXXIV. VI. 11

35. SAGLIO, E., *Candela* (Daremberg-Saglio vol. I, p. 869)

36. ALLEN, D., *Candles and candle making* (J. Instit. Petroleum Techn. vol. XIX, 1933, pp. 155—175)
    BÜLL, REINHARD, *Zur Phänomenologie & Technologie der Kerze unter besonderer Berücksichtigung der Wachskerze* (*Vom Wachs, Hoechster Beitr. zur Kenntnis der Wächse* Bd. I, Beitrag 8/1, Frankfurt, 1965)

37. HOUGH, W., *Collection of heating and lighting utensils in the United States Museum* (U. S. Museum Bull. No. 141, Washington, 1928, pp. 14—18)

38. MALCOLM, FRASER H., *Beekeeping in Antiquity* (London, 1951) p. 121); SEIDENSTICKER, A., *Waldgeschichte des Altertums* (Frankfurt, 1886, Band. I pp. 323—327)

39. FORBES, R. J., *Studies in Ancient Technology* (Leiden, 1965, vol. V, p. 90) BÜLL, *Vom Wachs, Hoechster Beiträge zur Kenntnis der Wächse*, Band I, Beitrag 1—7/2 (Frankfurt-Hoechst, 1959—1963, 8 parts)

40. ARISTOTLE, *Hist. Anim.* V. 28; PLINY, *Nat. Hist.* XI. XV. 18; COLUMELLA IX. XIV

41. COLUMELLA IX. XVI; PALLADIUS, June VII

42. PLINY, *Nat. Hist.* XXI, XLIX, 83—85
43. DIOSCORIDES, II. 105 (edit. Gunther, Oxford, 1934)
44. FORBES, R. J., *Studies in Ancient Technology* (Leiden, 1965, vol. III, pp. 247, 256)
45. PLINY, *Nat. Hist.* XIII. 88
46. PAUSANIAS, *Phocica* X. 5
47. VIRGIL, *Ecl.* II. 32
48. JUVENAL III. 267; MARTIAL XIV. 40
49. *Ammian. Marc.* XVIII. 6
50. *Judith* 16.15; *Micha* 1.4; *Psalms* 22.15; 68.3; 97.5
51. *Schabb.* II. 1
52. *Schem.* R. 36(91a)
53. *Kel.* XVII. 17; XXIV. 7; *Tos. Schabb.* XI. 11
54. b. *Bab.* k. 85a
55. *Schabb.* VIII. 4; XXII. 3; *Tos. Ohal.* X. 8
56. CESARI, C., *La confezione delle candele nell'antichità* (Chimica nell'Industria vol. 9, 1933, pp. 232—234)
57. WOLHAUPTER, E., *Die Kerze im Recht* (Forschungen und Fortschritte vol. XIII, 1937, pp. 20—21)
58. *The Golden Legend or Lives of the Saints as Englished by* WILLIAM CAXTON (edit. Dent, London, vol. III, 1900, pp. 19—27)
58a. BEDINI, SILVIO A., *The Scent of Time* (*Trans. Amer. Phil. Soc.* vol. 53, 1963, part 5)
59. MACKAY, E., *Early Indus Civilisations* (London, 1948)
60. WALTERS, H. B., *Catalogue of the Greek and Roman lamps in the British Museum* (London, 1914)
61. WHEELER, SIR MORTIMER, *A symbol in Ancient Times* (In: *The Scallop, studies of a shell and its influences on humankind*, edit. Ian Cox, London, 1957, pp. 33—48)
62. HERODOTUS II. 133
63. DAVIES, N. DE G., *Rock Tombs of El Amarna*, vol. III. *The Tombs of Huya and Ahmes* (London, 1905, Plate VII)
    DAVIES, N. DE G., *Rock Tombs of El Amarna*, vol. IV. *Tombs of Penthu, Mahu and others* (London, 1906, Plate XV)
    DAVIES, N. DE G., *Rock Tombs of El Amarna*, vol. II. *The Tombs of Panehesy and Meryra* (London, 1905, Plate VIII)
64. GARDINER, SIR ALAN, *Egyptian Grammar* (London, 1950), Sign R 7
65. ROBINS, F. W., *The lamps of Egypt* (J. Egypt. Archaeol. vol. 25, 1939, pp. 184—187)
66. Most terms for lamps are written with the "brazier" ideogram (Gardiner, sign Q 7). We have ḥdwj.t, "the white" (Erman-Grapow, Wörterbuch, III. 213,23) written with the flask ideogram; and nḥb (II. 308.12 with the "brazier" ideogram), also used metaphorically for the moon. Then there are three later terms: ḫ(3)b(3)ś (III.230.3 with the "brazier" ideogram) Coptic ʜ ϧⲥ ʜ ϧⲥ and śt3.t (IV. 333.15, from śt3 (IV. 333.12, fire flame) indicating a metal (lotusform) lamp. The term ḫ3w (III. 221.11) means "part of a lamp" and is related to a term meaning sweet-smelling ingredients of unguents and incense.

67. ROBINS, F. W., *Graeco-Roman lamps from Egypt* (J. Egypt. Archaeol. vol. 25, 1939, pp. 48—51)

SHIER, L. A., *Roman lamps and lamp makers of Egypt* (Amer. J. Archaeol. vol. 57, 1953, pp. 110—111)

68. HOMBERT & PRÉAUX, *Comptes du temple de Soknopaios* (Chron. d'Egypte 1940, pp. 134—136)

69. ERMAN, A., *Christliche Lampe aus der Fayum* (Z. Aeg. Sprache vol. XXVIII, 1890, p. 63)

70. CROWFOOT, G. M. & HARDEN, D. B., *Early Byzantine and later glass lamps* (J. Egypt. Archaeol. vol. 17, 1931, pp. 196—208)

TOWBRIDGE, M. L., *Philological Studies in Ancient Glass* (Univ. of Illinois, 1930, pp. 190—191)

FORBES, R. J., *Studies in Ancient Technology* (Leiden, 1965, vol. V, p. 191)

71. CONTENAU, G., *Everyday Life in Babylonia and Assyria* (London, 1954, p. 32)

BERGHE, L. VANDEN, *Archéologie de l'Iran ancien* pl. 115,

Fouilles de Telloh vol. I, pp. 89, 144

LANGDON, S., *Excavations at Kish I*, pl. XXV, 2

Iraq XXI, 1959, pl. IIb

STEIN, A., *Ruins of Desert Cathay*, Fig. 117, no. 23

SALONEN, A., *Die Hausgeräte der alten Mesopotamier* (Helsinki, 1965, pp. 130—138)

72. FORBES, R. J., *Studies in Ancient Technology* (Leiden, 1964, vol. I)

73. *Exod.* 25,6; 27.20; 35.8.14.28; *Levit.* 24.2; KENNEDY, C. A., *The Development of the Lamp in Palestine* (*Berytus* vol. XIV, 1963, pp. 67—115); ZUSSMAN, V., *Some Lamps from Gadot* (*Yediot* vol. XXVII, 1963, pp. 192—194

74. *Schabb.* II. 1.2; *Tos. Schabb.* III. 3.4; *Siphra* 103b

75. *Jerem.* 25.10; *Relev.* 18.23

76. *Prov.* 31.18, *Isa.* 42.3; 43.17, *Matth.* 12.20

77. pištâ, Syr. linon or kettâna; *Isa.* 42.3; 43.17, *Matth.* 12.20; later also called petîlâ; *Schabb.* II. 1.2; *Tos. Schabb.* II, 1; *Ter.* X. 9

78. *Luke* 12.35

79. *Matth.* 5.15; *Mark.* 4.21; *Luke* 8.16; 11.33

80. *Schabb.* III. 6

81. Greek lychnia, Hebrew menôrâ, menâstâ; 2 *Ki.* 4.10; *Exod.* 25.31; 37.17; *Num.* 8.2; 1 *Ki.* 7.49; 2 *Chron.* 4.20; *Sir.* 26.17; 1 *Macc.* 4.49; 2 *Macc.* 10.3

82. *Exod.* 25.38; 37.23; 2 *Chron.* 4.21

83. *Kel.* II. 4; *Tos. Kel.* B. *m.* II. 7; *Kel.* B. *b.* VII. 11

84. *Kel.* XI. 7

85. 1 *Ki.* 7.49; 2 *Chron.* 4.7; *Zech.* 4.2; 1 *Macc.* 4.49

86. *Tam.* III. 6.9; VI. 1; *Siphra* 103 d

87. *Tos. Schabb.* II. 7.8; *b. Schabb* 67 b

88. *Luke* 15.8; *Shir.* R. 1.1(3a)

89. *Zeph.* 1.12; *Matth.* 25,1,3

90. *Ps.* 119, 105

91. *John.* 18.3

92. *Judges* 7.16
93. *Revel.* 21.23; 22.5
94. *Prov.* 6.23; *Ps.* 119.105; *Ecclasiasticus* 18.4; *Prov.* 20.27; 21.4
95. TOUTAIN, J., *Lucerna* (Daremberg-Saglio vol. IV, pp. 1320—1339)
96. VARRO, *De Ling.Lat.*V. 119; POLLUX,*Onom.* X. 115; MACROBIUS, *Sat. Vi.* 4.18
97. HOMER, *Odyssey* XIX. 34
98. ALEX. CLEMENT, *Strom.* I. 16
99. HERODOTUS II. 62, 130, 133
100. JOSEPHUS, C., *Apion* II. 39
101. WALTERS, H. B., *Catalogue of the Greek and Roman lamps in the British Museum* (London, 1914)
    LEPAPE, A., *Les lampes gréco-romaines* (Etudes Classiques vol. III, 1934, pp. 299—304)
    MILLER, J. M., *Die Beleuchtung im Altertum* (Würzburg, 1895)
    BRONEER, G., *The terracotta lamps* (Corinth vol. IV/2, 1930)
102. HERODOTUS VII. 215
103. ARISTOPHANES, Eccl. 1; POLL. VI. 103; X. 122
104. PAUSANIAS I. 26.7
105. ANTHOL. PALAT. VI. 148
106. MARTIAL, *Epigr.* X. 38; XIV. 39; PROPERTIUS, *Eleg.* I, II, XV
107. ARISTOPHANES, *Knights* 739, 1315; *Schol. Aristophanes*, Wasps 1007; Nub. 1065; ATHENAEUS DEIPN. XI. 474 d; POLLUX VII. 178
108. POLLUX II. 72
109. PLINY, *Nat. Hist.* XXVIII. 11.47; XXXV. 50
110. POLLUX VI. 103
111. PAUSANIAS I. 26.7
112. PLINY, *Nat. Hist.* XIX. 3
113. PLINY, *Nat. Hist.* XXIII. 4.41
114. HERODOTUS II. 62; PLINY, *Nat.Hist.* XXXI. 39; XV. 7; DIOSCORIDES I. 38; IV. 164
115. PLUTARCH, *Life of Alexander cap.* 35
116. HERODOTUS II. 94, STRABO XVII. 2, cap. 824; DIODOR I. 34, PLINY, *Nat. Hist.* XV. 7
117. PLUTARCH, *Quaest. Rom.* 75, *Quaest. Conviv.* 702 D
118. JUVENAL VII. 22
119. MACROBIUS, *Saturn.* VI. 4.17—18
120. MARTIAL XIV. 41
    FREMERSDORF, FR., *Das Beleuchtungsgerät in römischer Zeit* (Mainz, 1924)
    DÉONNA, W., (Bull. Corr. Hell. XXXII, 1908, pp. 133 ff)
121. WOLLMANN, H., *Antike römische Taschenspielerlampen* (Mitt. Dtsch. Archaeol. Instit. vol. 44, 1929, pp. 87—90)
122. DÉONNA, W., *Zoologie antique et lampes romaines* (Revue Etud. Anc. vol. 27, 1925, pp. 297—306)
123. NILSON, M. P., *Lampen und Kerzen im Kult der Antike* (Opuscula Archaeol. vol. VI, pp. 96—111)
124. HERODOTUS II. 130
125. HESPERIA vol. II, 1933, p. 346

126. PERSIUS V. V. 179

127. C.I.L. II. 4969; XV. 6196—6210

128. PETRONIUS, *Satyricon* 124

129. CHRYSOSTOM., JOH., *Homel.* 12, in *epist. I ad Corinth.*

130. C.I.GR. III. 4380; APULEIUS, *Metam.* XI. 245

131. C.I.L. II. 2102

132. FFEMERSDORF, FR., *Römische Bildlampen* (Bonn, 1922)

133. LOESCHKE, S., *Lampen aus Vindonissa* (Leipzig, 1919)

LOESCHKE, S., *Bearbeitung der antiken Lampen* (Arch. Anz. 1910, pp. 203—211)

134. MILTNER, FR., *Die antiken Lampen in Eisenstadt* (Jahresh. Oesterr. Arch. Inst. vol. XXIV, Beiheft, 1929, pp. 145 ff)

MILTNER, FR., *Die antiken Lampen im Klagenfurter Landesmuseum* (Jahresh. Oesterr. Arch. Instit. vol. XXIV, Beiheft, 1930, pp. 114 ff)

MENZEL, H., *Antike Lampen im Römisch-Germanischen Zentral Museum zu Mainz* (Mainz, 1954)

WINTER, A., *Brennende römische Ton-Lampen* (Saalberg-Jahrbuch vol. XIV, 1955, pp. 80—82)

NOLL, R., *Eine neue oberitalische Lampentöpferei* (Jahresh. Oesterr. Arch. Inst. vol. XXX, Beiheft, 1936, pp. 109—120)

135. ATKINSON, D., *A Hoard of Samian Ware from Pompeii* (J. Roman Studies, vol. IV, 1914, pp. 27—29)

136. P.O. 188

137. OSBORNE, A., *Lychnos et Lucerna* (Soc. Royale d'Archéol. d'Alexandrie, 1924)

138. GAUKLER, V., *Les fouilles en Tunésie* (Rev. Archéol. vol. II, 1902, p. 37)

CARTON, L. B. C., *Les fabriques de lampes dans l'ancienne Afrique* (Bull. Soc. Géogr. Arch. Oran, vol. XXXVI, 1916, pp. 64—67)

CARDAILLAC, F. DE, *Histoire de la lampe antique en Afrique* (Bull. Soc. Géogr. Arch. Oran, vol. X, 1890, pp. 241—324)

HAUTECOEUR, L., *Les lampes romaines du Musée Alaoui* (Gazette des Beaux-Arts vol. I, 1909, pp. 265—285)

CARTON, L. B. C., *L'art indigène sur les lampes de la Colonie Thuburnica* (Mém. Soc. Ant. France, 1913, pp. 141 ff)

HÉRON DE VILLEFOSSE, A., *Lampe de la Collection Barone* (Mon. et. Mém. Piot, vol. V, p. 180, fig. 44)

HOWLAND, R. H., *Lamps found in the agora* (Amer. J. Archaeol. 1937, pp. 110 ff)

139. C.I.L. VIII, 914 ff, 2211 ff

140. Bull. Comm. 1891, p. 547

141. C.R. 1908, p. 601

142. C.I.L. VIII. 22644, 260; X. 8053, 165, 247, 251

143. Notiz. Scavi 1891, 403

144. PACE, B., *Camarina* (Catania, 1927, p. 123)

145. C.I.L. II. 4969, 16, 17, 37, 41; 6256, 7, 9, 39, 54

146. C.I.L. II. 4969, 28, 35; 6348, 2

147. C.I.L. II. 4969, 19, 24

148. C.I.L. II. 4969, 31, 46; VIII. 22642, 1, 2

149. C.I.L. X. 8053, 102, 151, 243
150. I.G. XIV. 2405, 18
151. C.I.L. X. 8053, 105
152. C.I.L. X. 8053, 27, 160
153. C.I.L. X. 8053, 83
154. BLOCH, W., *Vom Kienspan bis zum künstlichen Tageslicht* (7. edit., Berlin, 1924)
155. ARISTOPHANES *Eccl.* 7, LUCIAN, *Golden Ass* 12. c. 51; LYSIAS, *de caede Erat.* 14; MARTIAL XIV. 39; MORETUM 10 ff; APULEIUS, *Metam.* V. 102—103
156. PLUTARCH, *Cimon*, cap. 6; PLUTARCH, *Pelop.* cap. 35; XENOPHON, *Hell.* VI. 4.36
157. THUCYDIDES IV. 133; PAUS. II. 17; ARISTOPHANES, *Plut.* 668
158. PLATO, *Symp.* 34; XENOPHON, *Symp.* cap. 5.2; LUCIAN, *conviv.* cap. 15, cap. 14; PLUTARCH, *Alexander*, cap. 38
159. PLUTARCH, *Demosthenes* cap. 11; LUCIAN, *Philos.* 31; LUCIAN, *adversus indoctum* cap. 13
160. DIODOR III. 12
161. TOUTAIN, J., *Laterna* (Daremberg-Saglio, 924—925)
     LOESCHKE, S., *Antiken Laternen und Lichthäuschen* (Bonner Jahrbücher vol. 118, 1909, pp. 370—430)
     TAILLARDAT, J., *Les sens d'amorgos et les lanternes dans l'antiquité* (*Rev. Etud. Grecq.* LXXII, 1959, XII—XIV)
162. VALERIUS MAX. VI. 8.1; ISID. *Orig.* XX. 10.7; PLAUT, *Aul.* III. 6.30; MARTIAL, *Epigr.* XIV. 61, 62; EMPEDOKLES, frag. 84; ARISTOPHANES b. Phot. p. 238, 7 (s.v. lychnouchon)
163. ATHENAEUS, *Deipn.* XV. 699; PLAUT, *Amph. prol.* 148, 149; *Cicero in Pis.* IX; VALERIUS *Max.* VI. 8.1
164. PLUTARCH, *Lycurgus* XII; XENOPHON *d. r. p. Lac.* V. 7
165. XENOPHON, *Hell.* V. 1.6; DIODOR XX. 75; LIVY XXIX. 25
166. PHILO, *mech. synt.* B. V. 93, 5—8; CICERO, *ad Qu.* fr. 3.7; PHRYNICH (edit. Bekk. Anecd. I. 50); *Chron. Casin.* III. 57
167. ARISTOPHANES, *Plut.* 816; ATHENAEUS, *Deipn.* XV. 699; *Photius* p. 238; PLAUT. AMPH. I. i. 185 (341); LUCRETIUS II. 388; PLINY, *Nat. Hist.* XI. 126; MARTIAL XIV. 61; POLLUX X. 117; ARIST. *Meteor.* VI. 49; CICERO *ad Attic.* VI. 3.5
168. EMPEDOKLES fr. 84; ARISTOPHANES acc. to PHOTIUS p. 238,7; ARISTOTLE, *Hist. Anim.* IV. 5; PLAUTUS, *Aul.* III. 6.29; MARTIAL XIV. 62; JULIUS AFRIC., *Kestoi* cap. 69
169. PLAUTUS, *Bacch.* III. 3.42; MARTIAL XIV. 62
170. EMPEDOKLES fr, 84; PLAUTUS, *Bacch.* III. 3.42(466); CICERO *ad Attic.* IV. 3.5
171. ISIDORE, *Etym.* XX. 10.7; S. ANSELMUS, de laude virgin. (J. BASNAGE, *Thes. mon. eccl.* ... Amsterdam, 1725, I. 717)
172. PLUTARCH, *Quaest, rom.* 72
173. ARISTOPHANES, Eccl. 49, 978, 1150; PLUT. 1194; VESP. 218; LYSIS 1003; THEOPHRAST, *De igne* 27; ARISTOPHANES, *Thesm.* 655, 280, 917; *Ranae* 340, 350, 1087, 1098, 1362; AELIAN, IX. 29; PLUTARCH, *Pericles* cap. 5

174. Plutarch, *Vita Anton.* 26; Suetonius, *Caesar* 37; Dio Cass. 63.4
175. Suetonius, *Caligula* 18, *Domitian* 4
176. Lampridius, *Sev. Alex.* 24
177. C.I.L. XV. 6221
178. Böhm, R., *Zur Geschichte des Beleuchtungswesens* (Prometheus vol. 28, 1917, pp. 260—263, 270—278, 296—299)
179. Ammianus Marc. XIV. 1; Libanius, *Antiochia* 266; but see also Procopius *Anecd.* 26
180. Breccia, E., *Bull. Soc. Archéol. Alexandrie* vol. XX, N.S.V. 3, 1924, pp. 239 ff

    Breccia, E., *Terrecotte figurate*, vol. I, 1930, p. 72

    Otto, W. and Bengtson, H., *Zur Geschichte des Niederganges des Ptolemäeereiches* (Abh. Münch. Akad. N.F. vol. XVII, 1938, p. 155)

    Hombert, M. & Préaux, Cl., *Papyri Fond. Reine Elizabeth* (Chron. d'Egypte vol. XXIX, 1940, p. 145)
181. Spano, G., *La illuminazione delle vie di Pompeii* (Atti Acad. Napoli, N. S. vol. 7, 1920, pp. 1—128)

    Lamer, H., *Strassenbeleuchtung im späteren Altertum* (Ph. W. vol. 47, 1927, p. 147)
182. Ruinaart, *Acta martyrum* 479; Hieronymus in *Isa.* 672
183. Tertullian, *Apologeticum* 35; *Ad uxorum* II. 6; *De idol.* 15
184. Codex Theodos. XVI. 10.12
185. Herodotus II. 44; Augustinus, *De vic. dei* XXI. 6; Lucianus, *De dea Syria* 32
186. Pliny, *Nat. Hist.* 37.5.е7
187. Bouteville, M. R., *L'éclairage public à Paris des origines à la fin du XIXe siècle* (Revue Scientifique vol. LXXI, 1933, pp. 609—615)
188. Riepl, W., *Das Nachrichtenwesen des Altertums* (Leipzig, 1913, pp. 13—120)
189. Livy 22.28; Plutarch, *M. Crassus* 11; Sallustius, *bell. Ing.* 49.68
190. Caesar, *Bell. Gall.* 2.7.4; Plutarch *Eum.* 15; Livy 44.9.3
191. Caesar, *Bell. Gall.* 5.48.10; Plutarch, *Camill.* 34; Appian V. 35; Polybius, 2.26.2
192. Livy 31.38.10, 27.42.10, 22.42.11, 43.1, 22.41.9; Sallustius, B. Iug. 106; Polybius 9.5; Appian 1.90; Diodor 19.38; 20.17
193. Caesar, b. Gall. 5.49.7; Livy 7.38.8; 27.47.2; 21.32.12
194. Livy 9.43.19; 10.43.11; 40.31.9
195. Livy 22.16.6; Appian, *Hannibal* 11
196. Caesar, b. Gall. 6.29.5; Appian, *Hannibal* 15
197. Caesar, b. Gall. 6.29.5
198. Vegetius 3.5; Livy 9.43.12; 10.48.8; 10.41.6; 21.46; Caesar, b. Civ. 3.36.8
199. Herodotus IV. 134, 135; Thucydides VII. 80.3; Diodor VIII. 111; XV. 84; XIX. 38; Pausanias VII. 26.2; Arrian V. 11; Polyaen I. 12.46; Diodor XVI. 19; XIX. 37; XX. 18
200. Livy 29.25.11; Procopius, *Vand.* 1.13; Dio 42.43; Virgil, *Aeneid* 2.256
201. Livy 29.2.511

202. DIELS, H., *Antike Technik* (Leipzig, 1920, chapter IV, pp. 71—90)
PACHTLER, G. M., *Das Telegraphieren der alten Völker* (Innsbrück, 1867)
MILLER, G. M., *Die Beleuchtung im Altertum* (Würzburg, 1885)
MÖLLER, W., *Ueber antike Telegraphie* (Hum. Gymnasium, 1927, pp. 61—75)
MERRIAM, *Telegraphing amongst the ancients* (Papers of the Archaeol. Institute of America, Class. Series III. 1, 1890)
STILL, A., *Communication through the ages from sign language to television* (Rinehart, New York, 1946)

203. HOMER, *Iliad* XVIII. 211; EURIPIDES, *Phoen.* 1318; AESCHYLUS, *Agam.* V. 280; HERODOTUS, XI. 3; VII. 183; ARISTOPHANES, *Birds* 1160; POLYBIUS X cap. 43; THUCYDIDES III.22.7; II. 94; XENOPHON, *Anab.* IV. 6.20; VII. 8.15; PLUTARCH, *Alc.* 30; DIODOR XII. 49; XIX. 57; IPHICRATES III. 5; ARRIAN IV. 29; DIODOR XI. 61; AENEAS TACT. cap. 4; VEGETIUS 3.6; LIVY 4.27.12; 27.15.13; 32.12.1; 32.11.8; 9.23.11; 9.23.15

204. THEOGNIS (edit. Bergk) V. 549; HOMER, *Iliad* 4.275; ARISTOPHANES, *Birds* 1161; THUCYDIDES 2.94; FRONTINUS, *Strat.* 2.5.16; LIVY 22.19.6; 23.27.5; 44.28.8; 29.3; PLINY, *Nat. Hist.* 2.181; 35.160; CICERO, *Verr.* 2.5.35; POLYAEN. 6.16.2; PLUTARCH *Aem, Paul.* 25

205. VAB VII. 264; *r*II. 10. ff; the IZI-GAR, tipâru (torch) was often made of reeds, hence it is also called GI-IZI-LÁ, gizillû from GI, qanû (reed). Another equivalent is DÈ, DÈ-DAL(-LA), ṭitallu, nablu.
SALONEN, A., *Die Hausgeräte der alten Mesopotamier* (Helsinki, 1965, pp. 138—146)

206. TALLQVIST, *Die assyrische Beschwörungsserie Maqlû*, VI. 103

207. MEISSNER, B., *Babylonien und Assyrien* (Heidelberg, 1925, I)

208. DOSSIN, G., *Signaux lumineux au pays de Mari* (Revue d'Assyr. vol. XXXV, 1938, pp. 174—186)

209. Judges 20.38

210. JEREMIAH 6.1

211. TORCZYNER, *The Lachish Letters* (Lachish I, London, 1938)
TORCZYNER, H., *Te'udot Lakhish* (Jerusalem, 1940)

212. Rôš HAŠANÂH, II. 2; V. FLUSS, *Feuerpost im Altertum* (Wiener Blätter f. Freunde der Antike vol. VII, 1930, p. 77)

213. Xenophon, *Cyr.* 3.2.1; FRONTINUS, *Strat.* 2.16

214. HOMER, *Iliad* 18.207—213; 4.275; ODYSSEY 4.524; EURIPIDES, *Rhes.* 55, 128, 694; EURIPIDES, *Hell.* 11.25, 1130; VIRGIL, *Aen.* 2.254; PAUSANIAS 2.54.3; DIODOR 4.50—52

215. AESCHYLUS, *Agam.* V. 280—316

216. DIELS, H., *Antike Technik* (Leipzig, 1920, pp. 71—90)
HENNIG, R., *Die älteste Entwicklung der Telegraphie und Telephonie* (Leipzig, 1908)
DARMSTAEDTER, E., *Feuer-Telegraphie im Altertum* (Die Umschau vol. 28, 1924, pp. 505—507)

217. HERODOTUS IX. 3

218. PSEUDO-ARISTOTLE, pseudo-kosmon cap. 6

219. JUSTIN 2.14

220. PLUTARCH, *Aem. Paul.* 25
221. THUCYDIDES II. 94; III. 22, 80; DIODOR 19.57; 19.97; POLYBIUS 10.42.7; LIVY 28.5.16; 28.7.1; APPIAN, MITHRIDATES 79; CICERO, pr. r. *Deiotaro* 8.22.25
222. LIVY 27.28.16; AENEAS TACTICUS 6.2; 22.9
223. Anonym. Byz. 8.5.6 (KÖCHLY-RÜSTOW, *Griechische Kriegsschriftsteller* II. 2, pp. 62 ff)
224. POLYBIUS 8.30.1; LIVY 25.9.10
225. POLYBIUS 10.43—47
226. POLYAENUS 6.12.2
227. REINECKE, G., *Feuertelegraphie im griechischen Altertum* (Archiv. f. Post und Telegraphie vol. 63, 1935, pp. 143—145)
228. EURIPIDES, *Orest.* 432; *Hell* 1126; DIO CHRYSOST. *or.* 7; APOLLODORUS, bibl. 2.1.5
229. POLYAEN. 3.56; LYSIAS *kata Agoraton* 67 (edit. Scheibe); PLUTARCH, *Alcib.* 30, LIVY 28.7.1; APPIAN, *Mithridates* 79; THUCYDIDES 2.94; DIODOR 12.49; THUCYDIDES 3.22; POLYAEN 6.19.2; FRONTINUS *Strat.* 2.5.16
230. SEXTUS JULIUS AFRICANUS, *Kestoi* 77
231. SUETONIUS, *Tiberius* 65; TACITUS, *Ann.* 6.39
232. DIO 46.36; 65.18
233. CAESAR, bell. civ. 44.3; 65.3; 67.1
234. RICHMOND, I. A., *A Roman Artificial Signalling System in the Stainmore Pass* (In: Aspects of Archaeology in Britain and Beyond London, 1951, pp. 293—302)
235. VEGETIUS 3.5
236. HOMER, *Iliad* XVIII, 207—213; XIX, 375—377; *Odyssey* X. 30—31
237. HERODOTUS II. 15
238. POLYBIUS I. 56.6
239. DIODOR IV. 50
240. STRABO III. 1. cap. 140
241. SEMPLE, E. C., *The Geography of the Mediterranean Region, its relation to ancient history* (London, 1932, pp. 613—637)
242. CAESAR, *Bell. Civ.* III. 112; PLINY, *Nat. Hist.* 36.12; STRABO XVII. 1.6
243. ISIDORE, Orig. XV. 3; HRABANUS MAURUS, *De Universo* XIV. 113
244. VIETMEYER, L. A., *Leuchtfeuer und Leuchtapparate* (München, 1900)
     ADLER, P., *Der Pharos van Alexandria* (Berlin, 1901)
     THIERSCH, H., *Pharos, Antike Islam und Occident* (Leipzig, 1909)
     LEHMANN-HARTLEBEN, K., *Antike Hafenanlagen*
     THIERSCH, H., *Jahrbuch D. Archaeol. Instit.* 1915, pp. 213 ff
245. SUIDAS CXX. 2. cap. 299
246. PROCOPIUS OF GAZA, *Panegyr. in Anast.* (edit. Migne) LXXXVII. 2818. XX)
247. JOSEPHUS, Bell. Iud. IV. cap. 10.5
     ASIN PALACIOS, M., *El Faro de Alejandria* (El-Andaluz vol. I, No. 2, 1933, pp. 242—292)
     DUKE OF ALBA, *The Pharos of Alexandria* (Proc. Brit. Acad. vol. XIX, 1933, pp. 277—292)

Sprague de Camp, L., *The "Darkhouse" of Alexandria* (*Technology and Culture* vol. VI, 1965, pp. 3, 423—427)

Tousoun, O., *Description du Phare d' Alexandrie* (Soc. R. Archéol. d'Alexandrie, Bull. No. 30, N.S. vol. IX, 1936, pp. 49—53)

249. Lucan, *Pharsalia* IV, 1004; Pliny, *Nat. Hist.* 36.12

250. Stevenson, D. Alan, *The Development of Lighthouses* (J. Royal Soc. Arts vol. LXXX, 1932, pp. 224—242)

251. Hennig, R., *Beiträge zur älteren Geschichte der Leuchttürme* (Beitr. Gesch. Technik Industrie vol. VI, 1915, pp. 35—54)

252. Josephus, *Bios* VI. 105

253. Suetonius, *Caligula* 46

254. Suetonius, *Claudius* 20; Dio Cassius LX. 11

255. Rollo, W., *Ostia* (Greece and Rome vol. IV, 1934/1935, pp. 46—47)

256. Seyrig, H., *Le Phare de Laodicée* (Syria vol. XXIX, 1952, pp. 54—59)

257. Betz, A., *Leuchtturm und Flottenstation Salonae* (J. Oesterr. Archaeol. Inst. vol. XXXV, 1943, Beiblatt, p. 129)

258. Robert, L., *Etudes anatoliennes*, p. 252

259. Solinus 32.43

260. Isidore, Orig. XV. 3

261. Hennig, R., *Zur Geschichte der Leuchttürme im frühen Mittelalter* (Prometheus vol. XXVI, 1915, pp. 241—244)

INDEX